# Perpetual Movement

THE SUNY SERIES

HORIZONS OF CINEMA

MURRAY POMERANCE | EDITOR

# Perpetual Movement

Alfred Hitchcock's *Rope*

Neil Badmington

Published by State University of New York Press, Albany

© 2021 State University of New York

All rights reserved

Printed in the United States of America

No part of this book may be used or reproduced in any manner whatsoever without written permission. No part of this book may be stored in a retrieval system or transmitted in any form or by any means including electronic, electrostatic, magnetic tape, mechanical, photocopying, recording, or otherwise without the prior permission in writing of the publisher.

For information, contact State University of New York Press, Albany, NY
www.sunypress.edu

### Library of Congress Cataloging-in-Publication Data

Name: Badmington, Neil, author.
Title: Perpetual movement: Alfred Hitchcock's Rope / Neil Badmington.
Description: Albany : State University of New York Press [2021] | Includes bibliographical references and index.
Identifiers: ISBN 9781438484150 (hardcover : alk. paper) | ISBN 9781438484167 (pbk : alk. paper) | ISBN 9781438484174 (ebook)
Further information is available at the Library of Congress.
Library of Congress Control Number: 2021938491

10 9 8 7 6 5 4 3 2 1

*For Felix, Dylan, and Maria, who toiled tirelessly
in the swimming pools of Los Angeles,
while I splashed around in the Hitchcock archives*

*To the memory of Catherine Belsey (1940–2021)*

# Contents

| | |
|---|---:|
| List of Illustrations | ix |
| Acknowledgments | xi |
| Note on Archival Sources | xiii |
| Introduction: Entangled | 1 |
| 1  Operation *Rope* | 19 |
| 2  Inside | 37 |
| 3  Entrances, Elsewheres | 53 |
| 4  In the Bedroom | 63 |
| 5  Just Plain Something | 83 |
| 6  Miss Sashweight of the Blunt Instrument Department | 93 |
| 7  From OR to "We" | 101 |
| 8  Two Small Fugitives from a Bowl of Alphabet Soup | 113 |
| 9  Faking Freud | 123 |
| 10  Cat and Mouse | 133 |

| 11 Arrest Indicated | 139 |
|---|---|
| Postscript | 149 |
| Notes | 153 |
| Bibliography | 191 |
| Index | 203 |

# Illustrations

| | | |
|---|---|---|
| 2.1 | Phillip and Brandon, nose to shoulder. | 42 |
| 2.2 | Brandon and Phillip—"charm." | 48 |
| 4.1 | Shot 4 begins. | 65 |
| 4.2 | Phillip and Brandon—criss-cross. | 65 |
| 4.3 | Janet is revealed. | 66 |
| 4.4 | Mrs. Wilson is revealed. | 67 |
| 4.5 | Brandon's inclination. | 71 |
| 4.6 | The death of David. | 73 |
| 4.7 | David and Janet in the publicity trailer for *Rope*. | 74 |
| 4.8 | Kenneth and Phillip greet Mrs. Atwater. | 75 |
| 4.9 | Back cover of the 1948 novelization of *Rope*. | 80 |
| 6.1 | Frames within frames. | 97 |
| 6.2 | Three spaces, three scenes. | 98 |
| 7.1 | OR outside the window. | 104 |

7.2  Brandon leaning.                                    111

8.1  The Reduco advertisement in *Lifeboat* (1944).      117

9.1  Proximity.                                          124

# Acknowledgments

I am grateful to the following people for help, advice, suggestions, conversations, and general support during the writing of this book: Areej Al-Khafaji, Kate Belsey, Ivan Callus, Michael Campochiaro, Rafael Chaiken, Chu-chueh Cheng, Ned Comstock, James Corby, Carl Distefano, Rob Gossedge, Camille Hale, Ann Heilmann, Dawn Knight, Rebecca Lemon, Anthony Mandal, Emma Mason, Irene Morra, Becky Munford, Eileen Nizer, James Peltz, David Skilton, Andy Stafford, Julia Thomas, Richard Vine, Damian Walford Davies, Chris Whiteoak, Martin Willis, Charles Wilson, Michael Wood, and Anthony Zegarelli.

Every working day I miss having Iain Morland as a colleague, but our conversations continue over dinner and I benefitted greatly from talking through this project with him—just as I have with every book that I've written.

The staff at the Margaret Herrick Library of the Academy of Motion Picture Arts and Sciences, Beverly Hills, made me feel welcome and helped me to navigate the institution's archives in April 2018; I am particularly grateful to Louise Hilton, Marisa Duron, and Stacey Behlmer. Meanwhile, Brett Service was a patient guide and generous supplier of blank index cards when I visited the Warner Bros. Archive at the University of Southern California, Los Angeles, in March and April of 2019.

Amanda Glover took care of travel, and Mel Griffin and her team at Griffin Books, Penarth, always managed to get hold of things for me far more quickly than her global internet rivals ever could.

Attending a meeting of the Futures of Literature Network at the University of Malta in October 2017 helped me at a crucial moment to think more clearly about the style and mood of this book. During that visit, Marija Grech explained Maltese bus routes to me and thereby accidentally engineered the strange encounter that I relate in my introduction.

I have learned a great deal about *Rope* by discussing it with the students of my Hitchcock module at Cardiff University over the years, and it was a similar joy to talk about aspects of the director's work with pupils at St. David's Catholic Sixth Form College, Cardiff, in January 2018. Lisa Newman, Pip Jones, and Liz French made this visit possible and pulled out all the stops to have my name emblazoned on an orange traffic cone in the car park.

Introducing a special screening of *Rope* at Snowcat Cinema, Penarth, seventy years to the day since the film's premiere will always be one of the highlights of my career. Ben Rive made this event possible and would win the Academy Award for Best Owner of an Independent Cinema every year if such a thing existed. Public discussions of Hitchcock's films at Snowcat have since become a regular part of my life, and one that I treasure.

I am particularly grateful to the two anonymous reviewers who read an earlier version of *Perpetual Movement* for the editorial board of SUNY Press and made various helpful, thoughtful suggestions.

This book could not have been written without the time and funding made available by Cardiff University's Research Leave Fellowship Scheme. I thank the institution for its support.

Murray Pomerance was receptive, encouraging, challenging (in only a good way), and understanding from the outset. I could not have asked for a better editor and guide.

NB<br>
Cardiff, May 2020

# Note on Archival Sources

This book draws extensively upon material preserved in two archives: the Warner Bros. Archive at the University of Southern California, Los Angeles, and the Margaret Herrick Library at the Academy of Motion Picture Arts and Sciences, Beverly Hills. For the sake of convenience, I will refer to these simply as "Warner Bros. Archive" and "Margaret Herrick Library" throughout this book.

# Introduction

## Entangled

I SPENT A YEAR TANGLED UP in *Rope*.
My working days during those months were ones of "pleasing monotony," to borrow a phrase from Thomas Mann.[1] Every morning I would make coffee, sit in a chair, and watch Alfred Hitchcock's experimental film of 1948 about two young men named Brandon and Phillip, who murder one of their friends in the name of art, intellectual superiority, and "the perfect crime."[2] I would pause the action every so often to make notes, to read a relevant text, or to pen paragraphs towards the book that you are now reading. Outside, the seasons came and went, bringing difference to the view from my window. But inside, the routine remained flatly the same day after day: *Rope*, *Rope*, and more *Rope*. A line from Philip Roth's *The Ghost Writer* often haunted me: "And I ask myself, Why is there no way but this for me to fill my hours?"[3]

It was a strange, disorienting experience—a claustrophobic experiment inspired by a claustrophobic experiment. By the time I became a "sojourner in civilized life again" and handed over the first version of the typescript of *Perpetual Movement* to the publisher in the summer of 2019, I had spent hundreds of hours watching a film that runs for a touch under eighty minutes.[4] I often felt lost or trapped in *Rope*, as if I were a friend of Phillip and Brandon, an unacknowledged guest at their macabre party. (On more difficult days I wished that I were inside their fine wooden trunk with only the corpse of David Kentley for company.) The word "diegesis" lost a little of its differentiating hold, as did the familiar distinction between life and text. I sometimes dreamed about the film and occasionally caught myself imitating a character's mannerisms or style of speech (Brandon, usually, for the record). I found myself unconsciously mouthing the dialogue with the actors while I watched. Sometimes I would utter lines from the script involuntarily before they had been spoken on screen—a case of the entangled critic as prompter. I still do not feel, though, that I have managed to free myself from *Rope*, to escape from its textual bind. I lived daily with and within the film for a year, and I have devoted an entire book to it, but the pages that follow do not claim to pronounce a final shrugging verdict, a burying assessment; I have no interest here in what Roland Barthes once called "the monster of totality."[5] *Rope* comes out on top.

## Why?

Why did I sacrifice a year of my life to a film about a sacrifice? What was the point? What did I discover? What, now that the experiment is over, do I have to report?

I found myself facing something like these questions a couple of months into the project. Examining duties took me briefly to Malta, where my hosts invited me also to attend a meeting of their "Futures of Literature" seminar during my final full day on the island. The topic for discussion was "creative criticism," and all those participating were asked to read in advance the introduction to Stephen Benson and Clare Connors's field-defining anthology on the subject.[6] On the afternoon before the seminar, after my work as examiner was completed, I made precise plans: catch the bus from my hotel in Attard to the ancient walled city of Mdina, see the sights, read the set text for the seminar in a café, travel back down to Attard, and meet my hosts for dinner. It all seemed so simple, so perfectly prepared. "You always plan your parties so well; it's odd to have anything go wrong," as Rupert says to Brandon at one point in *Rope*.

But things did go slightly wrong. Five minutes into the journey towards Mdina, the driver slammed on the brakes to shout furiously at a gang of teenagers who were playing music on their phones and shouting through the windows at pedestrians. As the bus set off again, I must have unconsciously muttered some kind of weary middle-aged approval. "You're English?" asked the man sitting next to me; he was perhaps twenty years my senior. I explained that, no, I wasn't quite English, but that English is nonetheless my native tongue. He wanted to know why I was in Malta. I said that I had been examining at the university. "Which department?" he asked. "English," I replied. "Ah," he cried. "So you teach English, you speak English, and you *look* English, but you say that you're not English. What kind of scam is this?" I laughed, and he then asked about my specialism. I explained that I was currently working on film. "Which films?" he wanted to know. "Just one," I said. Just one film. All day, every day.

He had not seen *Rope*, he confessed, but he was keen to know why on earth anyone would write—or read—an entire book on a single film. I was about fifteen seconds into a defensive soliloquy when he held up his hand and told me that his stop was approaching. He pressed the button to alert the driver. "If I see you on the bus later, you can finish your story," he said, rising from the seat. "I need to be persuaded that your book isn't a waste of time." The bus came to a halt. My companion stepped down into the street and waved fondly as the engine roared and we moved uphill towards Mdina.

He was not on the bus when I traveled back down to Attard several hours later. This was particularly disappointing because I had just read the introduction to Benson and Connors's *Creative Criticism* anthology on the sunny terrace of a café and been bowled over by its propositions. I was inspired, illuminated, ready to defend my book and to give a thrilling lecture on the practice of criticism that would, no doubt, have had the whole bus spellbound. The paragraphs that follow in this introduction are, in essence, what I would have said to my inquisitive traveling companion. I hope that my words somehow find their way to Malta, where they took shape.

I was struck first by Benson and Connors's claim that "while there is much to be said for getting things in on time, it does not follow that we should therefore keep quiet about how we have spent our days" (p. 35). Setting aside an entire year to living with or within a single text is an activity whose aims are perhaps not immediately apparent, particularly in times of cruel austerity and urged institutional efficiency. This is precisely why *Perpetual Movement* begins with an open, explicit marking of time, of my time: *this is how I have spent my days, and I will not keep quiet about it*. That does not, of course, explain *why* I did what I did. A year, yes, fine, but for what possible reason?

Benson and Connors's introduction also helped me to address this crucial question. (If we are unable to give an account of why we do what we do as critics, we are, it seems to me, doing something wrong.) Creative criticism, the authors propose at one point, "registers the way works of art don't just passively lie there, all before us, as the world did to Adam and Eve, but come at us in some way. We are surprised, or stolen up upon, find ourselves caught. It needn't be immediate; it is what turns out to have happened. It could take the form of an obsession, perhaps. We have to keep going back" (p. 37). As these words stole up, surprised, and caught me beneath the bright Maltese sun, I saw in them an account of my odd, obsessive relationship to Alfred Hitchcock's *Rope*.

I first saw the film as an undergraduate in the early 1990s. I returned to it occasionally in the years that immediately followed, but not with any kind of obsession. When I came to write *Hitchcock's Magic*, which was published in 2011 and about six years in the making, I did not feel the need to say much about *Rope*, though it rose up in a few places to shed light on other films by the director, notably *Rebecca* (1940).[7] After that, however, *Rope* just kept coming at me, to use the vocabulary of Benson and Connors, and I felt a need "to keep going back," as they put it, to meet the film head on. *Perpetual Movement* is an account of this experience.

I do not mean "account" in the mere sense of telling a tale, as I have spent much time doing so far in this introduction; this is not an autobiography, though I remain committed to the belief that academic writing should tell a story and should acknowledge the lived investment of the critic. I mean "account," rather, in the sense of accounting for the way in which I have found myself pulled back to Hitchcock's film as it, in turn, came at me. What I want to address in the following pages is, in short, textual tenacity—the way in which this particular film, this *peculiar* film, remains alive, engaging, alluring, entrancing, enveloping, and engulfing, even when, thanks to repeated viewings and many pages of existing scholarship, there really ought to be nothing left to see or say. Benson and Connors point out that each piece in their anthology "has been impassioned in different ways by its encounter with what it has read or seen"; such an encounter, they add, is a "being-with" an artwork (p. 5). My "being-with" *Rope* lasted for a year in its most intensively obsessional phase, and this book is, by way of response, an impassioned reckoning with the encounter, with the daily touch of the text. Why did I go back for more, and why did the film keep coming at me?

The final element of Benson and Connors's introduction that leapt out at me is their discussion of distance. A section entitled "On" opens on the following note:

"Write an essay *on*." "What are you writing *about*?" The vocabulary of criticism tends to limit itself to these two prepositions.

They position us as standing apart from a text or artwork, facing it, a subject confronting an object from which it is distinct and aloof. (p. 18)

Creative critics, however, they propose, "invent a more flexible prepositional vocabulary, to capture the mesh of their involvement in and relationship to the art they encounter" (p. 19). They turn briefly to Eve Kosofsky Sedgwick's "criticism of 'beside,'" which they find persuasive in part, but, spurred on by their intervention, I have come to see this book not as being *on* Hitchcock's *Rope* or *about* Hitchcock's *Rope* or even *beside* Hitchcock's *Rope*. It is, rather, a book that finds itself *in* Hitchcock's *Rope*. This is a text by a captured critic, a bound critic.

I am, however, clearly a critic who can still move, can still put pen to paper. The film has a hold, but not a stranglehold. How the rope is tied makes all the difference, I think. Too tight, immobility and death follow—as David Kentley discovers in the opening minutes of the film. Too loose, the bind is lost, and there is no hold. Hitchcock's *Rope*, I will argue in what follows, walks a tightrope. On the one hand, the film pulls us into its narrative and holds us in suspense as we wonder if the "perfect crime" that we have witnessed will be discovered and the killers brought to justice. Our seeing the murder take place at the start of *Rope* is crucial to this suspended entanglement: from the very outset, the camera permits viewers to see and to know in ways denied to characters in the film. Most notably, until the final reel only we and the two murderers know what has happened and are therefore aware that there is a body in the wooden trunk in the living room throughout the party.[8] I will examine this textual quality closely in the chapters that follow. *Rope* reels us in, then, and holds us tight until its final scene comes, at which point we are released from the agonizing suspense because we see the crime uncovered and the burden of our bleak knowledge at last shared.

On the other hand, however, one of the central arguments of this book will be that *Rope* never completely releases its audience. The textual knots are loosened with the conventional Hollywood arrival at narrative resolution, of course: Rupert lifts the lid of the trunk, sees the body of David Kentley, denounces the killers, and alerts the police by opening a window and firing a gun. This finally undoes suspense with revelation and knowledge: the viewer need no longer wonder anxiously if or how the crime will be detected. But this late loosening never goes as far as a complete release into full knowledge. *Rope* retains a hold upon us for, while we see and know with special clarity throughout the film, we are also reminded repeatedly that we are *not* seeing and *not* knowing certain details, certain elements of the taut world in which the tale unfolds. This is particularly surprising because, with the exception of a sole exterior shot beneath the opening credits, the whole of *Rope* takes place in a single apartment and in real time.⁹ For around eighty minutes, the camera glides majestically around the limited interior space and offers intimate, nuanced access to conversations and details. This is all part of the film's apparent commitment to creating a position of knowledge and overview for the audience—a position of "dominant specularity," to take a phrase from Colin MacCabe's classic account of realism in cinema and literature.¹⁰ But, as I will discuss in detail in the following chapters, there are moments in every one of the film's shots at which it becomes clear that we are being denied access to something. Each roaming possession of the mise-en-scène, that is to say, finds itself interrupted and undermined by an acknowledgment of an *elsewhere*: something that the camera could perhaps in principle show us but does not; something that lies beyond the embrace of its prowling, unearthing gaze. "Dominant specularity" meets oversight.

## Perpetual Movement(s)

The film pulls, and pulls us, in two directions at once. This way: narrative closure, knowledge, and mastery. That way: openness, unknowing, and mystery. My year in *Rope* persuaded me that this movement cannot be stilled: it is a perpetual movement.

I should explain this phrase; it is the title of my book, after all, and I have already used the words in this introduction without comment. Over the opening credits of *Rope* we hear an orchestral arrangement of a piece that will appear repeatedly in the film: the first section of Francis Poulenc's *Trois mouvements perpétuels*.¹¹ This three-part composition was originally written for the piano in 1918 and performed for the first time by Ricardo Viñes in February 1919.¹² A popular phonograph recording was released in 1928, and by the time that Hitchcock's *Rope* appeared two decades later, Poulenc's name was well known in the United States, "where his choral works were more frequently performed than in his native country."¹³ The archives show that Hitchcock was insistent on having Poulenc's music in *Rope* and that a fee of $1500 was paid for the necessary rights.¹⁴

When Poulenc wrote to Ricardo Viñes to ask him to perform the *Mouvements* for the first time, he called the pieces "easy enough for a child to play."¹⁵ The compositions, with their debt to Erik Satie, are certainly brief and might appear to be "easy enough for a child to play," but there is actually, again echoing Satie, a subtle complexity to the first part that makes its place in *Rope* both apt and significant.¹⁶ Scott Paulin offers the following concise description:

> Poulenc's *Mouvement perpétuel* No. 1 is remarkable for its opposition to the norms of classical tonal music—in short for its deviance. Over a moderately paced *ostinato* bass (the "perpetual motion" of the title) Poulenc writes a series of brief, unrelated melodies, some of which are highly chromatic and clash rather dissonantly with the unchanging bass. After a return "home" to the opening theme (Poulenc's one nod to classical form: a recapitulation) the music ebbs away, finally rising to close on a quiet but dissonant tone-cluster. The ending is tentative and inconclusive, and the pleasures of the work are those of momentary harmonic colors and shifts—not of a steadily building tension which is finally and cathartically resolved, as in classical tonal procedures.¹⁷

I will return repeatedly in this book to *Rope*'s incorporation of the first of the *Trois mouvements perpétuels*. What I want to isolate here at this early point are merely the "unresolved" and "dissonant" aspects of the music by Poulenc that runs through the film. I have given this book the title *Perpetual Movement* because one of my central points will be that the qualities of openness and dissonance found in Poulenc's music are also at work in Hitchcock's film. *Rope*, I want to argue, is as unresolved and dissonant as the music that frames it and is played on a number of occasions by one of its main characters. Like the first of the *Mouvements perpétuels*, *Rope* perhaps seems simple enough, straightforward enough: it is, after all, a mainstream Hollywood production with familiar narrative conventions that it is bound to follow. If Poulenc's music is "easy enough for a child to play," that same child could almost certainly understand Hitchcock's film. But appearances are deceptive: Poulenc's composition lets a distinct lack of resolution resonate, and *Rope*, I will argue in the ensuing chapters, follows suit. Hitchcock and Poulenc are a fine match: the *Trois mouvements perpétuels* and *Rope* are made for each other, a perfect couple, even if Poulenc was unaware that his work had been used in the film until he happened to attend a screening of it during his first North American tour in late 1948.¹⁸

## A Whole Book?

My companion on the bus in Malta wanted to know why I was writing an entire book about a single film. Why devote so many pages to just one of Alfred Hitchcock's many works? Why allow a discussion of *Rope* to tie up around 75,000 words of analysis when there are more than fifty other films by Hitchcock calling out for consideration and comparison? ("Six and only six films," writes Murray Pomerance, outlining the scope of *A Dream of Hitchcock* and stressing that "no claim will be found here that I uncover the deeper meanings of Hitchcock the personality, or a blueprint to his vast oeuvre."[19] One and only one film fills my pages, which are similarly uninterested in the personality of the director or a key to his work.) These are fine and fair questions, to which I have two broad responses.

First, while *Rope* has received a significant amount of critical attention over the years, and while some of that criticism has helped radically to reshape the study of Hitchcock's work, there has never been a monograph in English devoted solely to the film. Some of Hitchcock's other productions have found themselves the focus of dedicated volumes, but not *Rope*.[20] *Perpetual Movement*, then, is the first book of its kind, and it makes extensive use of archival material that has been underplayed or overlooked in existing criticism.

Second, and more significant, *Rope* requires space. Allowing my analysis of the film to unfold across an entire book enables me to draw attention to aspects of the film that have until now escaped the gaze of critics. There are many wonderful short discussions of *Rope*—in essays and in sections of books—but there is a textual density to the film that invites and requires extended discussion. *Perpetual Movement* will often engage with earlier analyses of the film, but it offers above all a new contribution to knowledge—one that is only possible in the context of an extended, obsessive discussion. *Rope* is set within a limited space, but critical analysis of the text cannot follow suit if it is to do justice to the tightly coiled richness of the film. Hitchcock "was master of the frame," as Murray Pomerance rightly notes, "and every nuance of his image is vital, no aspect decorative."[21] This book, accordingly, is an attempt, in the words of Roland Barthes, "to live according to nuance."[22] *Rope* does not take up much room, but analysis must.

There is a risk, of course, that my approach will summon shades of Vladimir Nabokov's *Pale Fire*, in which Charles Kinbote's discussion of a cryptic poem by John Shade far outweighs its subject matter and comes ultimately to drown it. In my defense, I would stress that I have no desire to be, in Kinbote's approving phrase, "the commentator who has the last word."[23] Even more laughable is Kinbote's suggestion that the reader consult his commentary before approaching Shade's work, then read the poem with the help of the analysis, and finally consult the critical discussion once again "so as to complete the picture" (p. 18). My attention to *Rope* will be close and precise—this is a work of academic scholarship, after all—but I will also conclude that Hitchcock's film of perpetual movement has the last word.

## *Rope* Guide I

Dante was guided through the realms of the dead by Virgil and Beatrice; I chose T. J. Clark and Roland Barthes to lead me on *la diritta via* through the tangled threads of *Rope*.

*The Sight of Death*, Clark informs us on the opening page of his book, "is not a manifesto."[24] It is, instead, a diary of textual obsession.[25] Clark relates how he arrived in Los Angeles in early January 2000 to take up a six-month position at the Getty Research Institute. The precise purpose of the stay was not apparent to him at the outset: "It was not clear what would occupy my time in Los Angeles, but the most likely bet was Picasso between the wars. Work on that subject had already begun. The notes and books for it were in the back of my car" (p. 1). But "a day or so" into his stay (p. 1), Clark found himself standing in front of two paintings by Nicolas Poussin in the Getty Museum: *Landscape with a Man Killed by a Snake* (1648) and *Landscape with a Calm* (1650–51). He began visiting the artworks repeatedly, taking notes in the form of a diary:

> It was not until several weeks into my note-taking that it dawned on me that the diary entries might make a book. Reading over what I had written then, I realized that if the notes were interesting it was primarily as a record of looking taking place and changing through time. Of course, bound up with that was the assumption, the truth of which I hoped would be demonstrated by the notes, that certain pictures demand such looking and repay it. Coming to terms with them is slow work. But astonishing things happen if one gives oneself over to the process of seeing again and again: aspect after aspect of the picture seems to surface, what is salient and what incidental

alter bewilderingly from day to day, the larger order of the depiction breaks up, recrystallizes, fragments again, persists like an afterimage. And slowly the question arises: What is it, fundamentally, I am returning to in this particular case? What is it I want to see again? (pp. 5–8)

I found myself standing in front of *The Sight of Death* quite by chance some months after my year-long entanglement in *Rope* had begun. While I am fortunate enough never to have suffered from writer's block, I often fall into deep despair while working on a book or even a short essay. Ink flows and fills the pages, yes, but the worth, direction, and dominion of the sentences are uncertain, unclear. "When I have laboured out a story, I suddenly see it in a light of such contemptible triviality," as Edwin Reardon says of his literary efforts in Gissing's *New Grub Street*.[26] I was in one of these states of wandering dejection when I happened to pick up a copy of *The Sight of Death* in a secondhand bookshop. I leafed through its smooth pages, and my eyes fell by chance upon the passage that I have just quoted at length. Looking at paintings is an activity that differs significantly from looking at films, of course, but I realized that Clark's questions about his obsessive returns to Poussin were, in effect, the questions that I had been trying to pose in my daily dealings with Hitchcock's film. *What is it, fundamentally, I am returning to in this particular case? What is it I want to see again?* In this chance encounter, *The Sight of Death* became the site of life, of new life, for my own uncertain undertaking, in which I would give myself over entirely "to the process of seeing again and again."

My conclusions about *Rope* are not the same as Clark's conclusions about Poussin's paintings, and I will sight death before I manage to write a book with the erudite elegance of *The Sight of Death*. But I take from Clark a spellbound interest in "what compels the return" (p. 142)—in what draws the gaze back again and again to a work of art. Around halfway through his analysis, while considering *Landscape with a Man Killed by a Snake,* Clark writes:

> [W]hat I want to talk about is why *Snake* bears repeated looking. Paul Valéry says somewhere that a work of art is defined by the fact that it does not exhaust itself—offer up what it has to offer—on first or second or subsequent reading. Artness is the capacity to invite repeated response. *Snake*, or my experience of *Snake*, is a strong case of that. (p. 115)

*Rope*, or my experience of *Rope*, is a strong case of that, too. Although the film begins and ends with moments at which characters have exhausted themselves, the text, for me, "is defined by the fact that it does not exhaust itself." My analysis of Hitchcock's film in the following chapters wrestles with this "capacity to invite repeated response," this textual tenacity, this open beckoning.

## *Rope* Guide II

On February 8, 1968, Roland Barthes began a new seminar at the École pratique des hautes études in Paris. The title of the course had been advertised in advance as "Recherches sémiologiques: analyse d'ouvrages récents, compte rendu et discussion de travaux en cours" ("Semiological research: analysis of recent publications, account and discussion of works in progress"), but Barthes announced at the start of the first session that he had since undergone a change of heart—as is "normal for all research," he added.[27] The stated title of the seminar, he explained, was now only "partly right":

> *Semiological research*? Yes, still [*toujours*].
>
> *Works in progress*? Maybe, after Easter, if we have time.
>
> *Recent works*? No, unless we decree that the plural is the singular and that the nineteenth century is the twentieth century. (p. 55)

The reference here to the singular gave a clue to the new direction of the seminar: "We will, in effect, *work* [. . .] on a single text and this text belongs to the nineteenth century," Barthes proceeded to explain (p. 55). The work in question was Honoré de Balzac's *Sarrasine*, a novella of around thirty pages, which forms part of the vast *Scènes de la vie parisienne*. The analysis of the tale would, Barthes noted, be slow and nonexhaustive, and it would proceed "*pas à pas*"—step by step (p. 74). He reserved for himself "the right to digression" (p. 75) and spoke of a "drugged reading" in which there would be a heightened sensitivity to the text under analysis (p. 79). The aim was not "deciphering" (p. 76) in the name of "*final* commentary on the work" (p. 79), and there would, Barthes stressed, be "no conclusion, truth, last word on *Sarrasine*" (p. 79). Barthes is no Kinbote.

So slow was the reading of the tale, in fact, that at the end of the seminar in Paris in May 1969, Barthes had made it no further than

*Sarrasine*'s prologue—barely twelve pages of text. The analysis came to a halt, and the seminar disbanded. When it reconvened for the following academic year, its focus was "La notion d'idiolecte: premières questions, premières recherches."[28] But Barthes's engagement with Balzac's narrative was not over: in 1970, he published a book entitled *S/Z*, in which he returned to *Sarrasine*—and finally made it to the end of the curious tale.

*S/Z* begins by denouncing forms of criticism that claim to reveal the truth of a text or, in classic structuralist fashion, attempt "to see all the world's stories (and there have been ever so many) within a single structure."[29] Such approaches, for Barthes, foster "indifference" on account of their ultimate lack of interest in the difference of each text.[30] He adds an immediate clarification:

> This difference is not, obviously, some complete, irreducible quality (according to a mythic view of literary creation), it is not what designates the individuality of each text, what names, signs, finishes off each work with a flourish; on the contrary, it is a difference which does not stop and which is articulated upon the infinity of texts, of languages, of systems: a difference of which each text is the return. (p. 3)

A difference that does not stop. Or, to phrase things differently, perpetual movement.

In *S/Z*, interpretation becomes a matter, not of "establishing a truth," but of "remain[ing] attentive to the plural of a text" (p. 11). The single tale by Balzac over which Barthes's analysis obsesses is, as an example of nineteenth-century realism, "committed to the closure system of the West" (p. 7) and, as such, apparently dissolves the central enigma which drives its narrative. There is a familiar fictional formula at work in *Sarrasine*: mystery is established—who is the little old man at the Lantys' party? what is the source of the family's wealth? who is Sarrasine?—and then, with the closing of the narrative, mystery is replaced by knowledge. The little old man, we learn in time, is La Zambinella, a once-famous castrato; the family wealth comes from La Zambinella's career on the Italian stage; and the figure who gives his name to the tale was a man who died for the love of La Zambinella. *Fin*.

But things are not quite what they seem. Balzac's apparently formulaic tale is, Barthes's painstaking analysis establishes, actually a story in which categories are undecidable, in which revelation occurs alongside reservation, in which narrative closure never quite comes. There is, contrary to first impressions, a disruptive plurality at work in *Sarrasine*. This plurality is "parsimonious" (p. 6), Barthes acknowledges, and is clearly not the kind of explicit undecidability found in the modernist fictions that took issue with realism—but it is a plurality nonetheless. To read *Sarrasine* as a story in which complete closure is achieved and all enigmas evaporate would be, *S/Z* concludes, to overlook the quietly nuanced complexity of the text.

Hitchcock's *Rope* is, like *Sarrasine*, a well-wrought case of realism. As a mainstream Hollywood production, it is required to move towards closure and resolution. The questions posed at the start of the film—will the terrible crime be discovered? will the body in the wooden chest be exposed? what was the motive for the murder? will the killers face justice?—are answered by the time that we reach the final reel. There is revelation, exposure of the truth, and, just before the final credits roll, the sound of the police approaching the apartment in which the killing has occurred. There is, in short, conventional closure: *Rope*, in spite of its striking formal innovations (to which I will turn in time), could not really be called an explicitly avant-garde film in terms of its narrative measure and movement.

But Barthes's *S/Z* watches over the pages of my book because the central argument of *Perpetual Movement* will be that *Rope*, like Balzac's *Sarrasine*, has a "parsimonious plurality," a subtle tendency to undo the categories and conventions upon which it nonetheless relies. Alongside the dramatic revelation and the classical closure, there are, I want to propose, ways in which the film tells another tale—a tale in which viewers are reminded repeatedly of the *limits* of their knowledge; a tale in which categories are unsettled; a tale in which an opening undecidability stems confident certainty.

Barthes draws out the muted openness of *Sarrasine* by breaking Balzac's text into 561 small pieces—*lexias*, he calls them—and reading these units in order to establish how "everything signifies ceaselessly and several times, but without being delegated to a great final ensemble, to an ultimate structure."[31] "If we want to remain attentive to the plural of a text (however limited it may be)," Barthes proposes, "we must renounce structuring this text in large masses, as was done by classical rhetoric and by secondary-school explication" (pp. 11–12). I remain persuaded by this approach, which Barthes elsewhere called "microanalysis," and I wondered while planning this book if I should divide *Rope* into hundreds of brief fragments for examination.[32] I quickly realized, however, that Hitchcock's film, unlike Balzac's novella, has a textual form that suggests a convenient way in which to separate the text for consideration: it is already divided, in effect, into eleven lexias.

## Form

Don DeLillo once called the family "the cradle of the world's misinformation." "There must," he added, "be something in family life that generates factual error."[33] It seems to me that DeLillo's claim also applies to discussions of Alfred Hitchcock's *Rope*, which repeatedly contain glaring errors about the form of the film. D. A. Miller, one of the very finest readers of *Rope*, summarizes the situation beautifully:

> The technical originality of Alfred Hitchcock's *Rope* has been so little neglected by serious-minded criticism that the latter may be considered almost definitively shaped by a ritual of recounting and assessing the director's desire to do the film, as he put it, "in a single shot," or at any rate, as nearly without benefit of montage as the state of the art allowed in 1948, when a camera only held ten minutes' worth of film. Yet this technicist bias has proven to be curiously distracted by the very shooting technique on which it elects to concentrate. For one thing, contrary to all reasonable expectations, it has hardly managed to generate a single accurate account of the technique in question. Again and again, for instance, we are told that each shot in *Rope* runs to ten minutes, whereas the shots range variously from roughly three to nine minutes; or that Hitchcock blackened out the action every time he changed cameras, though only five of *Rope*'s ten cuts are managed this way. It is as though *Rope* criticism aimed less at a description than at a correction of Hitchcock's experiment, for whose irregularities and inconsistencies there is substituted a programmatic perfection that better supports the dream of a continuous film (not yet to mention whatever wishes might find fulfillment in that dream) than Hitchcock's actual shooting practice.[34]

Given the strangely stubborn nature of such errors, it seems sensible to restate Miller's corrections here in as clear and prosaic a way as possible.[35] If the mistakes have been repeated over and over again, I can see no harm in rearticulating the reality; "I like people who face facts," as Uncle Charlie puts it in Hitchcock's *Shadow of a Doubt* (1943).[36] These, then, without a doubt, are the facts about the form of *Rope*:

- *Rope* was neither filmed in one take nor made to appear as if it were filmed in one take. Hitchcock might have had, as he once told François Truffaut, a "crazy idea to do it in a single shot," but such a thing was, as D.A. Miller points out in the quotation above, technically impossible in 1948.[37]

- *Rope* consists of eleven separate shots which range in length from roughly two-and-a-half minutes to nearly ten minutes.

- Half of the ten cuts between these eleven shots are "masked," in that there is some kind of attempt to hide the fact that a break in filming has occurred, but the other five cuts are perfectly regular, perfectly obvious. The ten cuts, whose style alternates, occur at the following moments:

    1. 0:02:24 (hard cut)
    2. 0:11:34 (masked cut)
    3. 0:19:06 (hard cut)
    4. 0:26:06 (masked cut)
    5. 0:32:58 (hard cut)
    6. 0:42:31 (masked cut)
    7. 0:49:49 (hard cut)
    8. 0:57:17 (masked cut)
    9. 1:06:59 (hard cut)
    10. 1:11:26 (masked cut)[38]

Critics writing in the years during which *Rope* was, for contractual reasons, withheld from general circulation can perhaps be forgiven for their oversights—they were, after all, working in the dark, from memory.[39] But anyone who writes about the film in our era of easy access and *still* claims that *Rope* is, or appears to be, one continuous shot is guilty of careless, casual scholarship.

Because *Rope* has an unusually small number of component pieces (Hitchcock's *Rear Window*, by way of comparison, contains nearly 800 shots), I have let the form of the film determine the form of this book, which, after this introduction, unfolds across eleven chapters—one for each shot.[40] In this respect, I have stuck with the plan that Geoff Dyer rejected when writing his brilliant, obsessive book on Andrei Tarkovsky's *Stalker* (1979)—another film, ultimately, about what happens in a room. "I had intended," Dyer explains:

> breaking this little book into 142 sections—each separated from the once preceding and following it by a double space—corresponding to the 142 shots of the film. That's a very low number of shots for a long film and it worked well at first but then, as I became engrossed and re-engrossed in the film, I kept losing track of where one shot ended and another began.[41]

I can see precisely why Dyer abandoned this approach, but *Rope* is considerably shorter than *Stalker* and, moreover, contains far fewer than 142 shots. I have, therefore, followed Dyer into a zone from which he retreated—and I have kept going. I will sometimes refer backwards and forwards, narratively speaking, in a given chapter—anything else would have been woundingly hermetic—but will for most of the time keep the focus of each part of the book trained obsessively upon its corresponding shot in Hitchcock's film. *Perpetual Movement*, in this respect, is a gradual movement through Hitchcock's film—*pas à pas*, as Barthes puts it. In the language of *S/Z*, I have treated *Rope* as a series of eleven ready-made lexias. When Barthes divided *Sarrasine* into 561 small units of analysis, he found himself having to choose at which points to "cut" the prose for inspection.[42] "This cutting up, admittedly," he added, was "arbitrary in the extreme" (p. 13). I, however, did not have to contend with such arbitrary impositions: I have cut my book where the film cuts; the filmic lexias were already apparent, already marked out in the fiction. *Rope* is roped off from the outset into eleven sections. Form follows form. "Form is everything," as a fictional Robert Frost puts it in Tobias Wolff's *Old School*.[43]

Introductions to academic monographs habitually conclude with summaries of the chapters that follow. Here, however, given the way in which the structure of the study mimics the structure of the film under analysis, there is little point in my offering a chapter-by-chapter overview. Chapter 1 addresses shot 1, chapter 2 considers shot 2, and so on. To continue in this vein would be laughably tautological (though I will point out here that most of the production history of *Rope* can be found in chapter 1).

I will, instead, bring this introduction to a close by returning to the heart of my project, to the desire that animates and orients each of the following chapters. My obsessively close analysis is driven by a wish to understand what it is in *Rope* that, in the words of T. J. Clark, "compels the return." This requires the use of a magnifying glass at times, but the aim is not, as Pascal put it long ago, to magnify small objects with fantastic exaggeration.[44] I have written to give an account of my time, of my curious year spent with and within *Rope*. But I have also written because my extended, obsessive engagement with this single text brought to light overlooked details and cast new light upon why Hitchcock's film will not release us from its hold. I have written, then, to describe how desire remains on the wing. This is a tale both of being held by *Rope* and of perpetual movement.

# 1

# Operation *Rope*[1]

## Transatlantic

As *Rope*'s first shot contains the opening credits, in which key figures involved in the making of the film are named, it seems sensible to devote much of chapter 1 of this book to production history. In the pages that follow, I will make extensive use of archival material to draw out elements of the film's history that have remained unknown, underdiscussed, or utterly misrepresented for over seven decades.

*Rope* was Alfred Hitchcock's first color production and also his first film since his contract of employment with David O. Selznick had come to an end.[2] Selznick had brought Hitchcock to Hollywood from Britain at the end of the 1930s, but their professional partnership—which began with *Rebecca* (1940) and ended with *The Paradine Case* (1947)—favored Selznick financially and creatively; Patrick McGilligan sums things up neatly when he refers to Hitchcock's "professional subservience" in the working relationship.[3] Hitchcock therefore chose not to renew his contract with Selznick once he had fulfilled its legal requirements. Even though he had been allowed to work for others while employed by Selznick, Hitchcock wanted greater creative freedom, and so, with the end of his contract in sight, he founded the independent Transatlantic Pictures with Sidney Bernstein, a prominent figure in the British film industry.[4] The deeds relating to Transatlantic were signed in early February 1946, making Bernstein's partnership with Hitchcock a legal reality, but the friendship between the two figures went back as far as the first half of the 1920s, when both were involved with the London Film Society, which Bernstein had helped to found.[5] Although Bernstein had known David Selznick since roughly the same period, he and Hitchcock began to plan their professional partnership while the latter was still employed by Selznick.[6] The initial suggestion came from Hitchcock in late spring 1945; Bernstein was at first reluctant, but soon changed his mind and accepted the invitation.[7]

At around this time, with the war still underway, Bernstein had proposed to the Treasury in London "a series of filmed plays, shot on stage and using an entire battery of cameras, featuring the best British actors and the masterpieces of British drama, largely as a propaganda exercise and to capture some of the excellent productions that John Gielgud was then staging at Stratford."[8] These plans came to nothing, but a clear trace of them can be seen in Transatlantic's inaugural production.[9] When Hitchcock and Bernstein met to discuss "the subject and nature of their first film, Hitchcock suggested to Sidney that they experiment with the technique of filming and try using single long shots, each of them the length of a full reel."[10] Bernstein was persuaded, mainly because Hitchcock informed him that such an approach would make for quick and relatively inexpensive shooting, and in time they settled on an adaptation of Patrick Hamilton's three-act play *Rope*. Hitchcock would direct, Bernstein would act as producer, and the film would, as I will explain later in this chapter, be distributed by Warner Bros.[11]

## Source(s)

Prior to the premiere of the play at the Strand Theatre, London, in March 1929, Patrick Hamilton was "a young novelist [. . .] [with] a small readership," as one of his biographers puts it.[12] But *Rope* was a major success and, along with the almost simultaneous publication of *The Midnight Bell*, it transformed Hamilton into a "public figure."[13] "I am known, established, pursued. The world, truly, is at my feet," he wrote to his brother in late May 1929.[14]

The play tells the tale of two young men, Wyndham Brandon and Charles Granillo, who murder their friend Ronald Kentley, hide his corpse in a wooden chest in their Mayfair flat, and throw a house party while the body is still within the trunk. The play unfolds in real time over the course of a single evening—"NB: The action is continuous, and the fall of the curtain at the end of each Act denotes the lapse of no time whatever," the stage directions stress—and builds to the discovery of the crime by Rupert Cadell, a somewhat eccentric poet who comes to suspect that all is not well in the flat.[15]

But if Hamilton's play is the immediate source of Hitchcock's film, it too has a source of its own. In May 1924, a little under five years before *Rope* was first performed on stage, two young and wealthy students at the University of Chicago, Nathan Leopold and Richard Loeb, kidnapped and murdered a fourteen-year-old boy named Robert Franks. Acid was poured over the genitals and face of the corpse, which was then buried in a culvert. Influenced by Nietzsche and seeing themselves as intellectually superior to others, Leopold and Loeb believed that they had planned and perpetrated "the perfect crime," but they were soon caught and charged. Their attorney, Clarence Darrow, persuaded them to enter a plea of guilty and thus avoid trial by jury, but the resulting legal proceedings nonetheless became a huge media spectacle; Hitchcock, Patrick McGilligan reports, followed the case with interest.[16] There were only one hundred seats available to the public in the court, but three thousand people tried every day to gain access to what was often called "The Trial of the Century" (even if it was not technically a trial). Leopold and Loeb managed to avoid the death penalty and were sentenced instead to life plus ninety-nine years. Loeb was killed in prison in 1936, but Leopold was released on parole for good behavior in 1958 and spent the rest of his days in Puerto Rico, where he died in 1971.[17]

Patrick Hamilton insisted that he had not been influenced by the Leopold and Loeb case. "It has been said," he wrote in a preface to a 1929 edition of the play, "that I have founded 'Rope' on a murder which was committed in America some years ago. But this is not so, since I cannot recall this crime having ever properly reached my consciousness until after 'Rope' was written and people began to tell me of it."[18] This claim is, as Sean French so neatly puts it, "simply not credible": if Hitchcock's *Rope* leads back to Hamilton's *Rope*, then the latter leads firmly further back to Leopold and Loeb.[19]

A trace of the real-life murder in Illinois surfaced during the making of the film, in fact. On February 20, 1948, while shooting was still underway, Barney Balaban of Paramount Pictures wrote to Harry Warner to report that a friend of his, Hugo Sonnenschein, had been contacted by Allen and Ernie Loeb. They had, Balaban related, heard about the new Hitchcock film that was in production with Warner Bros. and were, as relatives of Richard Loeb, worried about the distress that allusions to the Leopold and Loeb case could cause; they were also concerned that *Rope* might stir up antisemitism when released. (The murderers of Robert Franks were both Jewish.) Balaban's letter proceeded to urge Warner Bros., on Sonnenschein's behalf, to eliminate all direct invocations of the Leopold and Loeb case and to minimize allusions to Jews. Harry Warner passed Balaban's note to his brother Jack, who replied to Balaban on March 5, 1948. Hitchcock himself, he reported, had insisted that *Rope* had nothing to do with the murder of Robert Franks and that there were no Jewish characters at all in the film. Had the studio known of the echoes of the Leopold and Loeb case, Warner added, they would never have become involved with the project, but the film was now finished, and Warner Bros. had, he explained, a financial interest in it. On March 23, 1948, Balaban wrote back to say that Mr. and Mrs. Sonnenschein had recently attended a preview screening of *Rope*. They were pleased with what they saw.[20]

## Adaptation

Hitchcock enjoyed the original stage production of *Rope* in London in 1929 and immediately took an interest in directing an adaptation for the screen.[21] This came to nothing at the time, though he approached Patrick Hamilton in 1936 "to see if he had any interest in writing a film script for him" and then turned down the chance to direct a screen version of Hamilton's play *Gas Light* in 1942.[22] Sidney Bernstein was also impressed by Hamilton's play on stage, and it was eventually decided, as Transatlantic Pictures began to take shape, that *Rope* would be its first production.[23] Hitchcock's fee for directing was $150,000.[24] On March 20, 1947, Hamilton signed two contracts with Transatlantic. The first gave Hitchcock and Bernstein, for the price of £6500, the rights to film an adaptation of *Rope*. The second employed the writer for ten weeks to work on the project, traveling from the UK to the USA if necessary; for this, Hamilton would be paid £3000 (at a rate of £300 per week).[25] He began the process of adapting his play and visited Sidney Bernstein regularly at his apartment in Arlington House, in London's St. James's; further meetings took place at the Transatlantic offices.[26] Finding adaptation far more difficult than writing the original play, however, Hamilton ended up going on a "three-week drinking binge" and was sent to a nursing home suffering from alcoholic gastritis.[27]

Before that, in September 1946, Hitchcock had written to the Production Code Administration (PCA) in Hollywood to enquire about censorship issues that might affect Transatlantic's planned screen version of *Rope*. He enclosed a copy of Hamilton's original play with his letter to Joseph Breen, asking if it met the censors' general requirements.[28] Breen replied five days later to say that, while the play appeared to be broadly in keeping with the Production Code, it would be necessary, "in view of the very macabre basis of this murder mystery," for the script as whole to "stress very thoroughly the full compensating moral values necessary for the treatment of such a story on the screen." More specifically, Breen added, the play's "derisive" treatment of the Ten Commandments would need to be deleted, and he also urged Hitchcock to reduce the play's many references to the drinking of alcohol.[29] Breen's letter ended by inviting Hitchcock to send the screenplay to the PCA for consideration when it was ready.

Readiness took a while. After his initial period of collaborating with Sidney Bernstein on the adaptation, Patrick Hamilton learned in autumn 1947 that his contract with Transatlantic had been terminated.[30] (His name would appear in *Rope*'s credits when the film was eventually released in 1948, but he was so "appalled" by what he saw in a cinema in Britain in 1949 that he "got drunk and became depressed."[31]) With Hamilton out of the picture, the task of adapting the play for the screen fell first to Hume Cronyn (who produced a treatment) and then, more substantially, to Arthur Laurents, who was instructed by Hitchcock to "totally Americanize the play."[32] Laurents's retrospective account of the adaptation process makes light of Cronyn's involvement:

> On the screen, there is a credit to Hume Cronyn for his adaptation of the play. My agent, Irving (Swifty) Lazar, had to stop him from claiming credit for writing the screenplay in publicity interviews but I'm not even sure what the adaptation credit means; I was never shown what Hume did. I suspect, since he and Hitchcock were old friends, that he was used to help work out the details of Hitchcock's innovative plan to shoot *Rope* without any conventional cutting.[33]

Cronyn's own memoir, which was published nearly a decade earlier than Laurents's *Original Story By*, offers a slightly different version of events:

> [Hitchcock] wanted me to help him prepare a screen treatment of the Patrick Hamilton play *Rope*, a story based on the infamous Loeb-Leopold murder of a young man in Chicago. But why me? I had no screenwriter credits. A couple of my short stories had been published; I'd written and sold a screenplay that was never made and that I doubt he ever saw. Perhaps he just wanted someone to talk to, to use as a sounding board for his ideas. Whatever his reasons, I wasn't about to question an offer that almost any screenwriter would have jumped at. [. . .]
>
> I should make it clear that on both *Rope* and *[Under] Capricorn* I wrote only the "treatments." The screenplays were written by Arthur Laurents and James Bridie, respectively. I never knew Arthur well, but Bridie [. . .] became a great friend.[34]

Cronyn's book is no more precise than this about the nature of his contribution, however. Donald Spoto calls it a "prose treatment" but offers no further details, while Hitchcock, speaking to François Truffaut in 1962, said only that "Arthur Laurents did the screenplay and Hume Cronyn worked with me on the adaptation. The dialogue was partly from the original play and partly by Laurents."[35] There is no trace of Cronyn's treatment or his contract of employment with Transatlantic in either of the two relevant Hitchcock archives in California.

By November 22, 1947, Arthur Laurents had produced a full draft of the screenplay.[36] On December 1, Fred Ahern, production manager at Transatlantic, dispatched a copy to Joseph Breen at the PCA, reminding him of the earlier correspondence with Hitchcock in September 1946, and asking for a quick reply so that construction of the set could proceed.[37] Stephen S. Jackson of the PCA replied two weeks later and began his letter by referring to a meeting that had taken place recently at the Transatlantic offices in Los Angeles between Ahern and Vincent Peers (for Transatlantic) and, representing the PCA, Geoffrey Shurlock, Milton Hodenfield, and Jackson himself.[38] The event had been a "pleasant conference," Jackson recalled, but he went on to outline the censors' reservations about the script. "We stated," he wrote, "that we had some apprehension lest the picture come through as a dramatization of the perverted and distorted emotional enjoyment on a sadistic level by the psychopathic personality portrayed by Brandon." He then addressed an issue that had apparently not caught the eye of Breen's office on receipt of Patrick Hamilton's play in 1946: "a possible flavour in some of the dialogue that a homosexual relationship existed between Brandon and Phillip." This hint was, Jackson added immediately, "heightened somewhat by the fact that there is some degree of similarity between these two characters and Leopold and Loeb [. . .] We pointed out that such a treatment could not be acceptable under the terms of the Production Code."[39]

Ahern and Peers had clearly been eager to placate the representatives of the PCA at the meeting, for Jackson's letter went on to note that the censors had been pleased to hear during the discussions that Transatlantic would amend any dialogue implying same-sex relations and that the narrative emphasis would fall on the "intellectual phase" instead of "the emotional reaction" of the two main characters. Echoing Breen's letter to Hitchcock in September 1946, Jackson urged the filmmakers to be restrained in their references to alcohol. He signed off by encouraging Transatlantic to send a revised script to the PCA for consideration.

Arthur Laurents produced an amended screenplay the following day, and, on December 17, 1947, Fred Ahern forwarded what he called "the revised final shooting script" to the PCA, adding in his covering letter that filming was ready to begin and that a swift response would therefore be appreciated.[40] Jackson wrote back on December 22, informing Ahern that "the basic story seems to meet the requirements of the Production Code"[41] but also identifying a series of issues:

1. The strangling of David Kentley at the beginning of the film could not be shown in detail but should be done instead "even more by suggestion than it now is."[42]

2. The way in which Brandon wipes the glass from which David took his last drink, implying that he is removing fingerprints, was "unacceptable and should be omitted."[43]

3. Brandon's reference to the "exciting" nature of the inability to lock the wooden chest containing David's body implies a "perverted emotional reaction to the crime" and should therefore be altered; the PCA suggested the word "dangerous" as a suitable substitution.[44]

4. The phrase "We have a lovely excuse" should be amended in order to avoid "a questionable inference concerning the characters of Brandon and Phillip."[45]

5. There was still far too much emphasis upon alcohol in the screenplay. Jackson's letter identified ten offending pages and suggested that the filmmakers refer instead to *hors d'oeuvres* or "some such other prop" at these points.[46]

Further changes to the script were made in the light of Jackson's letter, and Fred Ahern sent the revised version, with the altered text on pink pages dated January 13, 1948, to the PCA on January 19; the archives show that it was received there two days later.[47] Ahern's covering letter articulated a sense of confidence that all the necessary amendments had now been made. Indeed, rehearsals for *Rope* had begun on January 12—a full week before Ahern dispatched the reworked screenplay to the PCA. But Jackson was not quite persuaded: his reply, dated January 23, complained yet again about the place of alcohol in the script.[48] Ahern responded the next day and opened his letter by saying that he appreciated Jackson's perspective and that Transatlantic was eager to avoid "any pitfalls." He then, having pointed out that Hitchcock was "photographing the picture one reel at a time without any cuts," observed that it could be "calamitous" to wait until the film was finished before seeking approval from the censors.[49] Perhaps, he continued, the PCA would be willing to scrutinize the first reel immediately for "any objectionable feature," with the completed movie then to be submitted for formal consideration in the usual way when the time came. Ahern ended by promising to telephone Jackson on Monday January 26 to receive the PCA's decision about this unusual request. The archives do not record the outcome of this conversation.

## Production #358; or, Rehearsing the Camera

Because Transatlantic Pictures had no production facilities of its own, it rented studio space for filming *Rope* from Warner Bros. in Burbank, California. The 57-page contract between the two parties was signed on January 6, 1948 and specified, among other things, that

- Warner Bros. would advance $250,000 towards the cost of production and would distribute the finished film.

- Transatlantic would borrow a further $500,000, with the help of Warner Bros. if necessary.

- The film's budget should not exceed $750,000, excluding a deferred sum of $600,000, and Warner Bros. reserved the right to seize control of production if expenditure should exceed $952,000 or if the film was not completed by July 1, 1948.

- The choice of writers, cast members, cutting, and editing lay with Transatlantic.

- Warner Bros. would own the rights to distribute *Rope* for ten years and would keep 20 percent of gross receipts in the USA, Canada, UK, and Ireland, and 25 percent of receipts from other territories.[50]

*Rope*—or production #358, as it was known internally—was filmed on Stage 12 at the Warner Bros. studio, with Stages 11 and 14 reserved for rehearsals and the recording of wild sound, respectively.[51] The set was built to accommodate a complex collision of technical demands: the film would be shot in Technicolor with a large camera that Bill Krohn neatly describes as a "square monster"; it was to consist of just eleven shots, some of which were nearly ten minutes long; and almost all of the action was to take place within a single apartment, around which the bulky camera would need to glide smoothly.[52] In a special photographic production notebook published by Warner Bros. in 1948, Hitchcock discussed the technical feat:

> Whole sides of the apartment slide away, and the camera follows the actors as they move through the apartment. In order to achieve successful production of this unique technique, a simplified method of securing dolly shots without crane, boom, or tracks was devised. [. . .] Truly, this could be termed "Operation Rope."[53]

The camera and the walls of the apartment were not the only things that could move, moreover: the furniture was mounted on rollers so that it could be wheeled out of the way when not in shot to make space for the crew and equipment.[54] "Tables and chairs had to be pulled away by prop men," Hitchcock explained to readers of *Popular Photography* in November 1948, "then set in place again by the time the camera returned to its original position, since the camera was on a special crane, not on tracks, and designed to roll through everything like a juggernaut."[55]

Hitchcock seemed to be most proud of all, however, of an aspect of the set that lay outside the apartment:

> [T]he most magical of all the devices was the cyclorama—an exact miniature reproduction of nearly 35 miles of New York skyline lighted by 8,000 incandescent bulbs and 200 neon signs requiring 150 transformers.
>
> On film, the miniature looks exactly Manhattan at night as it would appear from the window of an apartment at 54th Street and First Avenue [. . .]. And since all the major action of *Rope* takes place in the living room of this apartment, with the spectators constantly viewing the background, it was impossible to use process shots or a backdrop. Both would have been too flat. We had to remember the core of the arc of view. So we had to employ the scale cyclorama and devise a "light organ" that not only would light the miniature and its panorama of buildings, but also could give us changing sky and cloud effects varying from sunset to dark—all seen from the apartment—to denote the passing of time.
>
> In the 12,000 square feet of the cyclorama, the largest backing ever used on a sound stage, the spectator sees the Empire State, the Chrysler, and the Woolworth buildings; St. Patrick's, Radio City, and hundreds of other landmarks [. . .]. Each miniature building was wired separately for globes ranging from 25 to 150 watts in the tiny windows. [. . .] Twenty-six thousand feet of wire carried 126,000 watts of power for the building and window illumination—all controlled by the twist of an electrician's wrist, via a bank of 47 switches, as he sat at the light organ high up and far behind the camera.[56]

Three elements of the remarkable cyclorama posed particular problems for the crew: smoke, steam, and clouds. In the name of realism, bursts of smoke and steam were released from the chimneys of the miniature buildings, but it was quickly discovered that "the vapor left [. . .] too fast and rose too high for accurate perspective."[57] The problem was solved by one of the prop men, who placed dry ice onto the pipes as a retardant. "After that," Hitchcock reported, "the smoke trailed lazily into the sky at a rate of speed that was wholly in proportion to the size of the buildings in the miniature."[58] The quest for persuasive clouds, meanwhile, led Hitchcock to reject painting or projecting them onto the cyclorama or the backdrop; cotton was also ruled out because of how it looked underneath the studio lights.[59] In the end, "[f]ive hundred pounds of spun glass were woven by scenic artists into chicken wire moulds"; these were then suspended and moved slightly after each reel of the film had been shot.[60] For accuracy's sake, meteorological advice was sought from Dr. Dinsmore Alter of the Griffith Observatory in Los Angeles.[61]

The way in which *Rope* was filmed required extremely careful planning, as Hitchcock explained:

> *Rope* was a miracle of cueing. [. . .] Even before the set was built I worked out each movement on a blackboard in my home. Then in the studio, the stage (actually a stage within a stage, made noiseless by constructing a special floor one and one-half inch above the regular one, soundproofed with layers of Celotex and carpet) was marked with numbered circles. These indicated where each specific camera stop had to be made, and when.[62]

To make this complex choreography manageable, George Munaw, a grip on the production, would point a long bamboo stick at a number on the floor when cued by the script supervisor. This was the prompt for Morris Rosen, the head grip, to move the camera to its new position while the focus puller working on the crane adjusted the lens accordingly.[63] From a technical perspective, *Rope* was, for Hitchcock, "probably the most exciting picture I've ever directed."[64] James Stewart, however, was a little less impressed: Arthur Laurents reports in his autobiography that, at a carefully controlled press conference, the actor suddenly declared that "The only thing that's been rehearsed around here is the camera."[65]

Rehearsals, in fact, took up a fair amount of time at the Warner Bros. studio. As the production of *Rope* is often recounted incorrectly, it seems sensible to outline here, for the very first time in print, precisely how each day on set unfolded between January 12 and February 21, 1948 as the cast and crew progressed from rehearsals to filming. The table that follows is based upon careful scrutiny of the studio's daily production and progress reports from 1948 that are preserved in the Warner Bros. Archive in Los Angeles.[66]

| DATE | ACTIVITY | NOTES |
|---|---|---|
| January 12, 1948 | Rehearsal, 10 a.m.–6 p.m. | Pages 1–21 of the script rehearsed (reels 1 and 2). All cast except Dick Hogan and Cedric Hardwicke present. Hitchcock present 10 a.m.–6 p.m. |
| January 13, 1948 | Rehearsal, 9 a.m.–10 p.m. | Pages 21–32 of the script rehearsed (reel 3). Whole cast dismissed at 4.15 p.m. |
| January 14, 1948 | Rehearsal, 9 a.m.–10 p.m. | Pages 30–43 of the script rehearsed (reels 3 and 4). Cast dismissed at different times between 6 p.m. and 7 p.m. |
| January 15, 1948 | Rehearsal, 9 a.m.–6 p.m. | Pages 36–59 of the script rehearsed (reels 3 and 4). Cedric Hardwicke dimissed at 5.25 p.m.; rest of the cast dismissed at 6 p.m. |
| January 16, 1948 | Rehearsal, 9 a.m.–5.30 p.m. | Pages 56–74 of the script rehearsed (reels 6 and 7). |
| January 17, 1948 | Rehearsal, 9 a.m.–3 p.m. | Pages 74–85 of the script rehearsed (reels 7 and 8). |
| January 18, 1948 | DAY OFF | |
| January 19, 1948 | Technicolor make-up tests, 9 a.m.–5 p.m. | |
| January 20, 1948 | Rehearsal and set backing tests, 9 a.m.–6.20 p.m. | Rehearsal on Stage 11; set tests on Stage 12. No information available about precisely what was rehearsed on this day. |
| January 21, 1948 | Rehearsal, 9 a.m.–6.20 p.m. | Pages 1–12 of the script rehearsed (reel 1). Dick Hogan present on set for the first time. |
| January 22, 1948 | Rehearsal and shooting, 9 a.m.–6.35 p.m. | Pages 1–11 of the script shot (reel 1). Shooting began at 4.20 p.m. First two takes interrupted after 5 minutes and 4 minutes, respectively. Third take completed the shot in 8 minutes and 50 seconds. No information available about precisely what was rehearsed on this day. |
| January 23, 1948 | Rehearsal, 9 a.m.–5.45 p.m. | Pages 10–24 of the script rehearsed (reel 2). Camera blimp struck overhead door section, resulting in the breaking of gears in the camera head; company therefore dismissed early. |
| January 24, 1948 | Shooting, 9 a.m.–6.40 p.m. | Pages 12–21 of the script shot (reel 2). |

| DATE | ACTIVITY | NOTES |
|---|---|---|
| January 25, 1948 | DAY OFF | |
| January 26, 1948 | Rehearsal, 9 a.m.–6 p.m. | Pages 24–35 of the script rehearsed (reel 3). |
| January 27, 1948 | Shooting, 9 a.m.–8 p.m. | Pages 25–35 of the script shot (reel 3). |
| January 28, 1948 | Rehearsal, 9 a.m.–6 p.m. | Pages 36–46 of the script rehearsed (reel 4). |
| January 29, 1948 | Shooting, 9 a.m.–6.55 p.m. | Pages 36–46 of the script shot (reel 4). |
| January 30, 1948 | Shooting and rehearsal, 9 a.m.–6 p.m. | Pages 36–46 of the script shot (reel 4). Pages 47–56 rehearsed (reel 5). |
| January 31, 1948 | Shooting, 9 a.m.–6.45 p.m. | Pages 47–56 of the script shot (reel 5). |
| February 1, 1948 | DAY OFF | |
| February 2, 1948 | Rehearsal, 9 a.m.–6.10 p.m. | Pages 57–66 of the script rehearsed (reel 6). |
| February 3, 1948 | Shooting, 9 a.m.–6.40 p.m. | Pages 57–66 of the script shot (reel 6). |
| February 4, 1948 | Rehearsal, 9 a.m.–6.10 p.m. | Pages 66–77 of the script rehearsed (reel 7). |
| February 5, 1948 | Shooting, 9 a.m.–6.45 p.m. | Pages 66–77 of the script shot (reel 7). |
| February 6, 1948 | Shooting, 9 a.m.–6.40 p.m. | Retake of pp. 36–46 of the script shot (reel 4). |
| February 7, 1948 | Shooting, 9 a.m.–6 p.m. | Retake of pp. 36–46 of the script shot (reel 4). |
| February 8, 1948 | DAY OFF | |
| February 9, 1948 | Shooting, 9 a.m.–6.30 p.m. | Retake of pp. 47–56 of the script shot (reel 5). |
| February 10, 1948 | Shooting, 9 a.m.–7.55 p.m. | Retake of pp. 24–35 of the script shot (reel 3). Close-up footage of Joan Chandler, Constance Collier, and Cedric Hardwicke also shot on this day for use in the film's trailer. |

*continued on next page*

| DATE | ACTIVITY | NOTES |
|---|---|---|
| February 11, 1948 | Rehearsal, 9 a.m.–6 p.m. | Pages 78–87 of the script rehearsed (reel 8). |
| February 12, 1948 | Shooting and rehearsal, 9 a.m.–5.45 p.m. | Pages 78–87 of the script rehearsed and shot (reel 8). |
| February 13, 1948 | Shooting, 9 a.m.–6.15 p.m. | Pages 78–87 of the script shot (reel 8). |
| February 14, 1948 | Shooting, 9 a.m.–5.55 p.m. | Pages 78–87 of the script shot (reel 8). |
| February 15, 1948 | DAY OFF | |
| February 16, 1948 | Shooting, 9 a.m.–6.15 p.m. | Pages 87–92 of the script shot (reel 9). |
| February 17, 1948 | Shooting, 9 a.m.–6 p.m. | Pages 87–92 of the script shot (reel 9). |
| February 18, 1948 | Shooting and rehearsal, 9 a.m.–5.40 p.m. | Pages 93–95 of the script rehearsed and shot (reel 10). |
| February 19, 1948 | Shooting, 9 a.m.–6.40 p.m. | Pages 93–95 of the script shot (reel 10). Close-up footage of James Stewart also shot on this day for use in the film's trailer.[67] |
| February 20, 1948 | Shooting, 9 a.m.–9.10 p.m. | Retake of pp. 1–11 of the script shot (reel 1). Dick Hogan back on set today for this filming. |
| February 21, 1948 | Shooting, 9 a.m.–7.50 p.m. | Retake of pp. 12–24 of the script shot (reel 2). End of principal photography. |

## Release

Because *Rope* consisted of just eleven shots whose order was unchangeable, there was no need for a lengthy period of editing once filming came to an end on February 21, 1948: the movie was, as Hitchcock put it in conversation with François Truffaut, "in a sense, pre-cut."[68] The completed film was therefore ready for viewing by the censors as early as March 16 and was passed for general circulation without cuts, even though the PCA's typed assessment described Brandon as a "Psychopathic Young Man" and noted that there was (still) "Much display of liquor."[69] The official certificate of approval—number 13027—was sent to Victor Peers at Transatlantic on March 22.[70]

This was, however, by no means the end of *Rope*'s involvement with censors. Although the PCA had passed the film for release without alteration, some local censorship boards in the USA were less welcoming. *Rope* was banned in Spokane (WA), Seattle, Atlanta, Memphis, Worcester (MA), and New Bedford (MA), for instance, while Chicago imposed an initial ban before deciding instead to issue the film with an adult permit. Cuts, meanwhile, were required in Maryland, Ohio, and Pennsylvania.[71] The troubles continued abroad: *Rope* was initially banned outright in Germany, Italy, India, Holland, and was still prohibited in Germany as late as 1963 (presumably because of its allusions to Nazism).[72] In Canada, cuts were required in Toronto and Saskatchewan, while Vancouver and Calgary imposed an adult permit; Québec took a slightly different approach and added a written foreword in which "false and pagan doctrines" were denounced.[73] Finally, in the UK a preface headed "THOU SHALT NOT KILL" was inserted, and eighteen feet of film were trimmed from the first reel to remove the strangulation of David Kentley.[74]

Following preview screenings for the press, *Rope* received its official premiere in New York on August 26, 1948.[75] (By this time, Hitchcock was at work on the next Translantic film, *Under Capricorn*, at Elstree Studios in England.[76]) The release of the film was supported by a $450,000 marketing campaign, in which Hitchcock's formal innovation and the tenacity of the tale were stressed repeatedly through the recycling of the tagline "Nothing ever held you like Alfred Hitchcock's ROPE" from advertisement to advertisement.[77] A photograph of the St. Francis Theater in San Francisco, for instance, shows a counter at the cinema decorated with rope and a sign bearing the line; other images in the archives depict employees of movie houses wearing little tags emblazoned with the phrase and attached to their clothing with short pieces of rope.[78] Those keen on a more formal style of dress could purchase a *Rope* necktie from selected menswear stores.[79] Meanwhile, a pocket-sized novelization of the film's screenplay was published by Dell of New York in 1948 and had an initial print-run of 250,000 copies.[80] I will discuss *Rope*'s critical and commercial reception in the postscript to this book; I will refer to the anonymous novelization, which has many strange qualities, often in the following chapters.

## Outside the Apartment, David's Rope

I have spent much time so far in this chapter recounting the production history of *Rope*, for the simple reason that the film's first shot contains the opening credits—written records of the making of the movie. But this, of course, is not the end of the story: beneath those credits, we can see a prosperous one-way street in New York. (The sequence was filmed in Los Angeles on February 24, 1948, after principal photography had finished, using the "Brownstone Street" set on the Warner Bros. backlot.[81]) Little of consequence happens in the road while the credits are rolling, but just as the final printed words—"Directed by ALFRED HITCHCOCK"—pause in the center of the screen, Hitchcock makes one of his famous cameo appearances, walking along the road from left to right with a female companion. His presence is rather easy to miss: we cannot see his face, and the camera captures him only from an elevated distance. The cameo, in short, is cryptic and much less easy to spot than many of Hitchcock's other appearances in his own films (though nowhere near as obscure as his second cameo in *Rope*, as I will explain in time). So cryptic is it, in fact, that there has been some disagreement over the years about whether or not this strolling figure is Hitchcock.[82]

Following Hitchcock along the sidewalk are a policeman and two children. The officer steps into the road and stops the traffic so that the youngsters may cross. The scene seems serenely innocent, but the music takes on a more sinister mood at this point and, as Peter J. Dellolio has pointed out, the apparently benign representative of the law upon the screen is actually "another of Hitchcock's typically ineffectual policemen" because, as he reaches roughly the halfway point with the children, the camera, which has been stationary for around two minutes, pans to the left and stops to show a window whose curtains are drawn.[83] Suddenly, there is a terrible scream. ("It begins with a shriek. . . . It ends with a shot," as one of the taglines used in publicity materials for the film in 1948 put it.[84]) Its source is unseen at this stage, but shot 1 of *Rope* is approaching its end, and the beginning of shot 2 will soon bring us face to face with the origin of the cry. Or, to rope in an obsolete turn of phrase, we might say that *Rope* ties up its first shot with a "rope," for the signifier in question could, in Old and Middle English, be used to refer to "cries of distress and lamentation," the *Oxford English Dictionary* explains.[85]

Just before the panning movement of the camera comes to an end, however, something rather strange and striking occurs at the level of diegetic sound. The city street is now out of sight, but the soundtrack is suddenly marked by the noise of traffic, in the form of a vehicle's horn. In other words, moments after the end of its opening credits, *Rope* bears the sound of something that is not seen, for the simple reason that the camera is focusing on something else. The camera is *here*, showing *this* (the window), but the film simultaneously evokes an elsewhere that is unseen (the street where the horn has been sounded). We are allowed to hear something that would be visible to those down at ground level, but because our eyes can no longer see the street over which we gazed for around two minutes, the sound of traffic signals a limit to our sight.

I have paused on this marginal, easily missable moment because, as I will point out in the chapters that follow, every one of *Rope*'s eleven shots contains related points at which our knowledge and specular privilege are undermined by sounds of elsewhere, sounds of scenes that we cannot study, sounds of something that loosens the knots of knowing. Because these "elsewheres" figure so often in *Rope*, and because I want to tie them to my discussion of the film's tenacity, I will interrupt my own text with a bold abbreviation that signals each eruption: "**(E)**." "**(E)**" stands for elsewhere and will therefore interrupt *Perpetual Movement* whenever an elsewhere arises. Like this, here and now at the end of shot 1: **(E)**.

# 2

# Inside

## A Playful Little Prank

With the beginning of the film's second shot, the camera takes us inside and grants us access to the space obscured by the curtains at the very end of the previous shot. It will not leave this space for what remains of the film—a fact that leads Michael Wood to declare that *Rope*'s "subject is a situation rather than a story—its effect on us is rather like that of walking around an installation."[1] Having made this revealing leap from outside to inside, the camera will spend much of the rest of the film moving regally around the apartment in order to single out significant details and generally to provide viewers with crucial information that is often visibly unavailable to characters within the film. The camera is trapped from now on within a limited setting, then, but its behavior within that confined space appears to be in the service of unlimited access, as if its unspoken project were to create an enlightened, knowing audience. As Hitchcock himself noted, in a production notebook published by Warner Bros. to accompany the film's release in 1948:

> [T]he camera never stops. The story is ideally suited. It has no time lapses at all. It takes place in an hour and a half in one apartment (. . .) We have constructed a set that will take a camera into any corner of any room . . .[2]

Arthur Laurents went one step further by claiming that "the camera is the star" in *Rope*, and many critics have analyzed its remarkable performance in the film.³ Peter Conrad, for example, notes how it "prowls around" the apartment; D. A. Miller describes "the continuous mobile camera in *Rope*"; and Raymond Durgnat refers to its "incessant visual glissando."⁴ Richard Allen calls the camera "an all-seeing eye and ear that is eavesdropping in 'real time,'" while Lesley Brill draws attention to the film's "fluid camera work."⁵ Peter J. Dellolio sees "unchecked mobility" in operation, and for William Rothman "our sense that the camera is poised to move enhances our sense that it represents a palpable presence within the world of the film."⁶ Charles Barr, identifying a trace of F. W. Murnau's style in *Rope*, writes of an "unchained camera," while Angelo Restivo refers to the way in which the apparatus "obsessively monitor[s] the space of the penthouse."⁷ "*Rope*," Richard Allen concludes, "shows the audience everything there is to see, including the murder of Kentley, except the corpse in the caisson [*sic*] that harbors the dirty secret."⁸

These critics are not wrong, of course, to identify the fluid, searching movements of Hitchcock's camera. But what has been overlooked repeatedly in criticism, and missed completely in Richard Allen's suggestion that the film "shows the audience everything there is to see," is an awareness that *Rope*, for all its nourishing camerawork, regularly announces that something is *not* being seen, *not* being known, by the viewer. The camera glides and gives—yes, of course. But criticism has consistently ignored the many ways in which the camera also misses and masks. I want in this book to correct the oversight, to discuss in detail what has been left out of earlier analyses of *Rope*. The constant movement—a perpetual movement—between revelation and concealment lies at the very heart of Hitchcock's film and colors each of its shots. If the form of *Rope*, in Richard Allen's words, "seems to epitomize full disclosure or visibility," then the emphasis needs, I think, to fall firmly upon the signifier "seems."⁹ The film appears to be designed to deliver disclosure and visibility, but it actually undermines such outcomes with the hidden and the invisible. Peter J. Dellolio believes that Hitchcock's film is "a seamless whole" created by the mobile camera, but, for me, *Rope* is too contradictory ever to be whole or seamless.¹⁰ The film pulls against and away from itself. As my analysis unfolds in the following chapters, I will return repeatedly to this quality—a quality that, to return to T. J. Clark's compelling phrase, "compels the return."

The sudden and permanent passage from outside to inside—from light to dark, from public to private, from street to apartment—reveals the terror beneath the soft, serene surface of society, as Kristin L. Matthews has noted:

The beginning of *Rope* takes great pains to establish and subsequently undermine a sense of normalcy, signaling the importance of reading beyond, or beneath, surface appearances. The first shot is of an ordinary street on a spring afternoon. There are no distinguishing markers that would set this tree-lined street apart from any other—it could be anyone's neighborhood. The scream heard from behind closed curtains breaks the spell of normalcy and reveals the danger lurking beneath. Out of sight, laws are being broken. It is no coincidence that the murder weapon is a short length of "ordinary, household rope" which could be found in any home. The audience is drawn into a paranoia in which everyone could be dangerous and nothing is as it seems.[11]

This harsh swing from calm "normality" to violent terror brings us face to face with *Rope*'s two central characters, Brandon and Phillip, played by John Dall and Farley Granger, respectively. Granger, who was the lover of Arthur Laurents at the time, was on loan to Transatlantic from Samuel Goldwyn and would work again with Hitchcock on *Strangers on a Train* three years later.[12] John Dall, meanwhile, had been a Warner Bros. artist from July 1943 until May 1946.[13]

As we observe Phillip and Brandon with the limp body of David Kentley, we see, even though the interior space is in darkness, what no figure outside the apartment can. The camera has taken us into the hidden, private space from which the scream sounded. We are at the scene of a crime in the immediate aftermath of a strangling; although we do not witness the build-up to the killing or the moment at which the rope is tied around David's neck, we are afforded intimate awareness and access as we see David's body after he has cried out and then watch as his killers hide the corpse in a wooden trunk.[14]

In this respect, Hitchcock's film departs notably from Patrick Hamilton's original play, in which the stage directions describe the presence of "a large chest"[15] and then state:

> GRANILLO and BRANDON [. . .] are bending over the chest, intent, working at something—exactly what you cannot discern. The silence is complete. Suddenly the lid of the chest falls with a bang.[16]

*Exactly what you cannot discern.* The phrase is significant here. While Hamilton's dialogue soon has Brandon announcing "I have done murder"

(p. 14), neither the killing nor the hiding of the body is shown in the play. *Something* happens with the chest, clearly, but the crucial details are unknown. In the play, then, audience members are not witnesses to the crime or the concealment of the corpse; they arrive a little too late at the party, as it were. Hitchcock's adaptation, however, begins a touch earlier, and with inescapable clarity. As Hitchcock was planned to have said in a trailer for a rerelease of *Rope* in the early 1960s, the viewer of his adaptation is now "an eyewitness as two schoolboys perpetrate a playful little prank on an ex-classmate."[17]

## Leaning into the Afternoon; or, Innuendoing to the Converted

What we witness in this first glimpse of Brandon and Phillip (in addition to their "playful little prank") is an unusual closeness: the two men are positioned and framed in strikingly tight proximity. The camera itself lingers close to them, moreover, enhancing the sense of domestic intimacy. In a pioneering essay on *Rope*, D. A. Miller discusses the way in which the film repeatedly pictures Brandon and Phillip in precisely this manner:

> Sometimes [the] image, through an attenuation of depth perception, is able to suggest that Brandon and Phillip are actually touching, holding, or leaning against one another, when they are only occupying parallel spatial planes. More often and simply, it is content to capture the couple in less egregious, but also less disputable, infractions of the codes governing male homosocial space. In their tight framing by the camera, for instance, Brandon and Phillip always seem to be standing too close to one another; and what is already a transgression of the normally enforced boundaries between men's bodies promotes the fantasy that these boundaries will be even further breached—as indeed they twice are toward the end of the film: first, in the violent quarrel between the murderers, where the choreography of their bodies relies prominently on Hollywood conventions of romantic embrace; and second, in the struggle between Rupert and Phillip for the gun that tends to disappear under a show of passionate and prolonged hand holding.[18]

Leopold and Loeb were lovers, their legal hearing had revealed in 1924. Patrick Hamilton once claimed bluntly, meanwhile, that he saw the role of Rupert as being "really cut out for a pansy," but the powers of the Lord Chamberlain over the British stage meant that the play could not, in 1929, have openly identified any of its characters as gay.[19] Same-sex relations between men were illegal in the United States when Hitchcock came to direct his adaptation, and, following suit, the Production Code did not allow representations of homosexuality upon the screen. Arthur Laurents took it that he was writing a film about gay men—"Homosexuality was at the center of *Rope*," he recalls, and "its three main characters were homosexuals"—but the problem was that this could not be acknowledged in any open, explicit way.[20] The censors were, as I explained at length in chapter 1 of this book, watching closely for what they saw as perversion. Laurents continues:

> At Warner Brothers studio in Burbank where *Rope* was shot, homosexuality was the unmentionable, known only as "it." "It" wasn't in the picture, no character was "one." Fascinating was how Hitchcock nevertheless made clear to me that he wanted "it" in the picture. And of course, he was innuendoing to the converted. I knew it had to be self-evident but not so evident that the censors or the American Legion would scream. It's there; you have to look but it's there all right.[21]

In a climate of "compulsory heterosexuality," *Rope* does what many Hollywood films of the period were forced to do: it codes eroticism.[22] If same-sex desire is "there all right," as Arthur Laurents puts it, then it is there only in the form of veiled hints, winks, innuendo, and flicker. Everything must be "consigned to connotation" and held back from denotation, subject to "an abiding deniability," as D. A. Miller observes.[23] This means, Miller continues, that

> homosexuality is in fact extensively prevented from enjoying any such obviousness not only, of course, by the famously hard-ass Production Code in force at the time of the film's making, which strictly forbade the display and even denomination of homosexuality; but also, more diffusely, by the cultural surround of legal, social, psychic, and aesthetic practices (the last including those of spectatorship) that tolerate homosexuality only on condition that it be kept out of sight.[24]

As "the dominant signifying practice of homophobia," connotation works to ensure that same-sex relations in *Rope* never reach the realm of denotation—a realm ruled out by the PCA as a condition of cultural production.[25] In John Orr's phrase, a "cryptic gay intimacy" is all that we ever encounter—all that we *can* ever encounter—in Hitchcock's film.[26]

This careful connotative coding is at work as early the opening of *Rope*'s second shot. After secreting David's body in the wooden chest, Phillip and Brandon lean forward with their heads bowed, exhausted from their actions. Although Phillip is slightly further back in the mise-en-scène, the camera creates the illusion that his nose is touching Brandon's shoulder. This effect is precisely what D. A. Miller is referring to when, in the long passage that I have already quoted, he describes how *Rope*'s "attenuation of depth perception" can "suggest that Brandon and Phillip are actually touching, holding, or leaning against one another, when they are only occupying parallel spatial planes."

There are also, Miller notes, "postcoital nuances" in the verbal exchanges that take place between the two men in the immediate aftermath of the murder.[27] "Let's stay this way for a minute," pleads Phillip, who asks Brandon later in the shot, "How did you feel—during it?" Brandon continues the innuendo in what Peter Conrad calls "a panting whisper"

Figure 2.1. Phillip and Brandon, nose to shoulder.

when he says, "I don't remember feeling very much of anything—until his body went limp and I knew it was over [. . . and] then I felt tremendously exhilarated."[28] A further connotation of intimacy can be found in the moment at which Phillip, whose hands tightened the rope around David's neck, sits passively while Brandon touches him to remove the leather gloves worn to commit the crime. (Conrad suggests that it is as if Brandon is helping "to unpeel a prophylactic" at this point.[29]) I am unable to watch this surprisingly gentle incident without thinking of the moment in Edith Wharton's *The Age of Innocence* at which Newland Archer sits beside Ellen Olenska "and, taking her hand, softly unclasped it, so that the gloves and fan fell on the sofa between them." Ellen's response is to move away and to say, "Ah, don't make love to me!"[30] David Greven is not overstating things, I think, when he calls this early moment in *Rope* "one of the most explicit scenes of homoerotic exchange in classical Hollywood film," but, at the same time, Eric San Juan and Jim McDevin are right to stress that there is "just enough plausible deniability to escape the wrath of censors."[31] *Rope* swings both ways, and it has to. In the face of homophobia, the gloves must stay on even as they come off.

D. A. Miller's groundbreaking "Anal *Rope*" was published many years before Adriana Cavarero's *Inclination: A Critique of Rectitude*, but we might, I think, wish to extend Miller's discussion of enforced connotation in the light of Cavarero's book by examining the pose of Brandon and Phillip as they recover from the killing of David Kentley. When the two men rest upon the wooden chest, each is, in his own way, *leaning*. I am inclined to dwell upon this detail.

Cavarero describes how Western philosophy—and by extension Western culture—has tended to treat the act of leaning, of being inclined, with normative suspicion. In "the theater of modern philosophy," she writes, "center stage is occupied by an I whose position is straight and vertical."[32] This tradition, as a result, "does not appreciate inclination; it contests and combats it" (p. 1) because the norm is "the upright man (*l'uomo retto*)" (p. 2):

> The "upright man" of which the tradition speaks, more than an abused metaphor, is literally a subject who conforms to a vertical axis, which in turn functions as a principle and norm for its ethical posture. One can thus understand why philosophers see inclination as a perpetual source of apprehension, which is renewed in each epoch, and which takes on even more weight during modernity, when the free and autonomous self celebrated by Kant enters the scene. (p. 6)

This Kantian self, she adds, is "self-enclosed, it stands up on its own with no need for external support" (p. 27). It is not meant to lean towards others (p. 33).

To lean, then, is to deviate from this dominant Western tradition. If "the austere moral subject does not incline, not even in on itself" (p. 33), then leaning signifies being out of line, dubious, askew, at odds with conventional morality. It is not surprising, then, that *Rope* depicts Phillip and Brandon in a state of inclination near the beginning of shot 2, moments after they have first appeared upon the screen in the aftermath of their crime. I will turn in subsequent chapters to similar moments later in the film, some of which will again involve the wooden chest in which David's body is hidden.[33] At this point in *Perpetual Movement*, I wish merely to point out, in the light of the work of Miller and Cavarero, that pose signifies according to a long Western tradition; more precisely, it connotes when denotation is roped off, out of bounds. Brandon and Phillip lean towards each other, and, in doing so, they mark their distance from the dominant values (the heteronormative values) of the culture. These are not upright, upstanding figures, the film implies; they incline because of their inclination to kill and to desire other men, and both qualities put them at odds with the policed norms of the era. It is possible, moreover, to infer a link between their murdering of David and their homosexuality, as if the former followed from the latter. As Robin Wood put it so well in *Hitchcock's Films Revisited*: "*Rope* can be read as associating homosexuality with the unnatural, the sick, the perverse—with 'evil' and fascism. Nothing prohibits such a reading; Hitchcock and/or his writers may have thought that was what the film was saying."[34] Nothing prohibits such a reading, but I want to examine in *Perpetual Movement* how nothing guarantees it, either.

## Inside, Looking Out

So far, the action in the contained apartment has taken place in a darkened setting that is at odds with the bright sunlight glimpsed outside in the film's opening shot.[35] But this darkness is soon undone when Brandon crosses the room and opens the curtains covering the long main window of the apartment.[36] With the flood of light comes a spectacular glimpse of the Manhattan skyline—or, to be more precise, the remarkable cyclorama whose design I discussed the previous chapter of this book. The outside world of shot 1 has returned to the field of vision, then, but here we see it only from a distance: the camera will from now on only look out across the city from the window, never down into its streets. The existence of activity at ground level nonetheless registers at this point in shot 2 because, after the opening of the curtains, there are several notable soundings of vehicle horns.[37] The source of these everyday noises is never shown, however: they are no more than heard hints of an elsewhere that remains unseen, beyond the grasp of the camera (**E**).

Just four minutes into the film, a textual tension has made itself apparent. On the one hand, the camera has allowed intimate access to an illicit event that occurs within the closed, private, darkened space of the apartment. On the other hand, however, the soundtrack signals that there is something which is *not* seen, something which the camera is ignoring.[38] This curious state of affairs is by no means unique to this moment in the film; on the contrary, I will identify throughout this book the ways in which *Rope* repeatedly reveals as it conceals, screens as it screens. Often this a matter of further traffic sounds, but sometimes it is a question of how the film handles parallel conversations within the apartment while the macabre party is underway.[39]

## "S" Marks the Spot

Near the beginning of Virginia Woolf's *Mrs. Dalloway*, a skywriting airplane begins to spell out a message high above London. The novel never reveals precisely what the letters are, but those at street level quickly become interested in what is taking shape in the sky: "Every one looked up," we read, and different characters proceed to offer conflicting opinions about what is on view.[40]

I do not know if *Rope* is alluding consciously to Woolf's novel when the opening of one of the curtains on the right-hand side of the apartment unveils a large unlit neon "S." The letter is part of a sign on a neighboring building that spells out a word, or at least contains a series of characters, but the full sequence is not revealed. Further letters, sometimes lit, will be glimpsed later in *Rope*, and I will discuss them as they appear, but a complete word is never shown. No character in the film ever pays the slightest attention to the sign outside the window—it apparently lacks the celestial lure of the skywriting in *Mrs. Dalloway*—but I want to allow these neon letters to illuminate my analysis of Hitchcock's film from time to time.

In revealing only "S" here, the film signals that something is being withheld; a sign is glimpsed but is incomplete. Another element of the world outside the apartment has entered the straitened field of the visible, but only in part. We are allowed to see a fragment but are left guessing about other letters and what, when taken together, they might spell. We are allowed to know *something*, in other words, and the opening of the curtain fulfils the habitual function of revelation, but we are also made to see that we are not seeing everything, that the knowledge provided by the camera is partial, limited. Hitchcock himself revealed in an article published in *Popular Photography* in November 1948 that the neon sign spelled out the word "STORAGE," but this remains a conclusion to be drawn by the curious viewer; the full word is not something ever given to us by the film itself.[41] (Hitchcock, in fact, was not quite telling the truth: the drawings for the set design held in storage in the Warner Bros. Archive in Los Angeles reveal that only the letters S, T, O, R, and A were planned and built; because the G and the E would never appear in shot, it was decided, presumably for budgetary reasons, not to manufacture or even sketch them.[42])

## Distance, Harvard, Princeton

Once the curtains have been opened, a difference in mood and manner between Brandon and Phillip becomes apparent: while Phillip looks anxiously at the trunk containing the body, Brandon gleefully prepares a drink and jokes about the corpse—"the perfect victim for the perfect murder," as he puts it moments before adding that David's being a Harvard undergraduate "might make it justifiable homicide."

What are we to make of this passing reference to Harvard? It could merely connote social standing: the splendor of Brandon and Phillip's apartment has already signaled their wealth, and the suggestion now that they move in Ivy League circles adds to the aura of privilege. A glance at the history of the screenplay, however, reveals the possibility that a familiar, long-established rivalry between elite American universities is at work in Hitchcock's film. In Laurents's first draft of November 1947, we learn that Brandon and Phillip dropped out of Princeton in order to travel around the world; Kenneth, meanwhile, is referred to as a current student of the same institution.[43] David Kentley is also connected to Princeton, implicitly as an *alumnus*, when Brandon suggests, in response to a question about his mysterious absence, that he might be at the Princeton Club.[44] In the beginning, that is to say, all four figures were Princeton men. By the time Laurents produced the final draft of his screenplay on January 13, 1948, however, things had changed: Kenneth is still identified as a member of Princeton University, but David is now called "a Harvard undergraduate," and Brandon's remark about his absence specifies the Harvard Club instead of its Princeton counterpart.[45] (This line of dialogue was actually recorded during shooting but somehow came to the attention of the president of Harvard University, James Bryant Conant, who requested that it be removed from the film before release. Transatlantic obliged, and the offscreen line was changed to simply "the Club" during post-production.[46]) With these alterations to the script, there is suddenly scope for rivalry, for homosocial tension between the four men.

As the conversation in *Rope* continues, Brandon reveals the conclusion of their "perfect crime" when he says that "in less than eight hours" David's body will "be resting gently but firmly at the bottom of a lake." This, then, is the plan: having witnessed the crime, the viewer is now allowed also to know where the narrative, as imagined by Phillip and Brandon, is meant to end; already we are somehow implicated through the kind of sight and knowledge usually reserved for accomplices. As so often in Hitchcock's films, however, the carefully plotted scheme will fail.[47]

Phillip's anxiety increases when he moves over to the chest and discovers that it is not locked; both men once again notably incline away from an upright position at this point.[48] Gaston Bachelard once suggested that a lock on a casket or a chest "is a psychological threshold" linked to a "*need for secrecy*"; the problem, for Phillip, is that the lock on the wooden trunk in the apartment does not work and so cannot maintain the psychological and material threshold that he evidently desires.[49] Brandon, however, is thrilled by the detail that alarms Phillip. "All the better," he says. "It's much more dangerous." (As I noted in chapter 1, the word "dangerous" here was originally meant to be "exciting," but was changed at the insistence of the PCA.) Because both men are now by the wooden trunk, the camera can close in and once again record physical proximity. As they discuss alternative victims, their shoulders and upper arms nearly touch. Then Phillip turns suddenly to his right and looks directly into Brandon's face. Their eyes meet and Phillip refers, after an enhancing pause in his speech, to Brandon's "charm." No matter how many times I watched *Rope* during my year-long experiment, I always saw this moment as prelude to a passionate kiss that can never come.

Figure 2.2. Brandon and Phillip—"charm."

What the second shot of *Rope* has already established in terms of its two main characters, then, is a wavering between proximity and distance. Brandon and Phillip enjoy a degree of physical intimacy and closeness, but there is also a distinct distance between them in mood and manner. If they perhaps share a bed, they do not share a disposition. They planned and committed the crime together, but their responses to it are far from unified; they are "a pair of smiling conspirators," to borrow a phrase from Isherwood, who do not quite form a pair.[50] As the narrative unfolds, this movement between entangled intimacy and tense distance will become increasingly pronounced.

## Other Rooms and a Choice of Words

Brandon mentions that he has some champagne in the refrigerator, and the two men move away from the main living area. The mobile camera follows them and for the first time reveals other sections of the apartment: Brandon slides open two dividing doors, and the pair pass through the foyer and the dining room, still pursued by the camera, which eventually comes to a halt just outside the kitchen door while Brandon retrieves the champagne from the refrigerator within.⁵¹

What this movement establishes, of course, is that the apartment consists of multiple and separate spaces. (This might sound like an excessively obvious statement, but how the film treats these different spaces will become increasingly important as my analysis unfolds.) While most of the film's events take place in the large living room, other moments will play out—sometimes unseen or in part unseen—elsewhere. In fact, this spatial multiplicity is underscored moments after the movement to the kitchen when the two figures cross to the dining room while discussing the nature of their crime. Brandon struggles with the champagne cork, so Phillip intervenes and opens the bottle; his hands, after all, were the ones that squeezed the life out of David Kentley's neck, so they are perfectly suited to squeezing the stopper from the neck of a bottle. Phillip fills the glasses, and they toast their victim. (The look of approving surprise on John Dall's face when he takes his first sip is explained by the fact that Hitchcock—always fond of mischief—had changed the ginger ale used in rehearsals to real champagne for filming without telling the actors.⁵²) The camera, although now positioned in the dining room with the two men, shows the area beyond this space over Phillip's shoulder. There is an *elsewhere* in the mise-en-scène: the lone mobile camera could be *there*, but it is *here* instead, and it cannot, of course, be in more than one place at any given moment. A more distant elsewhere makes itself known, moreover, but not present to the eye, while the men enjoy their drinks, as sounds of traffic outside are once again heard (**E**).

The camera is soon on the move again. After Brandon and Phillip discuss their feelings during the act of murder, it backs away a little to reframe the two figures. Phillip wonders if they have been wise to throw a party in the wake of their deed. Is it, he asks, a "mistake"? Brandon assures him that it is "the inspired finishing touch to our work [. . .], the signature of the artist":

BRANDON: Not having it would be like, uh, uh . . .

PHILLIP: Painting the picture and not hanging it?

BRANDON: (*Laughing*) I don't think that's a very good choice of words!

PHILLIP: It may turn out to be a little *too* choice, thanks to the party.

Brandon's heightened sensitivity here to language, to Phillip's "choice of words," marks for the first time a phenomenon which will recur in *Rope*: a play on words associated with the killing of David Kentley. At this early point in the film, when Phillip and Brandon are alone in the apartment before our eyes, there is no irony, no difference in levels of signification: because the viewer and the characters upon the screen are all aware of the murder, no one is excluded from the double meaning of the word "hanging." Later, however, as I will discuss in more detail subsequent chapters, there is a split in signification, in the light of which we, as viewers, can enjoy a duplicity of the signifier that is hidden from those who are in the apartment but unaware of what is hidden in the apartment. The reference here to "hanging" also anticipates the film's final shot, in which Rupert, having at last figured out what happened to David, tells Brandon and Phillip that they will hang for their deed. A capital rope stretches from one end of *Rope* to the other.

## The Case of the Canted Candle

Cole Porter made it clear that champagne and candlelight go hand in hand. Brandon appears to be of a similar mind, for he begins to ready six ceremonial candles for lighting upon the dining table. Suddenly, he stops and extinguishes the flame of his lighter; as he does so, a vehicle's horn is heard in the distance (**E**). The sound of this elsewhere is followed by the movement of the camera elsewhere, for it now glides back through the dining room and foyer with the two men. Phillip does not quite know why he is being asked to carry the candelabra away from its neat place on the table, but, as so often in *Rope*, he follows Brandon's instruction and lead; as he passes from the foyer into the living room, another horn is heard from the streets below (**E**).

In a remarkable analysis of *Rope*, D. A. Miller takes a close interest in what happens during this sequence to the candelabra—or, in his phrase, "the case of the canted candle."[53] He writes:

> Just as Phillip is asking Brandon whether "the party is a mistake," Hitchcock's camera drifts over the dining table's nicely developing symmetry: two three-branched candelabra flank a floral centrepiece, with the silverware spaced evenly around. But the drift discloses a conspicuous imperfection: one candle, in contrast to its five companions, is drooping from its socket.

> We notice this lopsided candle right before Phillip pronounces the word "mistake," which almost seems to be capitioning the image; and yet, plainly, this cannot be the mistake he has in mind. Is it even a mistake at all? (pp. 57–58)

This canted candle becomes a point of obsession for Miller—"I want the droop to be recognized and righted," he declares (p. 59)—and it finds itself caught up in a reading which pursues, and waxes lyrical about, the film's strange "coincidence of art and mistake, of the touch and the flaw" (p. 62). "I have become," Miller confesses, "more obsessive and perfectionistic than Brandon, who boasts 'I would never do anything unless I did it perfectly'" (p. 64).

I am seduced by Miller's "eccentric" reading of *Rope*—the adjective is his (p. 62)—and I do not wish to challenge his conclusions about the canted candle which, as he shows, goes through a curious series of imperfections before it at last, when "seen from a frontal angle, finally looks acceptable" (p. 69).[54] His proposal that there is an "understyle" at work in the film, a "double status [to] so many of *Rope*'s continuity violations and technical faults" (p. 72), is illuminating, and *Hidden Hitchcock* invites us to see the director's work in charming new ways. I wish merely to offer a small footnote to the case of the canted candle—a footnote that leans back towards my discussion of Cavarero's *Inclinations* earlier in this chapter. When the rogue candle deviates from its upright position despite Brandon's best attempt to set things straight, it recalls the way in which the two murderers lean upon the wooden trunk into which they have just deposited David's corpse. This earlier bodily leaning signifies a deviation from cultural norms, from the upright values of *l'uomo retto*, and here, towards the end of the same shot, one of the ceremonial candles follows suit. Its becoming-canted occurs, moreover, just when the candelabra in which it sits is carried through the apartment to the location of the body, to the scene of the earlier symbolic inclination. A source of warmth and light, of enlightened existence, gives way a little in the terrible face of what has occurred in the darkened apartment. It inclines, even when adjusted, because of the obscure inclination of its bearer.[55]

## Making a Masterpiece

Brandon stops walking when he reaches the wooden trunk containing David's body. The camera is positioned to show this moment clearly, but it also leaves in view part of the foyer through which it has just passed (and in which it is therefore no longer located). We are *here* again, in the main living area, but we can see part of a space which is now elsewhere and therefore beyond full visual inspection; Hitchcock's framing is generous enough to grant this, to admit the other location. "What the devil are you doing?" asks Phillip. There has, it seems, been a deviation from the pair's precise plans. Brandon replies that he is "making our work of art a *masterpiece*," and the fraught distance between the two men once again makes itself known: Phillip declares that Brandon is "going too far" and begins to remove one of the candlesticks from the trunk. Their transgression, for him, has now become dangerously excessive and flamboyant. But Brandon, ever the dominant figure, wins out, and they continue to transfer items from the dining room to the trunk in the living room.

The work of the camera during this activity is striking. While it has roamed informatively around the apartment often in shot 2, it now remains by the trunk while the two men walk back to the dining room. Because it shifts position slightly as they move away, it shows multiple retreating spaces within the apartment: we watch from the living room as the men, still talking, pass through the doorframe into the foyer and then through a second frame into the dining area; a third frame (the doorway to the kitchen) is visible farther back in the apartment. Here, in the final seconds of shot 2 of *Rope*, the camera has ceased prowling, ceased following Brandon and Phillip, and instead pictures multiple elsewheres, multiple places where it could be but is not (**E**). The living space of the apartment is presented as a series of living spaces, in the plural, and the presence upon the screen of space within space within space confirms that the camera, for all its roaming revelation, cannot possibly show the viewer everything at once. In vision dwells division.

As Brandon picks up two books from close to the chest, he turns his back to the camera, which closes in on his jacket until darkness fills the screen, but not before it has allowed us clearly to see something unnoticed by Brandon: the rope used to kill David Kentley is hanging out of the side of the wooden trunk. The film cuts, bringing the shot to a masked end.

# 3

# Entrances, Elsewheres

## Cut to the Quick

As V. F. Perkins pointed out many years ago, the third shot of *Rope* begins a touch too quickly. While the break between shot 2 and shot 3 is masked in an attempt to create an illusion of perfect continuity, the effect "is spoiled by a sudden acceleration in the acting pace after the join."[1] Although Perkins does not single out sound specifically, the imperfection is most obvious at the level of dialogue: when Brandon says, at the start of the third shot, "After all, old Mr. Kentley is coming mainly to look at these books," his words flow rather more quickly than they did when, at the very end of shot 2, he uttered the line "What are you worrying about, Phillip?"

*Rope*'s very first concealed cut, that is to say, exhibits a faint fault; it fails to do its job properly, to hit the mark. In a brilliant discussion of the tension between perfection and imperfection in the film, D. A. Miller points out that Perkins identifies related problems with other hidden cuts in the film, and he concludes that "with *Rope*'s editing, Hitchcock has *systematically* integrated faultiness into the film's design."[2] I will, with Miller's help, turn in time to the later moments of faultiness and "self-undoing" in the text.[3] At this point, however, I wish merely to note that the first of *Rope*'s famous "hidden" breaks is not actually hidden at all. A quickness on the far side of the cut cuts perfection to the quick. (As does Brandon's haircut, in fact: a lock on the front left-hand side of his head comes loose between the shots.) The film is not quite what it seems.

Moments into the new shot, the discussion between Brandon and Phillip is interrupted by the ringing of the apartment's telephone. The sound comes from elsewhere—the phone is in the foyer, out of sight for now—and marks twice over what we can hear but not see. First, it is not until Brandon leaves the main room, crosses to the foyer, and lifts the handset that the precise source of the ringing becomes visible **(E)**. Second, the caller is clearly and necessarily outside the apartment in which *Rope* is unfolding: telephony of whatever kind implies distance, an elsewhere **(E)**. As the novelization puts it at this point, the noise signals "the presence of someone downstairs," and presence downstairs means absence upstairs, here in the apartment, within the realm of the visible.[4]

This eruption of an elsewhere that is about to enter the living space is accompanied by a more distant and extreme elsewhere: when Brandon puts down the books and walks towards the phone, we hear a vehicle's horn from the Manhattan streets below **(E)**. Another sounds very faintly when Brandon informs Phillip that Mrs. Wilson is en route **(E)**. Brandon now walks out of sight, while Phillip continues arranging the books by the wooden chest. When he leans over to pick up the volumes—a movement that once again marks his deviation from the figure of *l'uomo retto*—he finally notices what the viewer has already been allowed to see: the rope used to strangle David is hanging from the side of the trunk. Terrified and unable to act, he calls for Brandon, who returns to the room and, as the more dominant figure, pulls the rope roughly from where it is caught, leaning notably as he does so. He warns Phillip about "the crime of making a mistake." "Being weak," he insists, "is a mistake [. . .] because it's being ordinary." Before they can continue their heated conversation, however, the buzzer at the door of the apartment sounds. Mrs. Wilson has arrived.

## Downright Peculiar

Played by Edith Evanson, the character of Mrs. Wilson was based upon Hazel Church, a well-known caterer for Hollywood parties who was employed by Hitchcock as a technical advisor for *Rope* and was on set daily to help Evanson develop her role.[5] The entrance of Mrs. Wilson marks a turning point in the narrative. Until this moment, we have watched Phillip and Brandon closely while sharing their knowledge of what has taken place in the apartment and what is hidden in the trunk. We have, as it were, been alone with the killers, sharing their secret, following their every move, listening to their conversations. But Mrs. Wilson, like the guests who will soon begin to arrive for the party, does not share this knowledge. From this point onwards, in other words, *Rope* is able to exploit an explicit distinction between knowing and not knowing. Later, this will take the form of cruel *double entendres* in speech—second-level meanings that only we or the killers can grasp—but here the effect is a touch gentler. "If it weren't for the traffic, I'd have been here a half hour ago," says Mrs. Wilson. "Oh, it's just as well," says Brandon. "We didn't expect you back until now." His reply seems casual, but in the words "it's just as well," the viewer is able to hear a nuance unavailable to Mrs. Wilson: "it's just as well" *because if you hadn't been held up in traffic, you'd have caught us strangling David*. In several minutes, another character, Kenneth, will wonder if he has arrived too early for the gathering; here, the viewer can see that Mrs. Wilson has arrived a shade too late to be in the know.

The linguistic game continues as the three figures cross from the foyer to the main room, where Mrs. Wilson articulates her concerns about the men's decision to move the food from the table in the dining room to the top of the wooden chest—an action that she calls "downright peculiar," particularly with respect to the candlesticks, which she feels to be out of place. (Moments before she says this, just after Brandon has explained the reason for Mr. Kentley's visit, the sound of another place, an elsewhere, is heard in the form a vehicle's horn **[E]**.) Brandon replies to the objection about the candlesticks by saying that, for him, they suggest "a ceremonial altar, which you can heap with the foods for our, our sacrificial feast." It is likely, I think, that the viewer's attention will fall upon on the signifiers "ceremonial altar" and "sacrificial feast" at this point: the sacrifice of David has just been witnessed, after all, as has the placing of his corpse inside the wooden chest from which Brandon and Phillip are now preparing to serve the evening's food.[6] Mrs. Wilson, however, simply because she does not share the viewer's knowledge, ignores Brandon's loaded phrases and latches onto another part of his statement instead: "Hmm, 'heap' is right," she says. This practical consideration clearly matters to her in her professional role of housemaid, but her emphasis positions her, in plain sight, on the side of not knowing, not seeing the bigger picture, not sharing what we share with Brandon and Phillip.

In her fine book on suspense and humor in Hitchcock's work, Susan Smith describes how

> *Rope*'s strategy of privileging the viewer with knowledge and sight of the murdered man right at the beginning of the film

before he is hidden away [. . .] has the effect of demystifying the male body and making it a much less threatening object of suspense (which, in this film, is more to with the fear of discovery of the crime than of the body itself).[7]

Smith's analysis is compelling, and I do not wish to challenge it, but I would like to add here that the textual strategy of, as she puts it so neatly, "privileging the viewer with knowledge and sight of the murdered man" creates an uneasy tension: in reaching such an elevated position of superior insight, the viewer becomes implicitly aligned with the murderers, who see themselves as superior to the muddled mire of social convention and established ethics. The price of knowledge is a sharing of guilt. For Richard Allen, "our knowledge of the crime in contrast to the ignorance of the partygoers makes us complicit with wrongdoing"; for Michael Wood, meanwhile, "certain angles on the chest [containing David's body] make our knowledge almost unbearable, a secret we wish we had not been shown."[8] It is precisely this core complicity that raises its troubling head when Brandon refers to the "sacrificial feast" and the "ceremonial altar" in the presence of Mrs. Wilson: to grasp the full weight of words that pass her by is to be implicated, through knowledge, in the murder of David Kentley.

## An Ordinary Household Article

But it is not only a word or a phrase that can signify on different levels, the film soon reveals. While he is leaning in front of Mrs. Wilson (and away from the cultural coding of *l'uomo retto*) to place some plates upon the trunk, Phillip suddenly notices that Brandon is still holding the rope used to strangle David; the camera zooms in to emphasize the object. "Brandon, we've got to hide it," he says anxiously when Mrs. Wilson is out of earshot, but Brandon replies, "It's only a piece of rope, Phillip: an ordinary household article. Why hide it?" He is absolutely right in one respect, of course: it is an ordinary household article that need not normally be concealed. "Lots of people have knives and saws and ropes around their houses," as Lisa puts it in *Rear Window*—another Hitchcock film starring James Stewart and involving a murder in Manhattan.[9] But if observed from a certain position—a position of intimate inside knowledge—the object signifies otherwise: it is now a murder weapon, a piece of evidence; it is *extra*ordinary. While its physical form is fixed—49½ inches of braided cotton sash cord, with the ends frayed for effect, to be precise—its meaning can change with perspective or level of awareness.[10] This fluidity is emphasized, in fact, by the way in which Phillip spots the fatal rope just as he is leaning over Mrs. Wilson's parcel, which is tied up with a perfectly innocent length of string—"an ordinary household article" being no more than that. The latter is far thinner than the murder weapon, clearly, but there is a connection, a functional thread that runs from the one to the other.

I would not go as far as Peter J. Dellolio and suggest that the piece of rope "plays its own role as if it were another character" in the film; this is not an eponymous biopic.[11] However, its ability to signify as both ordinary and extraordinary ties it intertextually to many of Hitchcock's other films, where absolutely everyday objects come suddenly to resonate in unusual, often menacing, ways as the camera brings out what Lee Edelman calls "[the] latency, some might call it a queerness, that inhabits things that otherwise tend to pass without remark."[12] Notable examples here would include the following: the windmill whose sails revolve in the wrong direction in *Foreign Correspondent* (1940), the illuminated glass of milk in *Suspicion* (1941), door keys in *Notorious* (1946) and *Dial "M" for Murder* (1954), stitches in the sleeve of a jacket in *Saboteur* (1942), a cigarette lighter in *Strangers on a Train* (1951), Mrs. Thorwald's wedding ring in *Rear Window* (1954), and a tiny scrap of paper in a toilet bowl in *Psycho* (1960).[13] In *Rope*, the mundane household object that lends its name to the film is also a murder weapon, which Phillip desperately wishes to have kept out of sight. But precisely because the piece of rope has innocent everyday uses (and is not a gun or a bloody knife), it can, like Poe's purloined letter, remain in plain sight. This is the fundamental duplicity of *Rope*'s rope: it has a straightforward place in domestic life, but it is also the destroyer of life and domesticity. As so often in Hitchcock, death blooms in the everyday.

Brandon suggests that the piece of rope simply be stored "in the kitchen drawer," and this leads to a delightful textual flourish. He strolls away from Phillip, flamboyantly twirling the cord, flaunting the evidence with glee precisely because it can pass as "an ordinary household article." As he reaches the kitchen door, it opens, and Mrs. Wilson emerges. Brandon passes through, and the door swings closed just as he opens the drawer next to the refrigerator; our view of him is now temporarily blocked.[14] But because he has pushed the door with some force, it sweeps open again just in time to provide us with a brief glimpse of him dropping the rope into its storage place with a smile. In a film about artistic perfection, the timing of the performing artist here is perfect—and had to be, of course, if the entire take of shot 3 were not to be ruined. (There had been plenty of time to plan this moment, which Rohmer and Chabrol were right to see as a practical challenge: it was outlined as early as Arthur Laurents's very first draft of the screenplay.[15])

## Cometh the Kenneth

Artistic perfection is mentioned explicitly soon after this moment, in fact, when Phillip learns that Brandon has invited Rupert Cadell to the party. Rupert, Phillip frets, is "the one man most likely to suspect." Brandon does not disagree, but he finds the prospect "exciting" because Rupert is also "the one man who might appreciate this from our angle: the artistic one." For Brandon, it would have been "too easy [. . .] and too dull" to invite only the other guests and not to include Rupert. He adds that he had thought of asking Cadell to be present for the murder itself, but realized that Rupert "never could have acted." "That's where we're superior, Phillip," he insists. "We have courage; Rupert doesn't."

Rupert will not actually appear in the film for around another eleven minutes (in shot 5), but already, here at the level of dialogue in shot 3, he is marked out as somehow different from the other guests: they are "dull"; he is "brilliant." But this brilliance means, of course, that the crime is at risk of being discovered. Rupert's name already bears a value that no other guest's name does, and he was not mentioned by Brandon in the earlier discussion in the dining room of those who would be attending. *Rope* is unfolding in "real time," then, but its dialogue gestures forwards to what will be, to what (or *who*) will be different when all the guests are at last present.

Moments later, the door's buzzer sounds again. "They're here," says Mrs. Wilson. "Now the fun begins," Brandon adds confidently. But Phillip's mind is clearly not on fun: while Brandon disappears from sight to answer the door, the camera stays in the main room and shows Phillip fiddling anxiously with the lock on the wooden chest. Brandon and Phillip are partners in crime (and possibly in bed), but the distance between them once again presents itself: one speaks arrogantly of fun; the other is in a state of high anxiety. (So much so, in fact, that the novelization at this point has Phillip wishing "that it was he huddled and jammed inside the coffinlike box before him—yes, even with his own face distorted and horrible—and that David Kentley was out here standing where he was, waiting for guests, and alive, alive—."[16])

Because the camera does not follow Brandon to the door, the audience hears the voice of Kenneth Lawrence (in conversation with

Brandon) for around eleven seconds before he graces the screen for the first time.[17] Like David, that is to say, Kenneth is a voice before he is a body; both are briefly "acousmatic," in that the *acousmêtre*, as Michel Chion explains in his analysis of Hitchcock's *Psycho*, occurs "when the voice of a person not yet seen is involved."[18] As the film continues, there will be further ways in which David is linked explicitly to Kenneth; I will turn to them in time.

Kenneth worries that he has arrived too early at the party, but there is a sense in which he actually arrived a touch too late for *Rope*. For the first seven days of production, while the actors were still at the rehearsal stage, the character of Kenneth was played by Richard Crane. However, for reasons that are explained nowhere in the archives, on January 21, 1948, Douglas Dick took over the role.[19] Whether we view it as early (diegetically) or late (extradiegetically), the arrival of another figure who does not know what has happened in the apartment allows for further *double entendres*, and these now take on a bleakly comic quality. When Kenneth asks, for instance, on learning that champagne is to be served, if it is someone's birthday, Brandon says, with a smirk notably unseen by Kenneth, "It's, uh, really almost the opposite." Champagne here signifies a celebration of death, not birth—but Kenneth, unlike the viewer, is not in a position to see this. For him, the chilled alcohol bears no chill. Phillip then joins in the coded linguistic play when he says, referring to his imminent trip to Connecticut, that he is "to be, uh, locked up" to make sure that he rehearses for his forthcoming concert at Town Hall.[20] "I hope you knock 'em dead," says Kenneth in response; he cannot possibly be aware of the full significance of his colloquialism here, of course. However, we, like Brandon and Phillip, receive a second level of meaning. Kenneth is not playing the exclusive linguistic game in which Brandon and Phillip are participating, but the very existence of that game (and the knowledge upon which it relies) brings macabre connotation to his words.

For only the viewer and the murderers, of course. To be in on the joke, here and elsewhere in *Rope*, is to be in on murder. The grim comedy in the film, that is to say, comes at a price, as Susan Smith has observed:

> What makes the humour doubly insidious is the way that it in turn flatters our *own* sense of epistemic superiority as an onlooker privileged with crucial information withheld from the other characters and therefore able to understand the double entendres uttered knowingly by Brandon (and, occasionally, Phillip) and unintentionally by the guests.[21]

In Henri Bergson's classic account, comedy binds society together. "Our laughter," he writes, "is always the laughter of a group. [. . .] However spontaneous it seems, laughter always implies a kind of secret freemasonry, or even complicity, with other laughers, real or imaginary."[22] It certainly has a binding quality in *Rope*, but the main ties established are between the viewer and the two murderers who see themselves as above and outside established social conventions and morality.

The third shot of the film comes to an end with more double-edged dialogue and a significant variation on Kenneth's acousmatic arrival. Janet Walker, Brandon announces, will soon be joining the party. The camera closes in on Kenneth, who looks disappointed and says that he and Janet are "all washed up." Feigning a lack of knowledge, Brandon claims that he was unaware of the break-up, and just as Phillip is adding that he had heard "vague rumours" about the state of the relationship, the door buzzer sounds. Brandon and Phillip both look towards the foyer and the source of the noise, but whereas a more conventional Hollywood film might have cut to the door at this point, *Rope* keeps the camera focused tightly on the three men in the main living area. As Kenneth explains to Brandon and Phillip that Janet is now romantically involved with David Kentley, a new voice is heard offscreen to say, "Hello, Mrs. Wilson." Janet Walker has arrived.

The role of Janet is played by Joan Chandler, who had been a Warner Bros. artist briefly in 1945 and 1946.[23] For her work on *Rope* in 1948, she was employed by Transatlantic at the rate of $1500 per week for a minimum of six weeks. Her contract required her to provide her own clothes for the production and gave Transatlantic the right to re-engage her for four further films; the agreement was, however, terminated on May 31, 1949 and a release document was signed on June 8 of that year.[24] Janet's arrival at the apartment is, like the entrance of Kenneth and the murder of David, initially acousmatic, and these three figures thus form a triangle in sound as in romance—but it notably adds a quality not present earlier in the shot.[25] When Kenneth came into the apartment, his exchange in the foyer with Brandon was, although both men were unseen, perfectly easy to follow. Here, however, later in the same shot, Janet's offscreen conversation with Mrs. Wilson is audible but indiscernible. We can hear that they are talking, but we cannot make out their words for the simple reason that the sentences uttered in the living room (where the camera is) by Brandon, Phillip, and Kenneth obscure the dialogue taking place in the foyer.

This is the first occurrence of a phenomenon that will figure often in *Rope*: a parallel conversation in which one party's words are rendered unintelligible by those of another. V. F. Perkins draws attention to this distinctive use of sound in the film:

> Even when there are only two characters on the screen, we hear constant reminders of the others' presence through the wisps of conversation and laughter which drift in from other rooms.[26]

Perkins does not dwell upon this point—it is made in a very brief essay written for *Movie* magazine—but I want to draw out its significance for our understanding of how *Rope*'s perpetual movement works upon its audience. What we find here, with Janet's acousmatic and muffled arrival, is an explicit registering of the fact that the film is unable to give us clear access to something that it nonetheless acknowledges to be taking place within the apartment. We hear that Janet has arrived, but we do not see her entrance, and all that we can grasp of her exchange with Mrs. Wilson are, in Perkins's phrase, "wisps of conversation." *Rope* informs us that an event is underway elsewhere in the penthouse, away from the current focus of the camera, but it keeps that other scene enigmatic, beyond mastery, elsewhere (**E**). Janet is not merely reduced to the level of *acousmêtre*; she is also an *indistinct* voice from elsewhere with a body that is held back.

In fact, the third shot of *Rope* ends without actually showing Janet, for, having said to Kenneth, "I have the honest feeling anyway that your chances with the young lady are much better than you think," Brandon walks out of the frame, followed by Phillip, and speaks the name of the character whose voice has just been heard: "Janet." Kenneth is left alone in front of the camera, looking towards the foyer and the source of the sound, but before we can see Janet in person, the shot concludes with a conventional, unmasked cut. As in the case of David Kentley, we will have to wait to see the body that accompanies the voice.

# 4

# In the Bedroom

## From Art to Artifice

There is choreography here, but it is easy to miss.

In *Hidden Hitchcock*, D. A. Miller makes a compelling case for the "Too-Close Viewer" who obsessively detects secret elements of the director's work—a "perverse counternarrative" consisting of strange textual moments that do not nourish narrative coherence "but explode it."[1] This way of reading is made possible by developments in technology, by our being fortunate enough to have "that thaumaturgic genie successively known as a Betamax, VHS, or DVD player at our command" (p. 3). Viewers who saw Hitchcock's films in their original cinematic contexts—where rewinding, freeze-framing, zooming, and so on were impossible—were unlikely to have spotted the "hidden Hitchcock"; the viewing conditions were simply not conducive to the kind of "too-close" reading offered by Miller. But a modern viewer has the ability to pause the DVD, for instance, to zoom in upon a detail in the frame, and to discover something that does not fit, something that "takes the viewer out of the story and out of the social compact its telling presupposes" (p. 5). This "ability [. . .] to interrupt continuity," Miller notes,

> must be regarded as an anachronism, the artifact of a latter-day technology with the power to circumvent the twinned sine qua nons of classical cinema in the movie house: the irresistible movement of images and the irreversible momentum of the story. (p. 12)

The detail brought to light by the too-close viewing might, Miller explains, be "a small continuity error," or, in the startling case of *The Wrong Man* (1956), "a Hitchcock cameo fashioned so as *not* to be seen" (pp. 4–5). "It is as though," he concludes, "at the heart of the manifest style, there pulsed an irregular extra beat, the surreptitious "murmur" of its undoing that only the Too-Close Viewer could apprehend" (p. 5). I will often adopt the guise and the gaze of the Too-Close Viewer in this book.

A long chapter of *Hidden Hitchcock* turns its attention to *Rope*, and Miller's analysis is just as captivating as his earlier account of the film's depiction of homosexuality.[2] But Miller says nothing about the curious choreography at the very beginning of shot 4—a choreography that is only really visible if the film is paused and advanced frame by frame. (This is not a criticism of Miller: the "too-close viewer" is clearly not expected to be an all-seeing viewer.) I want to pause briefly upon this incident and advance frame by frame through its implications. *Pas à pas*, to recall Barthes.

The transition from shot 3 to shot 4 is obvious, as I pointed out at the end of the previous chapter of this book: there is no attempt whatever to hide the cut. Shot 3 ends with Kenneth staring towards the foyer, and the beginning of shot 4 glances in the direction of his gaze. (This is clearly not a point-of-view shot, though: the camera, without cutting, will soon show Kenneth himself once again.) At first, Phillip, seen from behind, almost completely obscures Brandon, who is standing further forwards, also with his back to the camera. The arrangement of color in the mise-en-scène is striking here. The brown of Phillip's jacket is echoed in the shade of the door in the distance that lies within multiple frames and the small painting on the right of the scene, above the lamp. Also visible on the canvas, meanwhile, is a fleck of blue, which corresponds with the color of Brandon's suit that emerges from the dominant brown by which it is surrounded. What is more, the painting contains a small streak of red, and this is echoed outside the frame of the artwork in the red spines on the bookcase at the very edge of the frame.[3] What we see here, in other words, is life within the apartment echoed at the level of color and composition in a piece of art upon the wall; this framed painting in turns corresponds with the framed doorway to the kitchen in the distance. Each element colors the other, undermining the film's apparent mimetic realism. This is evidently a work of art about a work of art—and a work of art about a work of art that contains a work of art.

This quiet allusion to the fact that *Rope* is art or artifice continues as the opening frames of the shot unfold. Although Brandon is slightly to the left of Phillip at first, he quickly moves to the right, while Phillip begins to walk to the left. ("Criss-cross," to quote *Strangers on a Train*—

Figure 4.1. Shot 4 begins.

Figure 4.2 Phillip and Brandon—criss-cross.

Hitchcock's film of 1951 in which Farley Granger would once again find himself roped into a case of strangulation.) This movement allows for the revelation of what—or, more precisely, *who*—has hitherto been hidden: Janet, announced but not seen at the end of shot 3, is finally visible. If she was earlier a voice without a body, here, fleetingly, she is a head without a torso, between men.

The continued movement of Brandon and Phillip also makes two further things visible. First, we see that Janet is wearing a dress whose color mirrors the red element of the art or artifice on the wall (which is still visible, despite Brandon's movement to the right); we see this, moreover, while Janet is shown within two (door) frames. Second, Mrs. Wilson can now be observed in the background. Her movement matches that of Brandon and Phillip (particularly the latter): she is walking in the same direction and, like the two men, has her back to the camera.

It is unlikely that this incident at the very beginning of *Rope*'s fourth shot would have been noticed by viewers of the film at the time of its release. The precise choreography is all over in about two seconds and only really becomes visible when, enlisting modern technology unimaginable in

Figure 4.3. Janet is revealed.

Figure 4.4. Mrs. Wilson is revealed.

1948, the film is frozen and advanced frame by frame. Manipulating the text like this reveals an aspect of *Rope* that, a little like the body of David Kentley, is both hidden and on display. What I have described above has always been a part of the film, but viewers have not always been able to see it—clearly or at all. Indeed, to the best of my knowledge, what I am calling the film's "choreography" at this point has been discussed nowhere in print until now. I have drawn attention to this strange moment because it pulls against the film's measured attempt to appear natural, to persuade us with its innovative form that we are there observing the events unfold organically and spontaneously in real time. The third shot of *Rope* began too quickly, as I discussed in the previous chapter, and, in doing so, it unsettled the smoothness that the hidden cut between shots 2 and 3 was meant to sustain. A little under eight minutes later, here at the beginning of shot 4, the film is so strikingly choreographed that its artifice once again becomes apparent. When the actors move, and move with such clinically orchestrated precision, it is as if we have just heard Hitchcock shout "Action!" to begin the well-rehearsed fourth shot. If a text is, etymologically speaking, something that is woven, *Rope* at this point lays bare its weave, its strands.

## A New Young American Primitive

Janet's arrival at the party allows for more dialogue in which a second shade of meaning can be heard by the viewer (and the murderers), but not by Kenneth or Janet herself. When she catches sight of Kenneth and is stopped in her tracks, Janet is in the process of referring to how Phillip's concert at Town Hall might lead to his becoming "horribly famous." She means something quite straightforward by this, of course, but we can detect a hint that Phillip and Brandon, if caught, will become "horribly famous" for a horrible crime—just like Leopold and Loeb. Janet then proceeds to tell the three men that her new job involves "writing that same dreary column on how to keep the body beautiful" for a magazine named *Allure*. (In the first two versions of Arthur Laurents's screenplay, incidentally, the publication was called *CHIC*, but this was altered to *Allure* at some point after January 13, 1948 because researchers at Warner Bros. had discovered that a real magazine named *CHIC* existed.[4] Hitchcock must have liked the change: ten years later, in *Vertigo*, we see that Midge has a cover of an issue of *Allure* displayed in her apartment as an artwork or perhaps as an example of her own handiwork.[5]) Again, Janet's words are perfectly straightforward and are spoken in response to an everyday question about her life. What she and Kenneth do not know, however, is that a body is decaying, becoming anything but alluring and beautiful, several feet away from where they are all standing.

When Janet is handed a glass of champagne by Brandon, we twice hear the sound of a vehicle's horn **(E)**. This reminder of what lies elsewhere and out of shot is reinforced immediately when Janet draws Brandon away from the others on the pretense of wanting to know more about a certain painting on the wall. (The artwork that is seen at the very beginning of the shot, in fact.) The camera now must make a choice—it cannot be in two places at the same time—and it decides to follow Brandon and Janet to the wall by the bookcase. Brandon leans towards Janet when he stands by the "new young American primitive," again signifying his deviation from what Cavarero calls "the austere moral subject."[6] They speak loudly at first and can clearly still be heard by Phillip and Kenneth, who laugh offscreen in response to Janet's remark about her three-year-old sister's artistic abilities. But then a more dramatic division occurs: Janet speaks *sotto voce* and leads Brandon further away from the others, out of the room and into the foyer. Although we can no longer see Phillip and Kenneth, the sound of their ongoing conversation remains in play on the soundtrack—but, crucially, in muffled, indistinct form.

By splitting the group and having the camera leave Kenneth and Phillip out of the frame, the film clearly privileges the conversation between Janet and Brandon, but it also makes us aware that we are not following a different conversation that is underway in the apartment. The "epistemic superiority" identified by Susan Smith in her analysis of the film is once again provided to the viewer, in that we are permitted to hear a clandestine exchange and to grasp the cruel *double entendre* in Janet's "I could really strangle you, Brandon." (She, of course, is completely unaware of how the signifier "strangle" resonates queasily here.) But, *at the very same moment*, we are reminded that there is an elsewhere to which we no longer have access **(E)**. The "epistemic superiority" is met and muddled by what might be called "epistemic inferiority." *Rope* is pulling in two directions at the same time: it takes precisely as it gives; it foils as it flatters.

Janet pretends in this sequence to point at a painting on the wall in the foyer where one does not actually hang, but while she and Brandon subsequently discuss her past relationships, a framed painting is visible above her left shoulder, and part of another can be seen reflected in the mirror (also framed) behind her other shoulder. (Why did she not point to one these artworks when she touched her finger to a blank part of the wall and said "This"?) The frames in this tightly composed moment are, I think, further material reminders of the fact that the act of looking is forever *framed*, always subject to limits.[7] The roaming camera in *Rope* might give viewers privileged access to certain spaces within the apartment—as it does here when it follows Brandon and Janet to the foyer—but closing in on one intimate conversation means ignoring another conversation, leaving it *out of the frame*.

## From Brandon to Kenneth to David

Brandon's discreet discussion with Janet away from the others provides a little back story and, in doing so, adds a layer of complexity to the relationship(s) between Phillip, Kenneth, David, Janet, and himself. By this point in *Rope*, we already know that Janet used to be romantically involved with Kenneth and that she is currently in a relationship with David. But the conversation in the foyer now reveals that Janet and *Brandon* were once a couple: "After me came Kenneth, now it's, it's David," he says, in a line that was not present in the first draft of the screenplay.[8] If the opening of shot 2 hinted in mise-en-scène and dialogue at sexual intimacy between Brandon and Phillip, the conversation here in shot 4 gestures towards Brandon as heterosexual, or bisexual, or pansexual (even if the latter two possibilities would have enraged the Production Code Administration in 1948).

Brandon's allusion to his past with Janet is fleeting, however, and he soon turns his attention back to the present moment when he suggests that she has chosen David for his money. (Janet's financial status is much more explicitly sketched in the first version of the screenplay, incidentally, where we are told that her family "was almost 400 and had money until just about the time she entered her teens."[9] Phillip also remarks in this draft that Janet "doesn't have a dime" immediately before Brandon states that she has "banked everything on hooking David."[10]) She takes offence at the comment about her motives for marrying into the Kentley family and moves back into the main room, followed by the camera. As the four friends gather in shot near the piano, they are framed tightly and the dialogue adds a further layer of personal history: Brandon explains to Janet that Rupert Cadell, who is soon to arrive, taught David, Phillip, Kenneth, and him at prep school. As Brandon mentions David's name, he looks in the direction of the wooden chest and smirks with an awareness that only we and Phillip can see or share.

## "David!"

When Brandon refers subsequently to his admiration for Rupert, Kenneth recalls how "Brandon would sit up 'til all hours at the master's feet" in conversation with their former teacher. Janet enquires about Rupert's unorthodox beliefs, and Brandon gives an instance of Cadell's "impatience with, uh, social conventions," leaning away from an upright position in an oddly forced manner as he does so:

> BRANDON: For example, he thinks murder is a crime for most men, but . . . [*glancing towards Phillip*]
>
> PHILLIP: . . . a *privilege* for the few.
>
> BRANDON: Yes.

This brief account of Rupert's worldview links him for the first time, at least at the level of philosophy, to the killing of David: Brandon and

Figure 4.5. Brandon's inclination.

Phillip were, it transpires, taught by someone who believes that murder is "a *privilege* for the few," and they have now put this theory into practice by strangling David—who was also one of Rupert's pupils, of course. *Rope* will later examine in much more detail Cadell's influence on the murderers and, by extension, his complicity in the crime, but the matter is dropped as soon as it is raised here in shot 4 for when Brandon says "Yes" to confirm Phillip's statement, the door buzzer sounds once again, leading him to move quickly away from the group into the foyer, followed by the camera, where he encounters Mrs. Wilson. As they speak to each other, their words overlap with the conversation that is still underway between Kenneth, Phillip, and Janet. Unlike the earlier moment in shot 4 at which Brandon and Janet retreat to the foyer and discuss their former relationship, here the volume of the conversation in the main room does not drop on the film's soundtrack, which means that *Rope* is at this point is aurally jumbled: for a moment there are two separate conversations competing with each other, and, while the camera visually privileges what Brandon is doing, the dialogue becomes impossible to follow. The film cannot present two distinct discussions at the same volume level simultaneously and remain coherent, so it refuses to choose between them. If realism involves placing and preserving the viewer in a position of knowledge and mastery, here the realism of *Rope* ties itself in knots and becomes paralyzed. There is simply too much happening in the apartment to be captured clearly on film, and the text makes no secret of this fact.[11]

The nuanced arrangement of the film's sound changes, however, when Brandon opens the door and greets Mr. Kentley and Mrs. Atwater, played by Cedric Hardwicke and Constance Collier, respectively. Both actors had some form of prior connection with Hitchcock: Hardwicke had played General McLaidlaw in *Suspicion* (1941), while Collier had written, with Ivor Novello, the play upon which *Downhill* (1927) was based.[12] The camera closes in as the two new arrivals enter the apartment and Mr. Kentley explains that his wife is unable to attend. In the background at this point, and also when Mrs. Atwater subsequently joins in the discussion at the entrance to the apartment, we can hear vague fragments of speech from the other room, but, as when Janet and Brandon moved to the foyer earlier in the shot, the volume is too low for sense to be conveyed **(E)**.[13] As if commenting further on the fact that it is clearly framing the action here (and thus limiting what is seen and heard), the film shows a framed picture on the wall in the hallway outside the apartment when the door is open.

It is not even the case that what takes place purely within the foyer at this point is conveyed with clarity. Realism stumbles yet again, for as Mrs. Wilson takes Mrs. Atwater's stole and gloves, the conversation by the entrance door—which had been singular—splits into two: Brandon speaks to Mr. Kentley, while Mrs. Wilson and Mrs. Atwater engage in an entirely separate discussion. It is possible to make out the occasional phrase—Brandon says "Oh, not really," for instance, and Mrs. Wilson utters the phrase "Exactly two years ago this summer I had one myself"—but the viewer's ability to follow with any kind of overall clarity is strikingly limited. As so often in *Rope* we catch glimpses, fragments, but evidently not the whole picture.

Perhaps noticing this disorienting clash of conversations, Brandon steers Mrs. Atwater way from Mrs. Wilson and into the living room. The camera closes in and tracks backwards in front of her, showing the upper part of her body.[14] She squints as she looks around, and her face suddenly lights up. "David!" she says in excitement. As Brandon says (partially offscreen), "Oh, no, uh, no, uh, this is, uh . . . you've made a mistake. This, this is Kenneth Lawrence," the camera swings around sharply to show Kenneth and Phillip. As Marc Raymond Strauss has pointed out, this is "[t]he first pan in a long while" in *Rope*, and, as such, "it alerts us that something important is about to happen."¹⁵

## The Curious Case of Dick Hogan

It is easy to see how Mrs. Atwater makes an error and takes Kenneth for David. *Rope* shows us very little of David Kentley, of course, but we do glimpse just about enough (in shot 2) to know that he is of roughly the same age and build as Kenneth, and that he also has short blonde hair. Dick Hogan, who plays David, does not utter a word in *Rope*, dies seconds after the opening credits have concluded, and then disappears into a wooden chest from which he will never emerge.¹⁶ (This was a dramatic farewell in another way, too: *Rope* was Hogan's final role in a rather brief film career; his obituary in the *Los Angeles Times* in August 1995 noted that he became an insurance agent in Arkansas after retiring from acting following his appearance in *Rope* in 1948.¹⁷) But while Hogan

Figure 4.6. The death of David.

had no lines in the film itself, he did speak in its rather unusual theatrical trailer, which was shot partly on location in Manhattan in May 1948.[18] The publicity clip opens with a shot of Central Park and the title "NEW YORK One Spring Afternoon." An orchestral arrangement of the first of Poulenc's *Mouvements perpétuels* plays.[19] There then follows a scene which appears nowhere in *Rope*: David and Janet sit on a bench in the park and discuss their planned engagement. As David mentions the need to leave for an appointment (with Brandon and Phillip?), Janet says that she will see him "tonight at Brandon's party." They kiss and he walks away. Janet looks on fondly, but suddenly the voice of James Stewart intervenes with the words, "That's the last time she ever saw him alive—and that's the last time *you'll* ever see him alive." The engagement will never come.

This promotional footage allows us to understand with greater clarity Mrs. Atwater's squinted confusion: it shows far more of David than the film itself ever does and, in doing so, underscores his striking physical resemblance to Kenneth. "In a way," Kristin L. Matthews writes,

Figure 4.7. David and Janet in the publicity trailer for *Rope*.

Figure 4.8. Kenneth and Phillip greet Mrs. Atwater.

"Kenneth and David are doubles: the schools they attend, women they date, and clothes they wear are the same, as is their physical appearance. Kenneth, therefore, continues to function as a double of David throughout the party."[20]

But the mirroring in shot 4 of *Rope* does not stop with the confusion between Kenneth and David because the camera, when it swings around from Mrs. Atwater to show roughly what she is seeing, doubles up on the doubling by revealing visual links between Kenneth and Phillip: each character wears a single-breasted, three-piece brown suit with a white shirt and dark tie; each sports a white pocket square (albeit folded differently); each holds a drinking glass.[21] Mrs. Atwater thinks that Kenneth is David, but because the film cannot now show us the latter to emphasize that particular doubling, it offers a living character (who is responsible, of course, for removing David from the realm of the living) and renders him a double. Phillip is at this moment the double of a double, to be more precise: he occupies, through displaced visual traces, the position of David. The novelization of 1948 is much more emphatic than the film on this point, in fact, for, when Mrs. Atwater wrongly greets David, we read:

> The name whiplashed into Phillip Morgan's mind; a curtain snapped up as he saw David Kentley standing there in the room; he himself was in the chest, and his muscles, stiff and cramped, cried out for relief. (p. 45)

In both the book and the film, the shock of the moment causes Phillip to snap the champagne glass, which cuts into his palm. One of the hands that strangled David Kentley now finds itself bleeding at the mere mention of the victim's name—a strange stigmata.

## C'est SA

When the camera pans quickly from Mrs. Atwater to Kenneth and Phillip, it takes in something beyond the figure of doubling for we suddenly see more of the large neon sign that was glimpsed through the window of the apartment in shot 2: the "S" has now been joined by an "A."[22]

In Jacques Derrida's *Glas*, "sa" is the abbreviation, or "siglum," for *savoir absolu*—the "absolute knowledge" of Hegel's culmination of philosophy.[23] Here, however, in the fourth shot of *Rope*, "SA" illuminates again the viewer's *lack* of absolute knowledge. In the immediate wake of Mrs. Atwater's error of seeing and knowing, two elements of a sign that is never seen in full mark the mise-en-scène with enigma, with curtailed knowing and a need to guess. As a complete word, "STORAGE" remains forever in storage, and "SA" here signals the savage strangling of "sa," of *savoir absolu*.

After the glimpse of "SA," the guests initially all gather at the drinks table in front of the apartment's main window. The group quickly breaks apart, though, when Brandon directs Mrs. Atwater towards Janet, who, while David's father stands at her side, is told by the astrologically minded Mrs. Atwater that her stars "indicate a marriage very soon to a tall, fair-haired young man." She then glances at Mr. Kentley and adds, smiling, "with a very lovely father." Mr. Kentley looks proud, but we know, of course, that the promised marriage between Janet and David can never take place: the murder of David, as Richard Allen puts it, "effectively kills off the possibility of the heterosexual romance."[24] Our knowledge allows us to see through their happiness and excitement; we see what they cannot.

But even this privileged knowledge is clearly not *savoir absolu* for it is quickly undercut. While Janet, Mr. Kentley, and Mrs. Atwater are talking and in full view, the offscreen conversation between Phillip, Brandon, and Kenneth makes its presence felt in the form of a faint murmuring; as before, it is not possible to understand precisely what they are saying. They are elsewhere, out of sight and out of reach (**E**), as is the vehicle whose horn sounds from the street below just after Mrs. Atwater subsequently says, "Oh, well, I suppose you did" (**E**). *Rope*, as so often, flatters us with knowledge but then quickly recoils and reminds us of what we do *not* know.

The tight framing of, from left to right, Mrs. Atwater, Janet, and Mr. Kentley as they discuss forthcoming nuptials is then interrupted when Brandon brings Phillip over to meet Mrs. Atwater. The camera moves backwards a touch to show the five characters—Kenneth remains out of shot—before Mrs. Atwater and Phillip begin to walk away in search of champagne. As they do so—as they go elsewhere—yet another horn sounds from outside (**E**). The camera remains with Janet, Brandon, and Mr. Kentley, and the latter asks if David is present in the apartment. Brandon has his back to the two guests at this point. We can therefore see something that Janet and Mr. Kentley cannot: Brandon is clearly unsettled by the question because the smile falls from his face as soon as Mr. Kentley enquires about his son. Brandon blinks rapidly and glances from side to side. When he speaks, his words are uncertain, stuttered: "I e-e-e-expected him to come with you." Our privileged access to knowledge withheld from others is yet again undercut, however, because the conversation between Mrs. Atwater and Phillip is continuing indistinctly in the background precisely when we are being treated to intimate knowledge about Brandon's state of mind: because we have closed in on *this* scene, we have turned away from *that* scene. *Rope* withholds knowledge as it bestows knowledge. As if to emphasize this point, when Brandon subsequently moves out of shot to prepare Mr. Kentley's drink, the camera closes in on the conversation between Janet and Mr. Kentley but now permits the discussion between Kenneth and Brandon to make a faint, unclear aural impression (**E**).

## A Room of One's Own?

Janet decides that she will ring Mrs. Kentley, who is unwell at home and worried about David, to tell her that her son has been detained en route and is therefore unable to call her as planned. As Brandon re-enters the frame, bearing Mr. Kentley's drink, we witness the following exchange (throughout which Brandon is leaning sharply away from an upright position):

JANET (*to Brandon*): May I use the phone?

BRANDON: Of course. It's in the bedroom.

JANET: How cozy!

BRANDON (*pointing at Janet's glass*): Aren't you, uh, ready for another?

JANET: I will be. (*She drains her glass.*) I am. Thank you.

"Aren't you ready for another?" Brandon's comment is, of course, about the drink that Janet has nearly finished. It comes, however, almost immediately after a reference to "the bedroom"—a space that, I will argue in this book, remains utterly enigmatic and that is embedded within the undecidable status of the central characters' sexuality. Taken as a whole, *Rope* raises a question—how many bedrooms are there in the apartment?—that it fails to answer in a clear and consistent way. At times—here in shot 4, for instance—there would appear to be just one, but later in the film there is, as I will discuss in time, a hint towards the existence of a second bedroom. "Aren't you ready for another?" Brandon asks Janet. He might well be referring to more than just a glass of champagne: to watch *Rope* is to find oneself having to be ready for another bedroom.

In his brilliant book on architecture in Hitchcock's films, Steven Jacobs points out that *Rope* provides "no indications about the whereabouts of bathroom and bedrooms. This omission is telling since the viewer sees the other spaces of the apartment in meticulous detail."[25] These rooms, in other words, are eternally elsewhere in the apartment around which the camera so relentlessly roams. While there is no allusion at any point in *Rope* to the bathroom, we encounter here in shot 4 the first of the film's various references to the bedroom(s), and what Brandon says in response to Janet's request to use the telephone gives the impression, as Robin Wood pointed out many years ago, that there is just one space for sleeping in the penthouse: "It's in the bedroom," Brandon says, enlisting the singular.[26] This implies, of course, as D. A. Miller notes, "that more than one person, of no more than one sex, must sleep there."[27] Indeed, Wood goes on to remark that Janet's "How cozy!" might "certainly be taken as the film's most loaded comment on the issue" of the two men's potential homosexuality.[28] If the film could never, because of the strict Production Code in operation at the time, explicitly identify Brandon and Phillip as a gay couple, it can at least offer this cryptic hint at the level of connotation.

I suspect, in fact, that the watchful eyes of the PCA were responsible for how Brandon's line identifying the location of the telephone changed as Arthur Laurents's screenplay evolved. In the first version of November 22, 1947, Brandon refers at this point to "the bedroom," but the rewrite of December 16 has him saying, "Of course. It's in my bedroom."[29] This alteration, made just one day after the PCA had complained about suggestions of homosexuality in Laurents's first draft, allows viewers to imagine that there is more than one bedroom in the apartment and that Brandon and Phillip therefore sleep apart.[30] (Heteronormativity can once again sleep at night.) The revised line remains in the final draft of the screenplay but was evidently changed back to its original incarnation at some point during shooting.[31]

If Brandon's reference to "the bedroom" in shot 4 of *Rope* is a sign of what Angelo Restivo calls "implicit homosexuality," it explicitly fails to correspond in any predictable way with the suggestion, some minutes earlier in the very same shot, that Brandon and Janet were once romantically linked.[32] If, taken in isolation, that earlier element of backstory implied heterosexuality, the reference now to "the bedroom" opens up a different possibility—one that leads us back to the strikingly intimate proximity and contact (whether real or illusory) between Brandon and Phillip at the very start of shot 2, when they are recovering from the killing. Does that remarkable bodily closeness and touching now come, in hindsight, to look even more like a hint that similar things happen between the sheets, in "the bedroom" (in the singular)?

This, in fact, is effectively how the novelization of 1948 imagines things on its back cover, where we find a handy plan of "THE NEW YORK APARTMENT WHERE THE ACTION OCCURS IN 'ROPE.'" Bizarrely, the sketch bears very little relation to the apartment depicted in the film, but it is adamant that there is just one bedroom within the penthouse. What is more, this single bedroom contains just one bed—a bed that would appear to be large enough for two. But if this curious, excessively fictional cover drawing supports a reading of Brandon's reference to "the bedroom" which would conclude that there is not a second such space in the apartment, the actual pages of the novelization point in another direction altogether, for, like the screenplays of December 16,

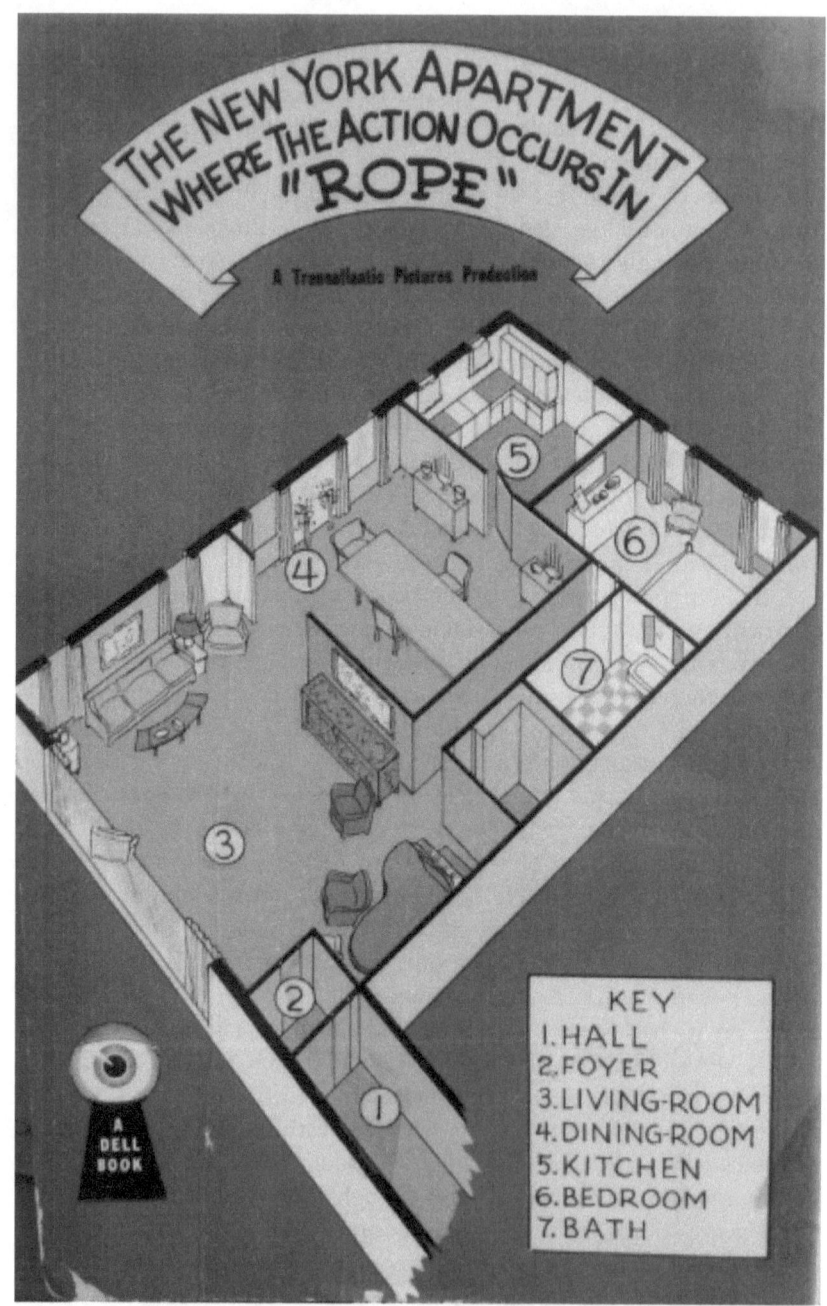

Figure 4.9. Back cover of the 1948 novelization of *Rope*.

1947 and January 13, 1948, they have Brandon speaking here of not "the bedroom" but "my bedroom."[33] If Brandon had stuck to the novelization or the revised scripts and said "my bedroom" in the finished film, the fourth shot of *Rope* would have contained clear and corresponding hints of heterosexuality near its beginning (when Brandon refers to his past with Janet) and close to its end. Things would have been knotted together, tied up, wedded with a greater degree of internal consistency. Instead, however, thanks to "the" instead of "my," *Rope* spins enigma from drift, from quiet inconsistency. My, my.

There is, moreover, a further reference to "the bedroom" (in the singular) at the very end of shot 4. Brandon pours a glass of champagne for Kenneth to take to Janet. "She's in the bedroom, telephoning," he says, pointing offscreen, pointing to the unseen elsewhere from which Janet is speaking to the world beyond the walls of the apartment **(E)**. The existence of this elsewhere is underscored by the faint traces of conversation in the background while the camera is focusing on Brandon and Kenneth. We hear that others in the living room are talking, but we can neither see them nor make out the details of their discussions **(E)**. Kenneth suspects that Brandon is trying to engineer an awkward social situation by asking him to join Janet in "the bedroom." "Then you'd like David to walk in," he says with a wary smile. "No," Brandon replies with a knowing smirk, "that'd be too much of a shock."

His expression is knowing precisely because, once again, he is exploiting and enjoying his elevated awareness; the meaning of his remark depends upon the position of its recipient. Kenneth would probably conclude that the signifier "shock" refers to the violation of contemporary social propriety that would occur if David were to discover Janet in a bedroom with her former boyfriend. For Brandon, though, and for the implicated viewer, there is an extra shade of sense at work. Because both know something that Kenneth does not, they can see why it would be "a shock" indeed for David to walk in: David is dead and lying in the wooden trunk several feet away. In other words, *Rope* has swung once more. (Perpetual movement is precisely that.) If the eruptions of elsewhere moments earlier are reminders of what the audience does not know and cannot see, here, as the shot reaches its end, lies a line which flatters the privileged knowledge derived by the viewer from an earlier act of looking.

Like shot 2, shot 4 closes with a sartorial hidden cut: as Kenneth moves in the direction of the bedroom with Janet's glass in his hand, the camera closes in on his jacket. When the darkness fills the screen, the cut comes.

# 5

## Just Plain Something

I N WHICH THE FINAL GUEST arrives, and *Rope* turns truly intertextual. When Kenneth moves in the direction of the bedroom with Janet's drink, the camera remains in the living room and turns its attention to Mrs. Atwater and Phillip, who are at the piano discussing astrology. While they consider the implications of Phillip's star sign as he leans away from an upright position, the faint sounds of an offscreen conversation between Mr. Kentley and Brandon can be heard. Their words are indistinct and impossible to follow; they signal once again, at the very beginning of this new shot, the existence of an elsewhere that remains beyond our grasp and knowledge **(E)**.

Apparently aware of the links between astrology and palmistry, Mrs. Atwater asks to see Phillip's hands. As the camera closes in on his upturned palms—which bear no trace of the bloody wound caused just minutes earlier—she offers her prediction: "These hands will bring you great fame."[1] Not long after *Rope* was released, Roland Barthes pointed out that astrology has a habit of being "a confirmation of the real world," in that its status as myth makes it more descriptive of things as they are than predictive of things as they will be.[2] Barthes's point is a political one and addresses the manner in which myths, such as astrology, seek to make alterations to the established way of the world utterly unthinkable. I suspect that Barthes would have had as little time for Mrs. Atwater as he did for Marlon Brando's character in *On the Waterfront* (dir. Elia Kazan, 1954): her belief in the stars puts her firmly on the side of bourgeois norms.[3] But it seems to me that Barthes's remark about astrology's "confirmation of the real world" can be taken somewhat out of context to describe what happens when Mrs. Atwater predicts that Phillip's hands will bring him "great fame" for she unwittingly confirms the murderous reality of which we, like Phillip, are aware. Knowing nothing about the murder of David, she is merely speaking in an abstract way about what she believes to have read in Phillip's palms. But for Phillip, and for us, there is an added connotation made possible by inescapable knowledge: "These hands will bring you great fame"—*if, like Leopold and Loeb, you are caught, and your crime is exposed*. Little wonder that he turns away in horror.

*Rope* then exploits our privileged narrative knowledge once again to give another innocent phrase a cruel connotation. When Mr. Kentley says, referring to Janet's phone call to his wife, "David wasn't there?" Janet replies, "No, he'll probably be here in a minute, though." As she utters this line, the camera tracks backwards to bring the wooden trunk containing David's corpse into view. Because we were watching when the murder occurred, we, unlike all of the guests at the party, can hear a bleak reality in Janet's words: David is already here, in a sense, but he is in no position to greet his friends and family. The wooden chest that occupies the frame when Janet speaks is, we know, a form of coffin.[4]

## Rupert, Special Pâté, Special Access

Phillip begins to play the piano.[5] He chooses the first part of Poulenc's *Trois mouvements perpétuels*; the orchestral reworking heard during the film's opening credits has been replaced by the original arrangement. (Farley Granger received musical tutoring before production began to make the movement of his hands upon the keys look more convincing. A budgetary document from the period notes that a total of $600 was set aside for these lessons.[6]) As the others in the room listen to Phillip's performance, the camera pans slowly to the left until it reveals a new character in the doorway. His arrival at the party, unlike those of the other guests, has been neither announced nor shown. (Mrs. Wilson is clearly aware of his presence, though, for she is glimpsed closing the door to the closet in the foyer, where his belongings have evidently been stored.) This mysterious character moves towards the piano and says, "Your touch has improved, Phillip." Phillip stops playing, and Brandon, who had been looking out of the main window, turns and says, "Rupert!"[7] Rupert Cadell, mentioned with enigmatic excitement in shot 2, has at last joined the party.

For playing the role of Rupert, James Stewart was paid a fee of $300,000 plus 7.5 percent of gross receipts in excess of $4,000,000. His contract stated, as was fairly common practice at the time, that he was responsible for providing his own clothes for filming.[8] As Rupert is introduced to Janet and Mr. Kentley—who remembers Mr. Cadell as the house master of Somerville, the school attended by David, Phillip, Brandon, and Kenneth—we first hear the vague sounds of another conversation (between Phillip and Mrs. Atwater) in the background **(E)**, and then, as Rupert says "Miss Walker," the distant sound of a vehicle horn **(E)**. A horn sounds again when Rupert speaks of justice **(E)**, and the indistinct traces of the discussion between Phillip and Mrs. Atwater continue when Rupert walks over to greet Kenneth **(E)**. When Kenneth says, "It's awfully good to see you again," yet another horn sounds faintly **(E)**. In short, *Rope* has swung quickly again from the emphasis of knowledge (we heard the connotation in the words of Mrs. Atwater and Janet) to the emphasis of elsewhere. We veer from knowing to not knowing.

The pendulum swings abruptly back in the direction of awareness and access, however. When Rupert walks towards the wooden trunk and speaks to Mrs. Wilson, they whisper to each other about the "special pâté" that she has bought for him. Although their voices have dropped in volume, the film allows the viewer to hear every word of their conversation clearly: we listen, in other words, to something that is probably inaudible to everyone else (to whom Rupert and Mrs. Wilson have turned their backs at this point). But *Rope* is a film of perpetual movement, so this imparting of knowledge is simultaneously undercut by the presence in the frame of something that the viewer cannot possibly grasp in full: while Rupert and Mrs. Wilson whisper by the chest, the camera shows us that the conversation between Phillip and Mrs. Atwater is still underway at the piano in the background. Because we have narrowed in on the intimate exchange about pâté, the other conversation is beyond our reach, visible and vaguely audible, but too elsewhere to be graspable entirely **(E)**. We see *and* we hear that we are not following in full. As if to drive home this point, the film then doubles the inaccessibility on screen by showing two further parallel conversations that lie beyond our mastery: when Brandon joins Mrs. Wilson and Rupert at the chest, the camera shifts position to reveal that Mr. Kentley and Janet are still in distant conversation by the window. When the latter subsequently rises and walks forward across the room, Mr. Kentley stands and strikes up a barely audible conversation with Kenneth near the drinks table **(E)**. Elsewhere upon elsewhere.

## Cassone

Noticing that candles are being lit upon what was earlier called "a ceremonial altar," Rupert gestures towards the object and asks, "Brandon, exactly what is this?" "A *cassone* I got in Italy," comes the reply.

*Cassone.* The word—which is heard at no other point in *Rope*—is far from neutral: the signifier is a chest filled with stories that wink anew towards the unspeakable relationship between Brandon and Phillip.[9] These stories coil back to the late fourteenth century in Italy, as Cristelle L. Baskins explains:

> Referring to a painted wedding chest as a *cassone* actually reflects a modern convention; in the fifteenth century such elaborately decorated pieces of furniture intended for the newlywed's chamber are referred to more frequently in documents as *forzieri*: great chests, or "strongboxes." The custom of providing containers for a bride's possessions can be traced to ancient Rome, but by the late fourteenth century Florentine patrician brides could expect to transport their *donora*, or marriage gifts, in a procession to their husband's home in a pair of lavishly decorated *cassoni* or *forzieri*.[10]

This is not the place to offer the gift of an intricate history of the *cassone*.[11] What matters here, in the specific context of a discussion of sexuality in *Rope*, is that *cassoni* were not ordinary wooden chests: they were specifically *wedding* chests and, as Baskins explains in fascinating detail, were part of the cultural organization of desire and domesticity. They were, above all, the property of *a married couple*. In the United States of 1948, of course, Brandon and Phillip could not possibly have married each other—and a sexual relationship between them would have been illegal—but Brandon's precise use of the signifier "*cassone*" is a veiled hint that the two men are more than merely old friends. As Heath A. Diehl puts it:

> On the one hand, Hitchcock's use of the term *cassone* [. . .] points up the socioeconomic privilege and the refined decadence commonly associated with aesthetes (which Brandon and Phillip are supposed to typify, in Hamilton's moving the Leopold and Loeb murder case of Chicago to Oxford [*sic*]). Additionally, the placement of the corpse of Janet's betrothed

in the traditional wedding chest underscores the violations of the institutions (heteronormative) of family, sex, and marriage wrought by the murder.[12]

If the *cassone* in Hitchcock's film is transformed in function from a wedding chest to a coffin—Peter Thornton notes, in fact, that many sixteenth-century *cassoni* had a decidedly tomblike appearance—it nonetheless retains, by being openly called a *"cassone,"* its roots in the formal union of sexual desire.[13] Just as the reference to "the bedroom" in shot 4 hinted that Brandon and Phillip sleep with each other, the uttering of the unusual term *"cassone"* here in shot 5 implies something similar. I can only presume that no one at the Production Code Administration was versed in the nuances of Renaissance-era Italian home furnishings.

## The Legend of the Mistletoe Bough

While the lighting of the candles on top of the *cassone* continues, Rupert tells Janet that Brandon was fond of bedtime stories involving chests during his schooldays. "'The Mistletoe Bough'—that was always your favourite tale, wasn't it?" he says, glancing at his former pupil, who smiles in recognition.[14]

"The Legend of the Mistletoe Bough" is a horror story that has been told and retold over the years in many different cultural forms—in print, in song, on stage, in illustration, and in film, for instance. It was particularly popular in the nineteenth century, thanks in part to its incarnation in Samuel Rogers's poem "Ginevra," which appeared in a volume entitled *Italy* in 1822, and in a later popular song by T. H. Bayly and Sir Henry Bishop that was often sung at Christmas.[15] By 1926, when Hitchcock was still in the early days of his career in filmmaking, three notable silent cinematic adaptations—all simply entitled *The Mistletoe Bough*—had been directed by, respectively, Percy Stow (1904), Edward J. Collins (1923), and C. C. Calvert (1926). I have found no evidence to confirm that Hitchcock ever saw any of these productions, but he was a keen cinemagoer, so it is not inconceivable that he encountered at least one of them; the Collins adaptation of 1923, in fact, was written by Eliot Stannard, who produced screenplays for many Hitchcock films later in the same decade.[16]

Rupert and Mr. Kentley summarize "The Legend of the Mistletoe Bough" for Janet, who has said that she is unaware of the tale:

RUPERT: I don't remember exactly how it started. It was about a lovely young girl . . .

MR KENTLEY (*interrupting*): She was bride-to-be, and on her wedding day she playfully hid herself in a chest.

RUPERT: Yes, that's right.

MR KENTLEY: Unfortunately, it had a spring lock. Fifty years later they found her skeleton.[17]

JANET: I don't think I'll get *that* playful.

But *Rope* is getting playful. I noted in chapter 1 of this book how the film is adapted from Patrick Hamilton's play of the same name and that Hamilton's tale, in spite of the author's denials, bore incriminating traces of the real-life case of Leopold and Loeb. What Hitchcock's film now reveals at this point in shot 5 is a debt to another oft-told tale: "The Legend of the Mistletoe Bough." And there is no attempt whatever to hide or downplay the line of descent: *Rope* is, in its dialogue, explicit here about its status as a text threaded together from other texts—a "fabric of quotations drawn from a thousand sources of culture," to take a phrase from Roland Barthes's classic account of influence, imitation, and impurity.[18]

"The Legend of the Mistletoe Bough"—the place of which in *Rope* has rarely been discussed in any significant way by critics—is not merely named and borrowed in Hitchcock's film, however; it is also given a playful textual twist, reknotted. In the traditional telling, as Mr. Kentley explains, it is the young bride who dies inside the chest. Samuel Rogers, for instance, spends much time celebrating the fifteen-year-old victim's youthful beauty in "Ginevra," and then has her absence first noticed "at the Bridal feast," where "soon from guest to guest the panic spread."[19] In *Rope*, however, the future *groom* is the one who occupies the wooden chest, and his wife-to-be (whose name—Janet—jangles with an echo of "Ginevra") utters her line about not becoming playful while she is eating from the trunk which contains the body of her beloved. David Kentley did not conceal himself inside the chest as part of a game, of course, and the fatal "spring-lock, that lay in ambush there" in Rogers's poem does not work properly in Hitchcock's film.[20] It will not, moreover, be a "[f]ull fifty years" until the body is found in *Rope*: Rupert will lift the lid of the trunk in a little under fifty minutes.²¹ Nonetheless, the textual debt is clear: *Rope* is a refashioning of "The Legend of the Mistletoe Bough" in which the *cassone* points at once to the impossibility of heterosexual romance (the murder of David is the death of the wedding) and the encrypted possibility of same-sex desire (the murder of David is conducted by two men who might be lovers). Traditional early modern *cassoni* bore elaborate illustrations, often of tales from texts such as Virgil's *Aeneid* and Boccaccio's *Teseida*; they were, as Cristelle L. Baskins discusses at length, fabulously textual objects.²² The wooden chest in *Rope* bears no narrative painting—a simple floral motif is all that we see—but it is profoundly textual in another way, an invisible way, for it positions Hitchcock's film within an ongoing telling and retelling of "The Legend of the Mistletoe Bough."²³

## Another Strand: That New Thing with Bergman

This open, explicit strand of intertextuality continues immediately when Mrs. Atwater joins the group at the *cassone* and asks the others if they have seen "that new thing at the Strand." (As she makes this remark, Brandon leans into the frame from the left.) Her reference here is to a large movie palace which one stood at the corner of 47ᵗʰ Street and Broadway in New York's Times Square. The theater, which was "designed and built exclusively to show movies," first opened on April 11, 1914, contained 3500 seats, and was described by *New York Call* as the "most imposing and impressive institution of its kind in existence."²⁴ The Strand became the Warner Strand in 1928 when Warner Bros. purchased the property, and the building was eventually demolished in 1987. In other words, when Mrs. Atwater refers to "that new thing at the Strand," *Rope* is subtly invoking the name of the Hollywood studio responsible both for its distribution and for housing the soundstage on which it was shot. As a phrase, "that new thing at the Strand" leads us, in effect, to "that new thing directed by Alfred Hitchcock and brought to the cinema screen by Warner Bros." (At the risk of tying myself in knots, I would also note here that each component of a piece of rope is called a strand.)

The film never openly names its director, of course, but there is a playful allusion in the dialogue that follows Mrs. Atwater's reference to the Strand. The guests' talk turns to actors, and Janet confesses a fondness for James Mason (who would appear eleven years later in Hitchcock's *North by Northwest*). When Mrs. Atwater says that she likes Mason "as much as Errol Flynn," Janet adds, "I'll take Cary Grant myself."²⁵ Mrs. Atwater shares the admiration, it transpires, and as she waxes lyrical Brandon once more leans into the shot:

> MRS ATWATER: Oh, he was thrilling in that new thing with Bergman. What was it called now? *The Something of the Something*. No, no, that was the other one. This was just plain *Something*. You know, it was, sort of, you know.²⁶
>
> RUPERT: It's right on, right on the tip of my tongue.²⁷
>
> JANET: Mine too. It was just plain *Something*, I'm sure. I adored it. And *Bergman*.

"Just plain *Something*." This is something of a plainly mischievous gesture towards Hitchcock's *Notorious*, in which Ingrid Bergman had starred alongside Cary Grant just two years before the release of *Rope*. The film had performed well at the box office in 1946, and it is likely that many of *Rope's* first viewers in 1948 would have seen through the "just plain *Something*" and grasped the reference. (Readers of the novelization, meanwhile, had things laid out far more clearly for them: Mrs. Atwater refers in its pages not to "that new thing at The Strand" but to "that new Hitchcock picture."²⁸)

What we find towards the end of the *Rope's* fifth shot, in other words, are three neighboring moments at which the film becomes openly metafictional and exposes its own status as a piece of fiction. When it explicitly invokes "The Legend of the Mistletoe Bough," it names an earlier, much-told tale that it is refashioning; when it summons the Strand it identifies a cinema owned by the studio where *Rope* was shot and that distributed the film for Transatlantic Pictures; and when it speaks of Bergman and Grant in "just plain *Something*," it summons up *Notorious* and has the characters in the present Hitchcock film allude to characters in an earlier Hitchcock film. The realism of *Rope* therefore unravels: a text made according to the conventions of classic realism does not draw attention to itself *as a text*, as something both created and created out of other fictions. In realism, as Colin MacCabe puts it, "[t]he real is not articulated—it is."²⁹ The task of the realist text is to allow readers or viewers to observe the world before them, as if it and they were really there, as if the words or the screen were merely a window (and not sites of meticulous inscription). Realism effaces the signs of its own articulation, but here in shot 5 *Rope* drifts in the direction of metafiction, and metafiction, as Patricia Waugh explains in her classic overview of the form, lays bare the illusion upon which realism relies.[30] Discussing the way in which John Barth's "Lost in the Funhouse" repeatedly undermines and exposes itself as a piece of fiction, Waugh notes that "[t]he effect of this is to lull the reader, not into acceptance of the scene as real, but into acceptance of its reality as *a sentence in a book*."[31] We might, I think, adapt Waugh's words to make sense of the layered metafiction in *Rope*'s fifth shot: *the effect of this is to lull the viewer of Hitchcock's film, not into acceptance of the scene as real, but into acceptance of its reality as a scene in a Hitchcock film that is reworking "The Legend of the Mistletoe Bough," and whose very existence as a film upon the screen relies materially upon Warner Bros.*

## Lazarus and the Chicken

After the discussion of Hollywood films, the characters shift positions in the room: Mrs. Wilson returns with more food; Phillip comes over to the *cassone* from the window, where his conversation with Kenneth had been only partly visible and audible (**E**); Rupert and Mrs. Atwater walk towards the piano; Mr. Kentley reappears and then joins Rupert and Mrs. Atwater. As the latter three characters stand with their backs turned to the camera, we hear that they are talking, but their words are too quiet to be clear and within our grasp (**E**).

Janet offers a serving of chicken to Phillip, but he says, after an anxious pause, "I don't eat it." "How queer!" says Janet.[32] In 1948, as now, the signifier in question—which occurs nowhere else in *Rope*—conveyed a range of possible meanings. It could simply mean "strange" or "unusual," but notably since the late nineteenth century had also been used (pejoratively) to refer to same-sex desire and activity.[33] Janet's remark—the opening "How" of which connects it to the "How cozy!" that she utters earlier on hearing that the phone is "in the bedroom"—therefore raises once more the possibility of a sexual relationship between Phillip and Brandon: something about the former's way of life is "queer."

Janet wonders why Phillip avoids chicken: "Freud says there's a reason for everything—even me," she remarks.[34] "There's no reason, Janet," Phillip replies sternly.[35] He turns away from her and walks to the others. Rupert, however, quickly suggests that Phillip, contrary to his dismissal, has "a very funny reason" for avoiding chicken, and he invites Brandon to tell the story:

BRANDON: Well, it happened about three years ago in Connecticut. Mother has a place there, you know. We were going to have chicken, so we, we walked over to the farm. It was a lovely Sunday morning in late spring. Across the valley the church bells were ringing, and in the yard Phillip was doing likewise to the necks of two or three chickens.

MRS ATWATER (*placing the chicken that she was about to eat back upon her plate*): Oh dear!

BRANDON (*rising to stand*): It was a task he usually performed very competently, but on this particular morning his touch was perhaps a, a trifle too delicate, because one of the subjects for our dinner table suddenly rebelled. Like Lazarus he rose . . .

PHILLIP (*interrupting, shouting*): That's a lie!

Phillip is presumably disturbed by the telling of this tale because he has recently participated in the wringing of David Kentley's neck: Brandon's bleak pun has struck a nerve.[36] But this is something that only he, Brandon, and we know, of course, so the extra level of meaning, of grim understanding, is not available to the other characters in the apartment. If Freud is right about there being "a reason for everything," as Janet puts it, then understanding the reason for Phillip's angry shout relies upon a privileged relationship to knowledge, to the bigger picture, in which David, unlike Lazarus and the chicken in Connecticut, will never rise.

With Phillip's dramatic outburst—"That's a lie!"—the fifth shot of *Rope* comes to an end. If his approach to the chicken's neck was "delicate," the cut here is anything but: it is utterly obvious, unmasked. No lie.

# 6

# Miss Sashweight of the Blunt Instrument Department

## The Art of Murder according to Rupert Cadell

THE SIXTH SHOT OF *ROPE* OPENS on Rupert and shows his reaction to Phillip's indignant shout of "That's a lie!" The camera remains focused tightly upon him for around twenty seconds while Phillip, Brandon, and Janet speak offscreen. His eyes flick from character to character, and he turns his head slightly to be in a better position to observe the nuances. Rupert is very much a silent observer here: he plays no part for now in the conversation that he is scrutinizing. We watch him studying something that is occurring out of our sight (**E**), and we watch his reactions to what he is witnessing: he frowns slightly and looks rather intrigued by Phillip's outburst and its aftermath. Although the three younger characters are off camera at this point, their voices are perfectly clear; this is not, in other words, another moment at which *Rope* leaves its acousmatic dialogue enticingly vague. We hear with clarity the words that Rupert is analyzing intently:

> PHILLIP: There isn't a word of truth in the whole story. I never strangled a chicken in my life.
>
> BRANDON: Now, look here, Phillip . . .
>
> PHILLIP (*angrily*): *I never strangled a chicken*, and you know it.

JANET (*laughing*): Forgive me, but it does seem very funny, you two being so intense about an old, dead chicken.

BRANDON: Sorry, we were ridiculous and very rude. I apologize for both of us and the story.

RUPERT: Well, is it all over?

BRANDON: I'm afraid so, Rupert.

RUPERT: Oh, what a pity. In another moment you might have been strangling each other instead of a chicken. (*He smiles.*)[1]

Has Rupert, whose scrutiny is as intense as Brandon and Phillip's disagreement, begun to suspect that something is awry? "His gaze thoughtful, Rupert Cadell watched the two," we read in the novelization, and the film in its own way privileges his reaction to the discussion following the outburst by holding the camera on him while the others speak.[2]

For a moment, it seems possible that Rupert is on the right path: when he moves across the room, he says that his former pupils appeared to be on the verge of "strangling each other instead of a chicken"; they have, of course, as we know all too well, recently strangled one of their erstwhile classmates. But his remarks soon head in another direction when he says, "Personally I think a chicken is as good as reason for murder as a blonde, a mattress full of dollar bills, or any of the customary unimaginative reasons," and his phrasing gives notable emphasis to the word "murder." Robin Wood pointed out some decades ago that two processes coincide with each other in *Rope*: Rupert's discovery of what has happened to David, and Rupert's discovery of "how deeply he is implicated" in the crime.[3] It is, of course, too soon in the narrative for Rupert to learn of David's fate—he can be on the right path, but he cannot yet reach the point at which the path ends in truth—so *Rope* must retreat temporarily from the moment of revelation and turn instead to the possibility that Rupert is to some extent complicit in the killing. It does this by having him move away from his discussion with Brandon and Phillip; instead, he now shares with the others his philosophy of murder as a form of art and as the solution to a series of everyday problems (such as, in his own words, "unemployment, poverty, standing in line for theatre tickets").

While *Rope* has previously featured moments at which the guests are split into smaller groups holding parallel conversations, Rupert's theories about the legitimacy of homicide are delivered to the entire group as he sits by the apartment's window, as if he were holding court. This is clearly a speech that everyone, including the audience, is meant to hear. Murder, Rupert explains, is not acceptable in all circumstances: "the privilege of committing it should be reserved for those few who are really superior individuals." While he speaks, the camera moves a little to the right to show Mr. Kentley and Brandon. There is a striking difference between their poses: David's father has turned away partly and stares out of the window—Robin Wood concludes that he is looking anxiously for his missing son—while Brandon looks eagerly in Rupert's direction and eventually chimes in to voice his support:[4]

> BRANDON: And the victims—inferior beings whose lives are unimportant anyway.
>
> RUPERT: Obviously.

A rope thus binds the murderous actions of Brandon and Phillip to Rupert's philosophy; his "obviously" is obviously a sign of connection and complicity. But as Rupert explains his opinions, it seems that holding such a position is something of a joke for him: his examples are delivered with a knowing smile, and Mrs. Atwater appears to be enjoying the macabre discussion of fantastic characters such as "Miss Sashweight of the Blunt Instrument Department."[5] However, when Mr. Kentley says, in response to Rupert's celebration of "Strangulation Day," that he does not appreciate the "morbid humor," Rupert insists that "the humor was unintentional" and proceeds to claim that he is "a very serious fellow." (He cannot yet know, of course, that there is a deadly seriousness in the precise moment at which Mr. Kentley has voiced his objection: the entire film unfolds on what is actually a strangulation day.)

The camera focuses on Mr. Kentley and Brandon as the latter fleshes out the philosophy proposed by Rupert:

> BRANDON: The few are those men of such intellectual and cultural superiority that they're above the traditional moral concepts. Good and evil, right and wrong were invented for the ordinary average man, the inferior man, because he needs them.
>
> MR. KENTLEY: Then obviously you agree with Nietzsche and his theory of the Superman.

BRANDON: Yes, I do.

MR. KENTLEY: So did Hitler.[6]

The final line in this exchange is striking even now, of course, but, as Peter J. Dellolio reminds us, in 1948, audiences would have encountered it "[a]gainst the contemporary background of the Nuremberg trials"; for Rohmer and Chabrol it was precisely this explicit—albeit brief—discussion of the legacy of Nazism that made *Rope* a political film.[7] Brandon tries to establish a distinction between himself and what he calls the "brainless murderers" of Nazi Germany by saying that the latter were "incompetents and fools" who deserved to be hanged for their stupidity, but when he attempts to enlist Rupert for support at this point, the latter senses that Mr. Kentley has become upset, and he refuses to take Brandon's side. *Rope* has established a connection between Rupert and the killers, then, but also a difference. Rupert eventually holds back, but Brandon presses on, and this determination pushes the discussion into awkward silence as Mr. Kentley stands and bows his head. Into the silence comes a sound of elsewhere when vehicle horns sound twice in the street below **(E)**.

Rupert, whose philosophies have produced this social unease, now changes the subject and suggests that Phillip show Mr. Kentley the rare books that have been laid out for his visit; literature, it seems, will distract and repair. As Phillip says the words "dining room," another vehicle horn can be heard **(E)**. Mr. Kentley's mood lifts on hearing of the first editions, and he leaves the main room of the apartment with Phillip. As they pass out of the frame, the camera moves to focus tightly on Rupert and Brandon. The other three characters remain by the window, and we catch a fragment of their ongoing conversation, but, as in previous cases in *Rope*, it is not possible to follow fully **(E)**. Rupert then moves away towards the books, and Brandon invites Mrs. Atwater to join him; he leans towards her as he speaks. As she walks in the direction of the dining room, she says that she "used to read quite a bit" when she was a girl. "Oh, we all do strange things in our childhood," says Brandon. Mrs. Atwater turns to him and looks puzzled, but reading—or the act of textual analysis—is indeed a "strange thing" at this point in *Rope* for, once again, offscreen dialogue in the other room can be heard in the background. Because there is speech, there is an invitation to understand it, to follow it, but sense remains withheld, out of reach, elsewhere **(E)**.

The soundtrack becomes even more complicated when everyone except Janet and Kenneth leaves the room. (Those who were brought together to hear Rupert's discourse on murder are now in different parts of the penthouse.) Brandon has suggested that Kenneth switch on the radio—"A little atmospheric music goes a long way," he says with a scheming smile—and the music that subsequently comes out of the speaker almost drowns out the conversation that is taking place off-screen, in the other room.[8] Almost, but not quite. The other characters' voices can still just about be heard, but there is now loud accordion music to distract the attention of the viewer.

## Framing of Frames

As Kenneth and Janet discuss their past together and her new relationship with David, they begin to realize that Brandon has been feigning ignorance and exploiting his knowledge of their personal lives. They cross to the doorway and call him over. While the three characters exchange angry words about Brandon's duplicity, the conversation between Mr. Kentley, Mrs. Atwater, Phillip, and Rupert can be both seen and heard indistinctly in the background, but the camera does not leave the living room to provide a closer view or full access to their conversation **(E)**. The film's use of perspective and framing at this moment of "elsewhere" is striking.

Figure 6.1. Frames within frames.

In the foreground, occupying much of the field of vision, we see Janet, Brandon, and Kenneth. They stand in front of the door frame, within which there is another open frame (marking the threshold between the foyer and the dining room), and then another (as Mrs. Wilson passes through the swinging door into the kitchen). Vision, in other words, is once again framed *as framed* at this point, and each retreating frame marks the presence of a space within the apartment in which the roaming camera could in principle sit, but in which it is clearly not sitting. By presenting space—living space and visual space—in this way, as explicitly framed, *Rope* quietly reminds us once more that the act of looking is necessarily partial. A frame isolates a scene for scrutiny, of course, but it also marks a limit to looking, the point at which the gaze is arrested. As Susan Sontag put it so memorably, "to frame is to exclude."[9]

When the discussion between Janet, Brandon, and Kenneth becomes particularly heated, Rupert breaks away from the discussion of the first editions in the distant dining room and makes his way towards the main living room. He pauses when he reaches the foyer. The camera now shows three distinct populated spaces within the apartment: the living

Figure 6.2. Three spaces, three scenes.

room, the foyer, and the dining room. Each space contains its own separate scene: the books are being examined in the dining room in the distance; Brandon, Janet, and Kenneth are arguing in the main room in the foreground; and Rupert is in between, looking with interest from the foyer towards the altercation. All of this is visible, but the camera, abandoning the "sense of entitlement" that Peter Conrad attributes to it for much of the film, does not leave the living room and, because of the formal commitment to long takes, does not cut away to the foyer or the dining room to offer more precise, intimate access to those other scenes.[10] We can only observe from *here*, and the limited presence of other spaces within the apartment underscores within the mise-en-scène just how much our looking and our knowing are constrained and contained.

Upset by the argument, Janet walks away from Brandon and towards the dining room, followed by Kenneth. They pass through the space occupied by Rupert and into the area where Phillip, Mr. Kentley, and Mrs. Atwater are inspecting the books, but, again, the habitually mobile camera does not follow them; they visibly move into a scene and a conversation that we can only study in part and from a distance. Another element of life within the apartment is elsewhere, beyond our grasp (**E**).

When Kenneth and Janet have walked away, Brandon is joined by Rupert in the living room. "Something gone wrong, Brandon?" he asks. Brandon glides past the comment and is on the verge of retreating to the dining room when he suddenly stops and turns. "Uh, what did you mean, 'Something gone wrong?'" he says. Rupert explains that he was merely thinking of how carefully Brandon plans parties and how Janet's being upset has disrupted this, but Brandon appears to suspect that Rupert appears to suspect that something is awry. There is suspicion of suspicion. (In the novelization, in fact, Brandon's voice is described at this point as "thin-edged with suspicion."[11]) The game of "cat and mouse," as Phillip will later call it, is underway.

*Rope*'s sixth shot comes to an end when Rupert notes that Janet is clearly missing David. When he adds, "As a matter of fact, I'm beginning to miss him myself," the camera closes in on the back of Brandon's jacket to conceal the cut between shot 6 and shot 7.

# 7

# From OR to "We"

## Just Desserts

IF THE ATTEMPT TO CONCEAL the cut between shots 2 and 3 of *Rope* fails because of an increase in speed, here at the beginning of shot 7 of the film there is double trouble for, as D. A. Miller explains in *Hidden Hitchcock*, we find two distinct continuity errors:

> [Philippe] Mather calls attention to the violation of spatial verisimilitude that occurs after the cut; Rupert is now standing on the other side of the entrance, where Brandon had just been. "There has been a 100-degree shift in the diegetic space, and yet it goes by relatively unnoticed." Mather offers some possible reasons for our distraction (the alleged "temporal confusion" of the blackout, the "ongoing conversations"), but one he doesn't mention is the more striking continuity error involving the desserts themselves. For the two desserts Rupert is holding after the cut are not the ones he was carrying before it. On the right dessert, for example, the chocolate glaciers have become thin and runny, while the pound cake has doubled in thickness and lies on the other side of the mold. In every point of resemblance to its predecessor, this presque-parfait is far from perfect.[1]

This lack of perfection is perfectly understandable, Miller proposes:

> Here is a continuity error that, if not exactly committed on purpose by Hitchcock, he would certainly have known he couldn't avoid if he placed a hidden cut between the desserts' presentation and their eating. These desserts are edible—else we should not see Rupert scooping one into his mouth after the cut; and by the time the following long take was set up—probably at least a day later—the originals would have been obviously unusable. Even to speak of originals at all is misleading; since each ten-minute take was filmed several times, there must have been a whole freezer's worth of replacements. *Rope*'s production conditions virtually mandate this fault; in no way could the desserts have ever been matched across a cut. (pp. 79–80)

My archival research for this book unearthed no information about well-stocked freezers, sadly, but it did lead me to a photograph taken on set on January 31, 1948 that shows a group of seven puddings laid out ready for their moment in the spotlight with Rupert.[2]

*Rope*'s dialogue even underscores the film's visual imperfection at this point, as Miller's delicious analysis proceeds to reveal:

> [C]lustered around the fault is an exchange that, far from distracting us from it, seems to be alluding to it. "Something gone wrong . . . what did you mean, 'something gone wrong'? . . . it's odd to have anything go wrong." And I've been saving the cream for last. At the sight of the second pair of desserts [i.e., the pair seen after the cut], Mrs. Wilson exclaims: "*Two* desserts, Mr. Cadell?" The ambiguity that she can't possibly be aware of uttering (two desserts, two sets of two desserts), we can hardly escape hearing.[3]

This odd textual hitch is, for Miller, another of *Rope*'s "off" moments" or "occult correspondences between the fiction and filmmaking, between the dialogue of the one and the devices of the other" (p. 81).

We might go further, I think. The problematic puddings conveyed by Rupert are more than just desserts: in their imperfection they gesture forwards in the narrative to the moment at which their bearer will finally solve the "perfect crime" and, in doing so, serve Brandon and Phillip with their just deserts. What Rupert gets his hands on in both instances is the unraveling imperfection that comes to light when apparent perfection is studied closely enough. The perfect crime is as flawed as the perfect pudding.

As imperfect as these desserts is the viewer's mastery of events when Rupert and Mrs. Wilson move first to the piano and then across to the corner of the room while discussing Brandon and Phillip. They are now the only two characters in the living room, but Mrs. Wilson chooses to whisper her words. The film permits us to follow this intimate conversation (in which she speaks out against her employers), but, as it has done repeatedly in previous shots, it also reminds us that another conversation, to which we do not have full access, is underway: even when Rupert and Mrs. Wilson are at the far end of the apartment, vague sounds of the discussion taking place in the dining room can be heard, but not clearly enough actually to be understood (**E**).⁴ Seconds into its seventh shot, in other words, *Rope* is once showing itself to be a film of perpetual movement and duplicity: on the one hand it allows the viewer to follow a quiet, discreet conversation between two characters; on the other hand it acknowledges, in the form of simultaneous offscreen sounds, an elsewhere that is not revealed in full. *Rope* swings sweetly from here to there.

## OR

As Rupert and Mrs. Wilson pass one of the small windows in the right-hand wall of the apartment, we catch a different glimpse of the neon sign seen partially in shots 2 and 4 of the film. At those earlier moments we saw "S" (in shot 2) and "SA" (in shot 4), but now we gaze upon "OR." We have struck gold. As I noted earlier in this book, Hitchcock explained in the pages of *Popular Photography* in November 1948 that the sign beyond the window spells out a single, complete word—"STORAGE"—even if "STORA" was all that the production sketches and studio set ever actually featured. But "OR," as seen here in shot 7, is also a word in its own right, of course, and its plural possibilities in both English and French are discussed by Jacques Derrida in a short piece on the work of Stéphane Mallarmé that was first published in 1974. Towards the end of his analysis, Derrida turns his attention to a text by Mallarmé which carries the title of, quite simply, "Or." In French, "or" can mean "gold," and Derrida observes that "gold is indeed, to a certain extent, the theme of this text, its 'signified,' as it were."⁵

Figure 7.1. OR outside the window.

Or is it? Having offered the obvious reading—"the theme"—Derrida proceeds to trace the ways in which Mallarmé's writing more generally suspends "[t]he act of naming, the direct relationship to the thing" (p. 122) by sprinkling "or" in so many ways that its meaning becomes impossible to settle—and not merely because the French language also enlists "or" as a conjunction to mean "now." At the end of a long list of quotations from Mallarmé that orchestrate "or" in various ways, Derrida poses a question:

> Is *or*, here, one word or several words? The linguist—and the philosopher—will perhaps say that each time, since the meaning and function change, we should read a different word. And yet this diversity crosses itself and goes back to an appearance of identity which has to be taken into account. If what circulates in this way is not a family of synonyms, is it the simple mask of a homonymy? But there is no noun: the thing itself is (that which is) absent, nothing is simply named, the noun is also a conjunction or an adverb. No more word:

the efficacy often comes from one syllable which scatters the word. There is, therefore, neither homonymy nor synonymy.

The classical rhetorician will be just as disarmed: we are not dealing here with any of the essentially semantic relations with which he is familiar. There is neither a metaphorical relation (there is no similarity between these instances of or); nor one of metonymy (besides the fact that the unities are not nouns, no identity is stable enough, of itself, to give rise to relationships of the whole and the part, of cause and effect, etc.).

Finally, why could not the critical treatment of a particular or play, at a distance, with its English homonym, or rather homogram, with the disjunctive versus which it enunciates? We know, and not only through his biography, that Mallarmé's language is always open to the influence of the English language, that there is a regular exchange between the two, and that the problem of this exchange is explicitly treated in *Les mots anglais*. For this reason alone, "Mallarmé" does not belong completely to "French literature." (p. 125)

Or, to put things differently, "or" has no clear and single signified or orbit in Mallarmé's writing: meaning, Derrida notes, "remains *undecidable*; from then on, the signifier no longer lets itself be traversed, it remains, resists, exists and draws attention to itself" (p. 114).

I am not for one moment proposing that Hitchcock was thinking of Mallarmé's playful textuality when he ordered his camera to isolate the third and fourth letters of "STORAGE" at this point in shot 7. But I do find it fitting that these two letters in combination—"OR"—should, given their aura of undecidability in Derrida's account, loom large in the mise-en-scène of *Rope*. "OR" marks a movement of meaning without end, without closure, without what Derrida elsewhere names the "transcendental signified."[6] Hitchcock's film, I have been arguing (and will continue to argue), has these very same qualities. Like "or," it is in perpetual movement. We gaze in awe upon golden undecidability.

## "We"

While she is discussing Brandon and Phillip's strange mood, and as she is passing the neon "OR," Mrs. Wilson makes a remark that hints gently yet again that Brandon and Phillip are a couple and that *Rope* might therefore be weaving what John Orr calls a "covert queer aesthetic."[7] "Both of them," Mrs. Wilson declares, "must have got up out of the wrong side of the bed."

On one level, the colloquialism—to get up out of the wrong side of the bed—is precisely that and is not meant to be taken literally. But *Rope*, as I have already established, is a film in which language plays in plural ways, and Mrs. Wilson's reference here to "the bed" (in the singular) winks back in the direction of the film's earlier allusions to there being just one bed or bedroom in the apartment. If both men "got up out of the wrong side of the bed," both men were in the lone bed beforehand. Mrs. Wilson's phrasing adds a further hint of intimacy, moreover, in its movement from "Both" to "the bed" as her sentence unfolds from beginning to end. Brandon and Phillip are brought together in a phrase that begins by blanketing them together within the signifier "Both" and then leads them to bed, to "the bed." Once again, the film, unable to be explicit, hints in passing in its dialogue that its two central figures sleep with each other.

Or do they? Mrs. Wilson's remark is made as the neon "OR" looms large in the background—"OR," the mark of undecidability; "OR," the suggestion of an alternative (this *or* that). Precisely because the Production Code prevents *Rope* from ever identifying Brandon and Phillip openly as lovers, Mrs. Wilson's remark must remain imprecise, veiled, deniable in the face of the censors. Its meaning, just like the central relationship of the film, is undecidable, in perpetual movement towards a plausible, palatable alternative. (Indeed, we will soon see, in the next shot of *Rope*, Mrs. Wilson utter a line that implies a living arrangement in which there is more than one bedroom in the apartment.)

Rupert, the figure and force of detection, needs to know why the day began in such a fraught manner for his former pupils, so he asks Mrs. Wilson to explain her remark—"prodding gently," the novelization specifies.[8] As she expands upon her statement about "the bed," the camera, which has been showing both figures, closes in slowly on Rupert. While he listens, his eyes move repeatedly from Mrs. Wilson to the dining room and back again. In an echo of the beginning of shot 6, he is studying the scene before him, weighing up the evidence, analyzing the sheer strangeness of the party and the actions of the hosts. While the others leaf through first editions some distance away, Rupert is here in the living room, at the scene of the crime, inches from David's body, moving gradually in the direction of discovery and exposure. Although the camera shows us clearly that Rupert is watching with intrigue what is taking place in the dining room, it does not need to reveal what he sees there as he is looking for clues in a mystery whose terrible truth *is already known to us*. We do not need to study Brandon and Phillip for tell-tale signs: we know what they have done with David.

## Like the Grave

But the moment of full knowledge and explanation cannot come just yet—the narrative still has work to do—so Rupert's questioning stalls when Mrs. Wilson says that even if she knew why Brandon and Phillip were "going at it hammer and tongs" when she returned to the apartment, she would protect her employers' privacy. "I'm like the grave," she says, unaware that her simile will have a grave second shade of meaning for the viewer who knows what neither she nor Rupert knows: while she speaks, she is standing, in effect, at David Kentley's grave.[9] Her refusal to answer any more of Rupert's questions is accompanied by the camera's retreat from its isolating focus upon him. Mrs. Wilson now appears in shot once again, but the camera continues its movement away until her conversation with Rupert becomes so faint that we can no longer follow what is being said. In the space of seconds, *Rope* has swung from intimate access to unknowing distance. Knowledge, first fed and flattered, is revealed once again to be precarious, partial, contingent.

The fading of the conversation between Rupert and Mrs. Wilson is accompanied by an increase in volume of the music on the radio and, more significantly, the voices of the other characters, who are still in the dining room. All except Phillip, that is: the tracking of the camera backwards across the main living area suddenly brings him into the frame. At first, he has his back turned to us. He is visible but not quite in focus, as the camera is still concentrating its gaze upon Rupert and Mrs. Wilson. But Phillip then turns and looks back through the foyer in the direction of the others. The camera pulls focus: he comes into view clearly while Rupert and Mrs. Wilson lapse into a blur. His expression is anxious, and he seems to be on the verge of speaking, but he remains silent.[10] At this point in shot 7, Phillip is positioned between two ongoing conversations, neither of which is completely clear to the viewer. For V. F. Perkins, the filmic technique here is a form of "subjective camera-work" because the "unintelligible whisperings which we now hear make us share in Philip's [sic] panic at what Mrs. Wilson may be revealing" inadvertently to Rupert.[11]

What we also see here, I think, is Phillip occupying a position similar to the one in which we, as viewers, have repeatedly found ourselves while watching *Rope*. He is torn between possibilities and has to make a choice: he can either return to the group in the dining room, or he can join Rupert and Mrs. Wilson by the window (through we can now see just two letters of the large neon sign—"RA"—as if they were ratifying the radical partiality of the predicament in which Phillip is caught). Even within the tightly enclosed space of the apartment, around which the camera so often glides, it is not possible for a single character or the viewer to have an overview, to have a complete grasp on what is taking place and being discussed. As Phillip shows so clearly at this point in the film, to be within the penthouse when the party is underway is to be compelled to make a decision about what to hear, what to see, and what to know. An individual, or the camera, can close in and single out an element of the whole, of course, but the whole itself remains ungraspable.

After a short pause, Phillip makes his choice and crosses the room to talk to Rupert and Mrs. Wilson; he is "carefully casual," the novelization specifies.[12] The sound of the conversation in the dining room fades a little but remains in play even when the camera moves in to frame Rupert, Phillip, and Mrs. Wilson tightly. The latter two characters explicitly refer to, and glance in the direction of, the dining room during the ensuing exchange, but, once again, the camera never shows the other scene; the lack of an eyeline match combines with the ongoing indistinct sounds of discussions to maintain the emphasis on what is elsewhere and beyond knowledge **(E)**.

When Phillip has urged Mrs. Wilson to serve the guests instead of lecturing them, he moves out of shot, and she makes a further reference to "the bed" (again in the singular): "We did get up on the wrong side of the bed, didn't we?" she whispers for Rupert's benefit. The phrasing, as so often in *Rope*, is intriguing, and it returns us to Mrs. Wilson's use of "both" earlier in the shot. On the one hand, the enlisting at this point of the signifier "we" is one of "a number of special uses" of the first-person plural pronoun in modern English, as Randolph Quirk, Sidney Greenbaum, Geoffrey Leech, and Jan Svartvik explain.[13] In some cases, they note, "we" can be employed to mean "you"; one of the examples that they give is of a doctor who, when talking to a patient, says, "How are we feeling today?"[14] The general effect of this, they conclude, is one of condescension but also "has an implication of sharing the problem with 'you' in the situation context of a doctor/patient or teacher/student relation, for example."[15] *Rope* certainly allows for such a reading of Mrs. Wilson's "we": there are moments in the film, after all, at which she treats her employers as if they were her somewhat exasperating children. But "the bed" (in the singular) is, as I have already established, one of the film's main coded hints that Brandon and Phillip sleep with each other, and here it finds itself lying cozily in a sentence alongside a "we" which might well, if taken at face value as a straightforward plural pronoun, cover and couple both Phillip and Brandon (in whose direction, and the direction of the bedroom, Mrs. Wilson happens to be looking when she speaks). Two men, one bed. We.

## That Thing

As laughter from the dining room carries across the apartment to the *cassone*, the camera closes in on Rupert, who is silent and apparently pensive. He appears to lose his appetite when he puts down the spoonful of dessert that he has been holding for nearly thirty seconds, places the entire plate onto the desk by the window, and walks towards the piano, where Phillip has once again begun to play the first of Poulenc's *Mouvements perpétuels*. The other characters are still out of sight, presumably in the dining room; we hear their voices but not their words **(E)**. Rupert, however, is interested in scrutinizing something else: he switches on the lamp that rests on top of the piano. Light shines into Phillip's eyes, as if an interrogation were about to begin. In fact, there is something strikingly forceful and direct about the way that Rupert immediately asks, "What's going on, Phillip?" He leans forward and bears down upon his former pupil. Phillip asks for the light to be switched off; Rupert obliges but accuses Phillip of trying to avoid being questioned. As Rupert says, "Yes, Phillip, I asked you a question," an emergency siren is heard in the street below. It is much louder than the noises of traffic that have been heard repeatedly up until this point in *Rope*; so much so, in fact, that both men turn their heads in the direction of the sound, which "knife[s] into the room with its insistent wail," according to the novelization.[16] This is the first time in *Rope* that anyone in the apartment has reacted to the sound of traffic from the streets outside. It is rather odd—yet perfectly common, in my experience—to look in the direction of a sound whose source cannot possibly be seen, but the actions of the two men here are a siren of their own, in that they call attention to yet another "elsewhere" in the film. We see Rupert and Phillip look, but we also see that they cannot possibly see something, the presence of which is nonetheless affirmed **(E)**.

Phillip's performance at the piano is, as Kevin Clifton points out in a brilliant analysis of the scene, "full of unmusical stops and starts, an aural analogue to Brandon's nervous stuttering heard throughout the film."[17] Rupert's interrogation of his former pupil continues after a brief pause for brandy. He picks up a metronome, sets it in motion, and gradually increases its speed until Phillip finally snaps: "I can't play with that thing," he says in a raised voice, turning away from the piano. "That thing," of course, is a device of regularity, norms, measured control; it is, as Paula Marantz Cohen notes, "a symbol of orderliness."[18] It establishes a tempo that the musician should follow; it is intended to stave off deviation, deviance, the irregular. Here in *Rope*, it is wielded by Rupert, who will later, in the film's final shot, present himself as the representative of order and societal regularity. His manipulation of the metronome poses problems for Phillip, whose playing—accomplished with the same hands that strangled David—falls out of step, out of line with the pulse of the machine, which "ticks at a tempo faster than Phillip's," Arthur Laurents's screenplay specifies.[19] Eventually, taunted by the ticking, Phillip's hands cease their work altogether, but not before, as Clifton observes, they have "freely repeat[ed] passages in an improvisatory manner," which means, in effect, that Phillip has "usurped Poulenc and elevated himself to the role of composer in an attempt to get the upper hand."[20] He "can't play with that thing," he tells Rupert, because the metronome represents the expected order, the imposed regularity, the norms from which he has so markedly deviated with his hands.

As the musical performance comes to an end, Mr. Kentley enters the frame from the left, carrying a pile of six books. Brandon has bound them together for him with the rope that was used to kill his son—"the device is worthy of the Jacobeans," notes D. A. Miller.[21] The reappearance of the murder weapon (last seen being dropped nonchalantly into the kitchen drawer in shot 3) alarms Phillip greatly: he stands and looks on in horror as Mr. Kentley walks away with his cruelly embellished gift. In shot 3, as I noted earlier in this book, Mrs. Wilson does not notice the murder weapon being twirled and stored by one of the killers: "It's only a piece of rope: an ordinary household article," Brandon says dismissively. At that earlier point, viewers catch a resonance to which Mrs. Wilson is utterly oblivious: we know, because we watched the murder, that it is anything but "an ordinary household article." Here in shot 7, however, things work differently: Rupert does not yet know the full truth, but he is evidently suspicious, and we watch him edging closer and closer to the moment of discovery.[22] "What's wrong?" he asks Phillip, looking puzzled and inquisitive;

no one else seems to have noticed Phillip's unease upon seeing the bound volumes. "I just think it's a clumsy way of tying them up, that's all," says Phillip after being questioned repeatedly. Rupert turns and looks at the bundle; the camera closes in on it, then moves back to show Rupert. He appears to have concluded something, but he says nothing.

However, when it is in the process of showing Rupert stepping closer to the truth, *Rope* reminds us that there are limits to our own knowledge, for, while Rupert is talking to Phillip at the piano about the tied books, the conversation between the others and Mr. Kentley continues off-screen. At first, this unseen parallel discussion is fairly easy to follow, but it quickly becomes indistinct behind the textually privileged exchange that is taking place between Rupert and Phillip. Rupert's attention is devoted to Phillip for obvious reasons, but this focus—on his part and ours—reminds us once again what happens when we single out a detail that is part of a larger, more complex picture: something is necessarily ignored, neglected, relegated elsewhere **(E)**.

The seventh shot of *Rope* concludes by allowing yet another elsewhere to grace the screen. When Brandon and Phillip meet at the drinks table and begin to argue, the conversation between the other characters is indistinctly audible in the background **(E)**. (Shortly before Brandon

Figure 7.2. Brandon leaning.

moves over to join Phillip, we see him leaning oddly in the background, just as Mr. Kentley says that he prefers "manners to femininity.") The tension between the killers surfaces again when Brandon tries to stop Phillip from having another drink. "Don't you ever again tell me what to do and what not to do," says Phillip angrily as he fills his glass. Rupert, who has joined them at the table, continues his interrogation, this time addressing both Brandon and Phillip, before they are interrupted by the voice of Mrs. Wilson. "Excuse me, sir," she says from off-screen. The three men look in her direction, and the film cuts without making any attempt to hide that it is tying up the shot.

# 8

# Two Small Fugitives from a Bowl of Alphabet Soup

## The First Bedroom

ALL BETS ARE OFF. IN THE opening seconds of *Rope*'s eighth shot Mrs. Wilson makes a remark that invites us to rethink the way in which Brandon and Phillip share their splendid penthouse. As I have already noted in *Perpetual Movement*, the earlier shots of the film, along with the strange plan of the apartment on the back cover of the novelization published in 1948, imply that the two men share a bed: everything that we have heard up to this point in *Rope* suggests that there is just one bedroom. But when, roughly ten seconds into the eighth shot of the film, Mrs. Wilson directs Mrs. Atwater to the telephone so that she can speak to Mrs. Kentley, she says quite clearly: "Uh, down the hall to your left, dear. The first bedroom."[1]

In Arthur Laurents's initial draft of the screenplay, dated November 22, 1947, the moment plays out rather differently: Mrs. Wilson refers simply to "the bedroom."[2] By the time we reach the second draft on December 16, 1947, however, the phrase has become "the first bedroom," and this is how it remained in the final revised script of January 13, 1948.[3] The archives record no reason for the alteration, but I presume that the line was amended in the light of ongoing discussions with the Production Code Administration about the homophobic demand to remove all hints of same-sex relations from the screenplay. After all, one day before the introduction to the script of the phrase "the first bedroom," Transatlantic had, as I noted in chapter 1, been informed in writing by the PCA that the censors had concerns about "a possible flavor in some of the dialogue that a homosexual relationship existed between Brandon and Phillip."[4]

*The first bedroom*. The phrasing suggests that, contrary to statements made earlier in the film, there is more than one bedroom: it makes no sense for Mrs. Wilson to specify "the first" if there is only one. "First" implies more than one: "so, there is a second, we may assume," as Steven Jacobs concludes in his study of architecture in Hitchcock's work.[5] And if there is indeed more than one bedroom in the apartment, the possibility that Phillip and Brandon sleep together finds itself thrown into doubt. Perhaps, the film now hints, they retire to separate rooms at night. Swinging suddenly towards this new possibility makes for undecidability: for the first fifty minutes of *Rope*, the viewer has been offered gentle suggestions that the two central male figures are a couple, but shot 8 undoes the earlier work of the text or at least undermines it by embedding an alternative. From this point onwards, then, *Rope* allows us to see its central relationship in two completely different ways: Phillip and Brandon are a couple; Phillip and Brandon are not a couple. There is textual evidence to support both readings, neither of which can be ruled out, for the simple reason that the film, as Jacobs observes, never shows us the apartment's bedroom(s).[6] Mrs. Wilson's contradiction in speech, D. A. Miller concludes, "reinforces the undecidability that keeps suspicion just that, a thing never substantiated, never cleared."[7]

## Lifting and Lowering the Lid

As Mrs. Atwater walks away towards "the first bedroom," one of the tensest scenes in the film begins; it is a moment which emphasizes with agonizing force the split between sound and vision and the way in which *Rope* often allows different scenes to play out in parallel. The camera watches Mrs. Wilson for nearly two minutes as she gradually clears the top of the *cassone*. She works without speaking and makes repeated trips to and from the dining room and the kitchen, removing crockery and returning books. While this is happening, the other characters (except Mrs. Atwater, who is in "the first bedroom," of course) stand just offscreen in conversation. Rupert is partly visible from time to time, but the others are represented only by their utterances—acousmatic voices from elsewhere **(E)**.

This makes the gap, or the difference, between what we can see and what we can hear—a gap which has often left its mark upon *Rope*'s earlier shots—particularly striking. In the field of the visible, the dominant element is evidently Mrs. Wilson innocently at work, clearing the *cassone* and coming closer to exposing the corpse. But the soundtrack while this is occurring relays a conversation between most of the other characters, all of whom, with the partial exception of Rupert, are out of shot. Their words address the whereabouts of David and make no reference whatever to what Mrs. Wilson is doing.[8] The scene, in effect, is therefore actually two scenes. In one, a maid clears up the remnants of a party thrown by her employers; in the other, the guests wonder why David has yet to arrive at the party (which is, as Mrs. Wilson's actions make clear, now winding down). The scenes are separate in a real sense, then, and this is emphasized by the fact that the conversation about David takes place offscreen. As implicated, knowing viewers, however, we are able to see the link between the two scenes and possibly to view them as one: because we know precisely where David is, and has been all along, we are aware that Mrs. Wilson is on the verge of bringing the whereabouts of David (and the terrible crime) to light inadvertently. What allows us to make such a link is, of course, knowledge.[9]

And yet, even as it spins a suspenseful scene out of our privileged awareness, *Rope* blatantly exposes the limits of that knowledge: while we can hear the characters' voices clearly, we are unable to see the individuals as they speak, which means that we cannot, as V. F. Perkins pointed out many years ago, tell if anyone is watching Mrs. Wilson as she comes closer and closer to discovering the body of David Kentley.[10] We see and know in one respect, then, but are unable to measure our seeing and knowledge against the center of things.[11] *Rope* gives and *Rope* reels away in perpetual movement.

Moments after Phillip reveals (offscreen) that he spoke to David on the telephone the previous morning, Mrs. Wilson's progress reaches the point at which even the ceremonial cloth and candles have been removed from what Brandon earlier called the "altar." She begins to open the *cassone* to place some books within. Rupert offers to help, so she lowers the lid and hands him the volumes before once again starting to open the chest. But before David's body can be discovered, Brandon enters the frame quickly to intervene. He places his hands on top of the *cassone* and the secret is preserved—for now, at least. Rupert says nothing, but he looks anxiously at the chest while Brandon speaks to Mrs. Wilson. How much does he now suspect?

Mrs. Atwater returns from the "first bedroom" and announces that David's mother is extremely worried about his absence. "She wants you to call the police," she says to Mr. Kentley. With those words, the camera swings around, passes Brandon, and pauses very briefly on Phillip, who looks horrified at the mention of the authorities. The sweep of the camera continues until Rupert is in roughly the center of the frame, with fragments of the neon sign visible behind him through the window. He is looking at Phillip and Brandon, and, as at earlier inquisitive moments, his eyes dart quickly around the room.

Worried by what he has heard from Mrs. Atwater, Mr. Kentley announces that he is leaving the party and accepts Janet's offer to accompany him. They move towards the foyer, along with Mrs. Atwater and Kenneth. Brandon reminds Mr. Kentley to take the bundle of books with him; as he passes them over, his right hand touches the rope around them—the rope that has, the viewer knows, been used to strangle the son about whom the Kentleys have become so concerned. The camera then lingers on Janet and Kenneth while they discuss how pleased they are to have "had that talk" about their past together. While we witness this moment of intimacy, however, we also hear a conversation between the characters who are now standing out of shot by the front door. Their words are audible but not understandable **(E)**. Privileged access sits again alongside distance.

## Reduco Redux

While Janet and Kenneth enjoy their brief closeness, between them, just above Janet's right shoulder, a red light can be seen flashing in the Manhattan skyline. It is almost certain that the first viewers of *Rope* in 1948 would, if they even noticed this winking light, have paid little attention to it. It is far away in the background and is little more than a colorful blur. It is impossible to make out the details, even with the recent benefit of high-resolution Blu-ray technology and the ability to freeze frames for closer inspection; D. A. Miller's "Too-Close Viewer" is defeated here.[12] But the red light is actually Alfred Hitchcock's second cameo appearance in *Rope*, and it is a curious appearance that marks another point of self-referential intertextuality in the film.[13] If shot 5 invoked Hitchcock's *Notorious* (1946), the flashing red light here in shot 8 ferries us back two years further to *Lifeboat*.

As I noted in chapter 1 of this book, although Hitchcock was under contract to David O. Selznick at the beginning of his Hollywood career, he was allowed, with Selznick's approval, to make films for others between

1940 and 1947. In 1944, he directed *Lifeboat* for 20th Century-Fox; Hume Cronyn, who would go on to write the initial treatment for *Rope*, played the role of Stanley Garrett. *Lifeboat* is an even more confined film than *Rope*.[14] It opens with the sinking of a ship that has been struck by a Nazi torpedo. The camera shows the burning vessel slipping beneath the waves and then focuses on a lone lifeboat, which is where the rest of the film will unfold. The extremely constrained setting posed an obvious problem for the customary Hitchcock cameo: how could the director possibly make an appearance in the middle of the ocean? The solution was inspired. Around twenty-three minutes into the film, a character named Gus was seen reading a newspaper. An advertisement on the page facing the camera heralded the properties of a slimming product called the "Reduco Obesity Slayer." "Before" and "after" pictures showed a portly gentleman transformed miraculously into a slenderer figure.[15] For the avoidance of doubt, a small text box in the lower left-hand corner of the panel printed the lucky fellow's name in bold capital letters: ALFRED HITCHCOCK.

Figure 8.1. The Reduco advertisement in *Lifeboat* (1944).

Although *Rope*'s setting is not quite as confined as that of *Lifeboat*, Hitchcock told *Popular Photography* magazine in November 1948 that he struggled once again to imagine how he could make a cameo appearance:

> It's traditional, with me at least, that I appear fleetingly in every one of my pictures. But *Rope*, with a cast of only nine people who never leave the apartment, looked like the end of the tradition. There was just no way that I could get into the act.
> Then someone came up with a solution. The result? The Hitchcock countenance will appear in a neon "Reduco" sign on the side of a miniature building!¹⁶

The "Hitchcock countenance," however, is impossible to see as such in the finished film. "Though the hidden caricature is unmistakable once you know it's there," writes D. A. Miller,

> in no format of *Rope* have I been able to read the word "Reduco": the blur is irresolvable. [. . .] "Reduco" would thus be the limit-case of a hidden picture: a thing so well hidden that, without ceasing to exist, it has become *invisible*.¹⁷

*Once you know it's there.* Miller's phrase is important. It is likely, I think, that many viewers of *Rope* have no idea precisely what is flashing in Manhattan skyline at this point in the film. Our eyes cannot bring the details of the light to light: we need to be given, by a critic such as D. A. Miller or by Alfred Hitchcock himself, the information and the explanation. To the best of my knowledge, moreover, there are no close-up photographs from the set of the Reduco sign either *in situ* or under construction. But the object certainly existed, even if its appearance in the finished film was far from clear: a sketch produced by the Art Department at Warner Bros. on January 12, 1948 provides a full-size rendering of the neon sign, which was roughly 20.5 inches high and 13.5 inches wide.¹⁸

This obscure flashing figure of intertextuality is there in *Rope*, then, as D. A. Miller is right to insist. What should we make of it as it winks between Janet and Kenneth, calling out for attention? Casey McKittrick offers one interpretation. For him, the neon weight-loss advertisement

> is significant, in that the body-under-surveillance becomes very important in the film. Of course, we spend the film wondering if the body secreted in the trunk will be discovered by the

guests. The boys' maid Mrs Wilson constantly monitors the guests' consumption. In a maternal pose she instructs the apparently frail Philip [sic], "You're too thin. Don't let them gobble up the paté [sic] before you get to it." Later, when the boys' friend Janet Walker, a writer who maintains a column about the "body beautiful," hungrily goes to the buffet (at the trunk), and is immediately checked by Mrs Wilson, "If I were you, I'd go easy on the paté, dear. Calories."[19]

I think that McKittrick is right to read the Reduco sign in this way: *Rope* is about the decay and discovery of a body as much as it is about the policing of bodies—whether those bodies are desiring food or homoerotic pleasure. I would merely add to this analysis a recognition that the neon advertisement is a further metafictional moment in *Rope*. Like the reference to *Notorious* in shot 5, the flashing sign here in the film's eighth shot shines a playful spotlight on another Hitchcock film and the familiar, full figure of the director himself.

## From Decay to DK

The departure of Kenneth, Janet, Mr. Kentley, and Mrs. Atwater is heard but almost entirely unseen because the camera has by this point in shot 8 turned to face Phillip and Rupert, who are still in the main room of the apartment. The latter begins to walk anxiously towards Phillip, but then he changes direction and heads for the foyer, where, while he looks back into the main room with a concerned expression on his face, Mrs. Wilson reaches into the closet to retrieve his hat. Or so she thinks. What she passes to him is a fedora that is far too small for his head. So distracted is he that he fails to notice the error until Mrs. Wilson alerts him to the mistake. While she turns back to the closet to retrieve the intended hat, Rupert looks at the incorrect one and notices the gold initials stamped inside: "DK."[20]

As Thomas J. Connelly has pointed out, Rupert's position within the frame at this point ensures that only we see his noticing the letters.[21] (Arthur Laurents's script was absolutely explicit about this effect as early as its first draft: "Note: The hat might be tilted so that the audience, too, sees the initials," it specified.[22]) The fedora, of course, belongs to David Kentley, and because the murder victim no longer has the same first name as he did in Patrick Hamilton's play (where he is called Ronald

Kentley), *Rope* is able to indulge in a macabre pun: DK is decay; the body of DK is beginning to decay in the nearby *cassone*.²³ When tattooed upon Kovac's body in Hitchcock's *Lifeboat*, initials signify desire and illicit sex. Stamped inside a grey hat four years later in *Rope*, they point only towards death, towards a youthful and desiring body that is now in the early stages of decomposition.

Cadell switches hats and leaves the apartment, clearly shocked by the implications of the "two small fugitives from a bowl of alphabet soup," as a 1962 script for a trailer to advertise a rerelease of *Rope* had Hitchcock himself calling the gold initials inside the fedora.²⁴ "Rupert," Arthur Laurents's script adds, "shuts his eyes with a sick feeling of horror: this is confirmation of his suspicions."²⁵

## From DK to P and Q; or, the Smile of the Satisfied Host²⁶

When all the guests have left, Brandon leans against the door and sighs with relief. He smiles as he places a cigarette in his mouth and makes his pleasure even more clear when, upon returning to the main room, he theatrically switches on a lamp and says, with a nonchalant wave of his hand, "Thank you for a lovely evening! Good night, good night. It's been charming!" He laughs, but Phillip is in a somber mood at the drinks table. Brandon believes that their party has been a success, but Phillip complains about Rupert's "prying, snooping, or just plain pumping." When Brandon says "About what?" the sound of a vehicle's horn rises from the street below **(E)**. A second such sound is heard just after Phillip says, "Tying up the books that way" **(E)**; a third follows as Brandon issues a stern reminder that Mrs. Wilson has not yet left **(E)**; and a fourth comes (very faintly) when Phillip refers to his potential hangover being "all mine" **(E)**.

The familiar difference between the two men becomes more pronounced as their discussion continues. Phillip is worried and convinced that their crime will be discovered—"I've been praying I'd wake up and find we hadn't done it yet," he says—but Brandon maintains his carefree, arrogant mood. If Phillip regrets the killing, Brandon remains committed to its artistic perfection and its bold statement against the dominant values of the culture. Suddenly, a sound from an unseen area of the apartment interrupts them **(E)**; they both look anxiously in its direction. It is merely Mrs. Wilson preparing to leave. She bids them farewell and urges them to mind their "Ps and Qs" while they are away in Connecticut. Her words and her general demeanor suggest that she sees them as slightly unruly children, errant boys in need of gentle correction, but what we know, of course, is that their brutal treatment of "DK" goes far beyond neglecting to remember Ps and Qs.

The shot comes to an end with a masked cut as the camera closes in on the back of Brandon's jacket while he lifts the receiver of the telephone in the foyer.

# 9

# Faking Freud

## On the Case

B UT THE PARTY IS NOT QUITE over. *Rope*'s ninth shot opens with Brandon ringing the garage and asking that his car be sent around: the killers are preparing to flee, preparing to move elsewhere altogether—out of the apartment, the city, the state. As if to suggest this imminent elsewhere, most of Brandon's phone call occurs while the camera is focusing on Phillip; in doing so, it shows part of the first two letters of the neon "STORAGE" sign through the window, out above the streets through which the pair plan to escape. We hear Brandon's voice clearly throughout the call—there are no longer any guests to be conducting competing conversations—but he is offscreen, as is the vehicle whose horn sounds faintly from the road below just as the call comes to an end (**E**). As Phillip walks to the drinks table, the Reduco neon advertisement can be seen once again through the main window of the apartment.

Brandon lifts the lid of the *cassone* a little and, for once, looks solemn. But he has second thoughts and suggests that they close the curtains before proceeding with their plan to remove David's body from the chest, transfer it to the car, and dispose of it in a lake. As they reach the windows, however, the telephone rings. Brandon quickly reassembles the books on top of the *cassone* and urges Phillip to pick up the receiver. Another vehicle horn is heard, this time a little more loudly (**E**). The bell rings again, and a further horn sounds in the street outside (**E**). Phillip answers the phone after the third ring and asks who is calling. Horrified by what he has heard, he places the receiver on the table (without ending the call) and rushes from the foyer back to the wooden trunk, where he informs Brandon that Rupert "wants to come up" to look for his misplaced cigarette case. Brandon accepts what he evidently views as a challenge—"Well, let him come," he says defiantly—but Phillip is thrown into a panic and frets that Rupert has "caught on" and is lying about the reason for wishing to return. They argue, and Brandon slaps Phillip's face before walking calmly to the phone to continue the conversation with Cadell.

By this late point in *Rope*, the difference between the two men that has figured repeatedly in the film has become a volatile gulf. Brandon remains mostly calm and composed, but Phillip is now drunk and despairing: "He slid without resistance into the morass of fear, and dark tendrils grasped at him, curling," the novelization notes.[1] Brandon, as so often, issues orders and even physically directs Phillip around the apartment. "Now, look," he says with some force. "I'm not going to get caught because of you or anyone else. No one is going to get in my way

Figure 9.1. Proximity.

now." The two stand very close to each other at this point, as they did at the beginning of *Rope* (in shot 2), but the proximity here is more about threat than erotic intimacy or being seduced by the other's "charm," as Phillip puts it in the earlier scene.[2] (Phillip, in fact, is slapped across the face by Brandon at this point in shot 9.)

The camera follows Brandon as he makes his way into the foyer to greet Rupert, but he suddenly changes direction and turns left, towards the bedroom(s). We never see *Rope*'s bedroom(s), of course, so the prohibited camera is forced to remain in the foyer and focus on the door. The buzzer sounds and, after a few seconds, the camera pulls focus to show Brandon in the foreground holding a revolver. "It's not loaded, is it?" asks Phillip. Brandon says nothing, but our privileged viewing position at this point allows us to see something that Phillip cannot: the cylinder of the weapon is indeed filled with bullets.[3] Brandon slips the gun into his pocket and opens the door.

Rupert enters, and the three men walk into the living room, where the hunt for the missing cigarette case begins. Well, almost. The object is not missing at all, and the work of the camera at this point allows viewers to see with complete clarity that Rupert is merely pretending to have lost it: he walks towards the camera with his back to Phillip and Brandon and, using his body to block their vision (but not ours), removes the case from his pocket, turns, and secretes it behind the books on the *cassone*. As he slides it into place on top of David's tomb, he conjures up a scene that could have come straight from Freud's *Psychopathology of Everyday Life*. "Completely unlike me to forget it, isn't it?" he says. "I suppose a psychoanalyst would say that I didn't really forget it at all: I unconsciously left it because I wanted to come back. But, uh, why should I want to come back?" Rupert has used his "missing" case to continue his investigation of the case of the missing David Kentley.

The reference to psychoanalysis is essentially a dead-end here, even if the allusion is accurate.[4] Freud's *Psychopathology* certainly deals with everyday instances of forgetting and even includes in its chapter on "symptomatic and fortuitous actions" an anecdote about a man who forgets his cigar case when he loses "quite a large sum of money" at a game of cards.[5] In *Rope*, however, we can see clearly that Rupert is *feigning* forgetfulness. There is nothing unconscious about his leaving of the cigarette case on the *cassone*: the act is calculated and fully conscious. He is, in effect, faking Freud in a mid-twentieth-century culture that had become familiar with a popularized version of psychoanalysis, thanks in part to Hollywood films like Hitchcock's earlier *Spellbound* (1945). This pretense of unconscious motivation is followed by a conscious taunt: why, Rupert asks, should he want to come back to the apartment? Why return to a party that is over?

## All Except One Guest

Phillip takes the bait—"Yes, why?" he asks sullenly from the drinks table—but Brandon seeks to calm the mood by saying that Rupert must have wanted to return "for the pleasure of our company or another drink." (The pleasure principle, of course, underpins much of Freud's account of human behavior. Is Brandon's remark a vague—but knowing—allusion to its workings in everyday life and therefore also a subtle signal to Rupert that two can play at this game?) Rupert moves closer to the wooden chest: this, he says, is where he last remembers having the cigarette case. Phillip, alarmed, drops the ice with which he is preparing Rupert's drink: the teacher is on the case in more sense than one.[6] After Rupert says, "And then what?" a vehicle's horn is heard from the street outside **(E)**. Rupert "finds" the cigarette case and apologizes, but Brandon and Phillip must realize that this is all a ruse: before Rupert returned to the apartment, they had completely cleared the lid of the chest.[7] Rupert therefore "discovers" the object where they know it could not possibly have been: this is all part of a terrible game that is moving in the direction of revelation and (more) death. When Rupert says, "After all, it was a party," a further traffic horn sounds from outside **(E)**. *Rope* positions us in a tense scene, then, but simultaneously reminds us of other scenes beyond the apartment where individuals are in the process of interaction, possibly in equally fraught ways.

Rupert's phrasing becomes even more knowing, confirming his gradual movement from ignorance to suspicion to discovery. Earlier in the film, as I have already noted, remarks by Brandon and Phillip carry connotations that viewers, unlike the various guests or Mrs. Wilson, can hear. But now, as the film moves closer to Rupert's grand exposure of the crime, it is he who utters lines with secondary levels of meaning. These signal to the killers that the game is up, that he now occupies the knowing position that once only they enjoyed:

> RUPERT (*sitting in a chair, sipping his drink, while Brandon and Phillip stand over him*): Please don't let me be in the way.

BRANDON: Of what?

RUPERT: Well, I know you have things to do.

BRANDON: What do you mean?

RUPERT: Well, packing, last-minute odds and ends. You are driving up to Connecticut tonight, aren't you?

BRANDON: Uh, yes, but we're all packed.

RUPERT: Oh, I see. All ready. All except one guest who must be gotten rid of.

"Things to do" is a perfectly ordinary phrase, but Brandon and Phillip know (as does the viewer) that the main thing that they must do very soon is transfer David's body from the wooden trunk to (presumably) the trunk of the car.[8] "Packing," likewise, could merely mean placing clothes and other possessions into a suitcase, but for those in the know, here it could also refer to the somber plan to pack the body into the vehicle before disposing of it in another state. (We have, after all, already seen David's body packed roughly into the *cassone*.[9]) But Rupert's most striking *double entendre* comes when he mentions "one guest who must be gotten rid of." He could merely be referring to himself—he is, after all, the sole partygoer who has returned to the apartment and interrupted the preparations for departure; he is currently an obstacle—but the film leaves open the possibility at the level of connotation that he is also alluding to David, the first guest at the party who has been lying in the trunk for around an hour and whose corpse "must be gotten rid of."

Rupert has already arrived twice at the apartment, at the scene of the crime; he now taunts his former pupils by delaying his second departure. "Well, I'll be off . . . ," he says, beginning to rise from his seat. But he then halts, adds ". . . as, uh, as soon as I've finished my drink," and sinks back into the chair. The drink in question, moreover, is "a long one" in a highball glass, in keeping with his loaded request, instead of the "short one" originally suggested by Brandon. A long drink will take longer to consume, of course, and will therefore defer the moment at which he leaves and allows the killers to return to their urgent secret plans; it is a toast to tarrying. He taunts Brandon and Phillip further when, back in his seat, he says that he might even stay long enough to see them off as they leave for Connecticut; if he does this, he will, of course, also watch the departure of David's corpse.

The strained conversation between the three men turns to the "strange" quality of the evening. The term is Rupert's and is not allowed to pass without comment. "What do you mean, 'strange'?" asks Phillip, drunkenly. Rupert turns his head towards Brandon and pretends not to recall using the word, to which Brandon says, "Well, you often pick words for sound rather than meaning." Rupert claims not to know what he meant by "strange," but then he adds, after a pause, "Unless I was thinking about David." Brandon's smile fades, and he looks anxiously towards Phillip, who was already in a state of extreme anxiety. The moment is one of high drama: Rupert has stepped closer than ever to exposing the truth about the character whose name he has just uttered and linked explicitly to the word "strange." The camera now embraces all three men in a tight shot. The teacher is seated, and his former pupils tower menacingly over him. Everyone else has left the apartment, but we, the viewers, are there to witness up close the exposure of the crime. We have intimate access, knowledge, insight—in a way that no guest at the party ever has (except for Rupert, eventually). And yet, even at this crucial late moment, *Rope* takes as it gives by reminding us that, for all our privilege, we still lack refined knowledge of something: the sound of a horn is heard from the streets below just after Rupert utters David's name **(E)**. We are watching *this*, but we are not seeing *that*.

## When It Happened

The tense verbal dance continues when the conversation turns to David's failure to appear at the party. Rupert wonders if he was "run over or held up," but Brandon immediately dismisses these suggestions: "In broad daylight?" he laughs, as if urging Rupert to venture another hypothesis. "That's right, I'd forgotten," Rupert replies. "Yes, it must have been broad daylight when it happened," he adds solemnly. Rupert's phrasing here implies a certainty of knowledge: the language is exact, and the use of the preterite tense leaves no real room for doubt. "It happened" identifies an event that took place at a precise moment in the past, not an event that *may* have taken place. If the puddings carried by Rupert at the start of shot 7 are not perfect, here his choice of linguistic tense comes closer. Brandon evidently realizes the implications of the phrasing, for the camera closes in on his hand as it reaches into the pocket where the gun is hidden. "When, uh, *what* happened?" he enquires as another vehicle's horn is heard faintly in the background (**E**).[10] (Even at this moment of high dramatic intensity and close camera work, *Rope* is gesturing once more towards an elsewhere that is ungraspable.) Because the movement of the camera cuts Rupert out of the frame, we cannot see precisely what he notices when Brandon reaches for the weapon, but his eyes seem to be cast in the direction of the danger when the camera shifts again and brings him back into view.[11] Indeed, Rupert now backs off a little: "When whatever did happen to David—nothing, probably," he says, gritting his teeth slightly.

But the film cannot leave things there. Governed in part by what Roland Barthes called the "hermeneutic code" of narrative, it must move towards closure and the dissolution of the enigma upon which the film is founded.[12] So, as Rupert rises from the chair, he relaunches his verbal attack; the temporary suspension of the movement towards disclosure is over. "Still . . . where is he?" he asks in a notably direct manner. The question is neither abstract nor posed casually to the world in general: it is aimed specifically at Brandon, who is now standing very close to Rupert. The discussion turns to Janet's theory, which is that Brandon kidnapped or somehow delayed David, and Brandon then invites Rupert to devise a hypothetical scenario to "get David out of the way." In a remarkable sequence that was not present in Arthur Laurents's first two drafts of the screenplay, Rupert sketches out his plan for killing.[13] In doing so, as Sam Ishii-Gonzáles points out, he makes his complicity in the actual murder of David Kentley strikingly clear.[14] He would, he says, first invite David to the apartment for a drink. "That's good, and no witnesses," says Brandon approvingly. "Then what?" Until this moment in the conversation, the camera has been focused tightly on the two men as they talk. But then, after Brandon's question and the sound of yet another vehicle's horn in the distance (**E**), it shifts to depict only Rupert while he smokes and gathers his thoughts. He begins to narrate the next part of his imaginary murder.

When he says that he would, "at the appointed time," make his way "out of the room, into the hall," the camera pans around roughly 180 degrees to show the empty hallway in question and then tracks slowly forwards.[15] Rupert continues by saying that he would take David's hat, and the camera shifts slightly to emphasize the closet in the foyer (where, of course, in shot 8 the audience has already seen David's initialed fedora). Rupert's next step, he says, would be to lead David into the main room and offer him a drink; the camera duly follows the imaginary route of the victim and comes to rest by the drinks table.[16] "Then he'd sit down," Rupert continues, as the camera crosses to the empty armchair in which Rupert himself sat some minutes earlier in the film. "Phillip would probably play the piano," he says, and the camera turns to show the instrument played previously by Phillip. Rupert proceeds to outline the hypothetical practicalities of the murder, pointing out that David was "quite strong" and would therefore need "to be knocked out." "So," he explains, "I'd move quietly around behind the chair and hit him on the head with something." The camera is positioned right behind the armchair as Rupert speaks this line, and when he adds that David's "body would fall forward on the floor," it moves to the left to show an empty space upon the carpet.

"Then where would you put him?" Brandon wonders. Even though it is not offering a point-of-view shot, the camera initially glances towards the *cassone*, recalling the way in which we have seen Rupert's gaze flit anxiously around the apartment earlier in the film. But a shadow appears upon the carpet while Rupert is stalling his narration. Brandon walks slowly into the shot, pictured from roughly the waist down. His hand is in the pocket of his jacket, where we know the revolver to be hidden. He positions himself between Rupert and the *cassone*, as if guarding the secret and the sacrificial altar. "Well, uh, well, let me see," says Rupert as Brandon thrusts his hand upwards within the pocket, emphasizing the outline of the gun. Before Rupert can go any further, however, the ninth shot of *Rope* comes to an end with an obvious, unmasked cut.

What has happened in the build-up to this cut is a remarkable demonstration of *Rope*'s perpetual movement between revelation and withholding. The sequence in which Rupert imagines killing David is, as Ned Schantz points out in his brilliant analysis of Hitchcock's "shadow scenes," at once "arresting," "ghostly," and an echo of the section of the director's first Hollywood film, *Rebecca* (1940), during which Maxim de Winter recounts to his new wife the events in the coastal cottage that led to the death of the first Mrs. de Winter.[17] While there are, as Schantz is quick to stress, "significant differences between the scenes" in the two films, there is also what he calls a "striking resemblance": each avoids a conventional flashback and instead narrates the past in the present; each allows the camera to retrace the steps (hypothetically, at least) of the murder victim; and each is narrated by the film's patriarch.[18] I do not wish to dwell extensively here upon the connections between these two key scenes in *Rope* and *Rebecca*; Schantz covers the ground memorably, and

I offered my own analysis some years ago in *Hitchcock's Magic*.[19] Of more relevance to the argument that I have been developing in this book is the way in which *Rope*, like *Rebecca*, shows us that *it is not showing us something*. At this point in shot 9, we witness in striking fashion the "fluid camera work" that I discussed at the beginning of chapter 2.[20] As if commanded by Rupert's words, the camera glides around the apartment, "tracing," as Schantz puts it, "the itinerary of an unseen figure past objects bristling with cryptic significance."[21] Schantz does not stress or linger upon it, but the signifier "unseen" is crucial to my reading of the sequence (and *Rope* more generally). While the roaming camera and narration by Rupert allow us to imagine what the minutes leading up to the murder of David Kentley might have involved, the camera is nonetheless, because of *Rope*'s formal unfolding in "real time," prohibited from offering a conventional flashback in which we would see the actual events preceding the crime. *Rope* must remain in the present, and in this present the living, talking, moving figure of David is necessarily absent. We get to see what might have happened when David arrived, but only during an uncanny, ghostly sequence in which David himself can never appear.

*Rope*'s perpetual movement, that is to say, leaves its mark upon the final part of shot 9. As the cut approaches, there is a striking sway from disclosure to withholding. We know that "it happened," as Rupert puts it, but we neither see "it" happen nor know *precisely* what happened. A degree of knowledge is provided, but it is shot through with enigma. *Rope* gives, *Rope* coils away.

# 10

# Cat and Mouse

### Return of the Rope

THE MOOD ALTERS, AND WITH it the pace of Rupert's narration. "Well, uh, well, let me see . . . ," he said slowly at the end of the film's previous shot, taking a brief pause in his murder story. But the subsequent sight of the gun in Brandon's pocket just before the cut evidently persuades him to change the direction of his narrative away from the *cassone* and therefore away from the truth. His words, which had been measured and leisurely, now become rushed as the camera sweeps away from the wooden trunk. He would, he says, seeking to bring his tale to a safe end, get Phillip to help him carry David "out of the room, down the back stairs, and the two of us would put him into the car."[1] As Rupert refers to his escape route, the camera rests its gaze on the distant doorway to the kitchen. The implication, I think, is that the rear staircase is somewhere beyond the door, but this part of the penthouse remains forever unseen, forever elsewhere (**E**), and was not included in any of the Art Department's plans for the set.

The conclusion to Rupert's tale does not, of course, match what actually happened in the apartment earlier that day: we know as well as the killers that David's body is still in the *cassone*. Brandon, accordingly, urges Rupert to rethink his murder plans, claiming that such an escape would have been impossible if the crime took place "in broad daylight." The conversation takes a new turn, though Brandon's hand is still in his pocket with the gun:

> RUPERT: Oh, that means I'd have to find some place to hide the body until dark.
>
> BRANDON: Yes, you would, but, uh, where, Rupert?
>
> RUPERT (*turning away from Brandon and walking towards the wooden chest*): Yes . . . yes. Where?

When Rupert approaches the *cassone*, the camera tracks backwards to bring the object into view at the bottom of the screen. In a discussion of imaginary hiding places for David's body, that is to say, the actual hiding place has become visible; deep in fiction, in performance, Rupert is within touching distance of the truth.

Phillip, who has been silent for some time, now reaches the end of his rope and loses his temper. "Cat and mouse! Cat and mouse!" he shouts as he throws his glass across the room.[2] "Only, which is the cat, and which is the mouse?" he adds, looking from Brandon to Rupert. This uncertainty about the difference between the two characters and their actions has already been hinted at in the film—Rupert has, after all, been identified as the teacher whose philosophies have inspired his former pupils to commit murder—and it will return in its most pronounced form in shot 11; I will, therefore, discuss Phillip's wondering about "which is the cat, and which is the mouse" more thoroughly in the following chapter of this book.

Brandon taunts Rupert further. "Uh, with him [Phillip] in this condition, though," he says, "there doesn't seem to be much point in your staying, Rupert. That is, unless you came back to find something besides your cigarette case." (Even though the film is approaching its climax, it nonetheless continues to mark itself with hints of elsewhere: vehicle horns sound outside the apartment either side of Brandon's saying "Uh" **[E]**.) Rupert states that he did not really believe that his former pupils could have kidnapped David until he noticed "fear of discovery" bulging in Brandon's pocket. "[I]t really scares me a little," he adds, but Brandon makes light of the weapon, saying that he needs to take it to Connecticut because there has been a spate of burglaries in the area. He tosses the gun casually onto the lid of the piano and walks out of shot to laugh with Phillip about Rupert's remark. We hear the voices of Brandon and Phillip at this point but do not see the two men themselves **(E)**, and this sense of acousmatic elsewhere is enhanced by the distant sound of vehicle horns, first when Brandon says, "He thought . . ." and laughs (**E**), and then again after he remarks, "We all do it, don't we, Phillip?" (**E**).

Rupert walks over to the main window. He turns his back on the killers, and the camera moves in to show us a familiar item: the rope that was used first to strangle David and then to bind Mr. Kentley's books together. Rupert had been hiding the object in the pocket of his jacket—just as Brandon had been concealing a gun in his—but now he tightens it between his fists. None of this, crucially, can be seen by Brandon and Phillip; *Rope* has shifted its allegiance and is now sharing visual knowledge between the viewer and the detective figure, and not, as in earlier shots, between the viewer and the murderers.

Rupert turns so that Brandon and Phillip can at last see the evidence stretched between his hands. Recalling Brandon's flamboyantly defiant twirling of the rope in shot 3, he rocks the murder weapon back and forth, as if taunting the killers; what he holds in his hands signals that he now has the upper hand and is ready to rope them in.[3] But he is clearly anxious about the confrontation that he is staging: his right hand trembles notably at one point.[4] As he turns, the neon "STORAGE" sign outside the apartment begins for the first time to flash.[5] It cycles through three colors—green, white, red—which creep oddly into the room. This sudden illumination is not as striking or unnatural as the eerie green glow that will envelop Judy and Scottie in a key scene at the Hotel Empire near the end of Hitchcock's *Vertigo* a decade later, but the sign has been dormant until now in *Rope*, so its sudden flashing heightens the drama when the detective figure confronts the killers with the murder weapon that they thought had been carried out of harm's way by the victim's father some time ago.[6]

In a fascinating discussion of color in Hitchcock's work, Richard Allen sees a link between jade and ghostliness and points out that *Rope*'s flashing neon sign will turn "Phillip's face, in particular, into a pasty, deathly green."[7] What, though, are we to make of the two other colors of the neon sign—red and white? It would be possible to see red as signaling "stop" (just as green suggests "go"), perhaps, but I am more interested in the simple fact that the sign changes color in perpetual movement as the film approaches its climax. Rupert is heading rapidly towards revelation and, as it were, illumination; the truth is nearly out in the open. But the neon "STORAGE" sign has a question in store as it offers three very different versions of illumination (green, white, red): what kind of enlightenment will Rupert reach and cast? How will the teacher whose philosophies inspired the crime respond to the discovery of the body and his own grave implication? What will be the tint and tenor of his reaction to the discovery of a body that would be breathing were it not for his lofty words?

## He Knows, He Knows, He Knows, He Knows

When Rupert utters the phrase, "You were right, Phillip: those books *were* tied clumsily," the camera (which had been emphasizing the evidence in Rupert's hands) begins to move slowly towards Brandon and Phillip until it comes to rest showing them in profile. Recalling the scene at the beginning of the film where they recover from killing David with the rope, they stand extremely close to each other. But now there is no erotic exhilaration: each man stares in horror at Rupert as he wields the murder weapon that, like Rupert himself, has returned to the scene of the crime.

"He's got it! He's got it! He knows, he knows, he knows, he knows!" cries Phillip as he grabs Brandon's discarded gun from the piano. The excessive repetition of "he knows" is in one respect merely a sign of Phillip's babbling desperation—"Stupid babbling drunk!" as Brandon will soon call him—but it also underscores the culmination of Rupert's long journey towards discovery and awareness: when he arrived at the party some forty minutes earlier, he had no knowledge of what had taken place not long beforehand in the apartment, but now, as the film enters its final minutes, "he knows, he knows, he knows, he knows." Instead of aiming the weapon at Rupert, though, Phillip initially points it at his partner in crime and says that he would sooner kill Brandon than his former teacher. As the neon lights continue to flash, Phillip more explicitly raises the question of knowledge that has run through *Rope*. "That's what you wanted, isn't it?" he says to Brandon. "Somebody else to know. Somebody else to see how brilliant you are, just like at school."

The remark touches upon a fatal tension that underpins *Rope*: what good is creating a perfect "work of art" (which is precisely how Brandon describes the murder in shot 2) if the perfection has no external observer to appreciate it? How can the brilliance be acknowledged without allowing an outsider to know what has been accomplished—and thereby ruining the perfection with discovery and exposure? William Rothman sums up this issue neatly:

In *Rope*, the John Dall character—collaborating with Farley Granger, who does his bidding—kills a young man in an act he conceives in purely aesthetic terms. He keeps the body in a trunk until he can properly dispose of it. But the creator is not satisfied that his work of art is complete and conceives of a perfect finish to his masterpiece: he invites his friends, including the boy's own father, to a dinner party and serves dinner from the top of the trunk. This is the artist's signature, the cream of the jest (as a line in *Notorious* would have it). Yet still he is not satisfied. His work remains unrecognized and unappreciated. He invites his old professor (James Stewart), whose theories about the prerogatives of superior men originally inspired him.[8]

For D. A. Miller, meanwhile, the duality of the killers' perception of the murder has a terrible flaw:

> It is in the art murder's twin status as "perfect crime" and "work of art" that its self-undoing lies. As an instance of perfection, the crime must be, in Brandon's expression, "an immaculate murder," without stain or other evidence to incriminate its author. To be an example of art, though, it must be marked with an intention, even a solicitation, to be recognized as one. In the art murder, then, perfection and art are radically at odds in their relation to the necessity of a signature. That is why most stories of the perfect crime, like *Rope* and Hitchcock's later *Dial M for Murder* (1954), are really stories of the perfect crime's failure; like so many fingerprints, those accumulated artistic touches eventually yield the forensic clues that give the game away. The recognition that the *artful* crime must do everything to secure, proves in the end but another name for the detection that the *perfect* crime has been designed to eschew.[9]

Brandon and Phillip are, in other words, doomed from the outset—and not merely because, at an extradiegetic level, the Production Code Administration demanded "full compensating moral values for the treatment of such a story on the screen" when discussing plans for *Rope* with Hitchcock in September 1946.[10] The young men cannot have it both ways:

the perfect crime cannot also be a work of art. "Open it" is the line that opens *Rope* when Brandon refers to the *cassone* in which David's body is to be placed. But what he and Phillip have already opened with their belief in perfection as a work of art is a road to ruin.

"Does a gun draw violence to it [. . .]?" the protagonist of Don DeLillo's *White Noise* wonders.[11] The revolver in *Rope* certainly does, for while Phillip is talking with the weapon in his hand, Rupert moves forward slowly and then lunges for the gun. In a sequence not added to the screenplay until the final draft of January 13, 1948, the two men wrestle for around twelve seconds, at which point the trigger is pulled.[12] No one is hit, but, the script and novelization both explain, Rupert's hand is grazed by the bullet; he wraps a handkerchief around the wound.[13] This bleeding hand recalls the cut in Phillip's palm earlier in the film; the two figures bleed into each other a touch.[14] (The injury posed a problem for the crew: how to make blood appear in the middle of an unbroken shot. Rehearsals with a small plastic container led to the liquid squirting up uncontrollably into James Stewart's face, so a perforated rubber vial was used instead. In the end, though, the blood is hardly visible during this shot.[15]) Phillip slumps onto the piano seat and leans forward onto the instrument. Rupert, who now holds the gun, takes control of the room.[16] He directs Brandon away from him and says that he is tired and does not wish "to fence any more."[17] He is, he announces, going to open the chest, which the camera duly brings into view by tracking backwards. "All right!" says Brandon. "Go ahead and look. I hope you like what you see!" Even now, the pupil longs for approval from the teacher, for appreciation and endorsement of the work of art. Although the *cassone* has become the center of attention—Brandon and Rupert are staring at it, and it is visible at the bottom of the frame—and although we are on the verge of a final dramatic gesture, *Rope* still allows a hint of elsewhere to surface for when Brandon says, "I hope you like what you see!" a vehicle's horn sounds from the street below **(E)**. At this most intensely focused of moments, in other words, the film acknowledges a scene that we are not witnessing; "I hope you like what you see!" is shot through with what you cannot hope to see.

As the two murderers look on aghast, Rupert steps forward and opens the wooden chest, sending the books tumbling to the floor; both the screenplay and the novelization specify that he lifts the lid "savagely."[18] The top of the *cassone* fills the screen with darkness—Robin Wood found the effect "electrifying," even though he disliked the film's disguised cuts—and the camera takes the opportunity to bring *Rope*'s penultimate shot to a masked end.[19]

# 11

# Arrest Indicated[1]

## Up Close and Personal

THE END IS CLOSE, BUT FOR now we are too close. The cut at the end of *Rope*'s tenth shot is, as I noted in the final lines of my previous chapter, masked when the top of the *cassone* fills the screen. When the camera moves away from the wooden lid at the beginning of shot 11, however, Rupert is notably closer than he was before the cut; the handkerchief around his wounded hand is far bloodier than it was when he opened the chest, too. Once again, an attempt to mask the fact that we are watching a film produced under conditions requiring a break in shooting is not entirely successful. Flow is flawed.

With this imperfection in mind, it is not quite clear why V.F. Perkins, writing in 1963, declared the transition between shots 10 and 11 to be the only one of *Rope*'s five concealed cuts which is "completely satisfactory."[2] Perhaps he simply missed the discrepancy: he was, after all, watching in an era during which close analysis and repeated viewings of films were far more difficult than they are now. Or maybe he was simply struck by the dramatic effect of closing in after the cut.[3] There is, it is true, a powerful image waiting for the viewer at the beginning of shot 11 when the camera rises above the lid of the trunk: not the lifeless body of David Kentley, of course, but an arresting close-up of the horrified face of the figure who has gazed upon it. This is not quite the screen-filling VistaVision countenance of James Stewart that startles Murray Pomerance in Hitchcock's *The Man Who Knew Too Much* (1956), but if we place an ear to the ground, we can almost hear the image in the later film approaching by bus from Marrakesh.[4]

"Oh, no, no," says Rupert in a voice that the screenplay calls "very low."[5] "I couldn't believe it was true," he adds. When Rupert claims that the killing of David Kentley cannot possibly be explained away, Brandon contradicts him. The former pupil, it transpires, believes that the master will understand and sympathize:

> BRANDON: Rupert, Rupert, remember the discussion we had before with Mr. Kentley?
>
> RUPERT: Yes . . .
>
> BRANDON: Remember we said the lives of inferior beings are unimportant. Remember we said—we've *always* said, you and I—that moral concepts of good and evil, and right and wrong, don't hold for the intellectually superior? Remember, Rupert?

At first during this exchange the two men are presented onscreen together, but as Brandon describes his perceived philosophical harmony with Rupert—a harmony connoted by both the framing and Brandon's use of "we"—the camera shifts position to show only Rupert, who looks shocked and distracted. He is implicated further when Brandon highlights the link between the act of killing and the philosophical endorsement of killing. He and Phillip have, he says to Rupert, "*lived* what you and I have talked." Theory has been put into practice; the dutiful disciples have enacted the teachings of the master. "I knew you'd understand," Brandon adds, "because you *have* to, don't you see, you *have* to."

But Rupert does not understand. He recoils from Brandon in horror and walks to the small desk by the window; he evidently wishes to distance himself from Brandon, literally and figuratively. The tense silence in the apartment is punctuated twice by the sound of a vehicle horn **(E)**. As Rupert sits weakly in the chair, the sound is heard on two further occasions **(E)**. Even here, even now, at this intense climactic moment, *Rope* gestures away from what it is showing in the direction of something else, something outside, something unseen.

Rupert then responds to Brandon's attempt to place him on the side of murder. He is on the ropes, so speaks with force and fervor in what

Amy Lawrence calls "a climactic outburst of the kind we have come to expect in a James Stewart movie":[6]

> RUPERT: Brandon, Brandon, until this very moment, this world and the people in it have always been dark and incomprehensible to me, and I've tried to clear my way with logic and superior intellect. And you've thrown my own words right back in my face, Brandon. You were right to: if nothing else, a man should stand by his words. But you've given my words a meaning that I never *dreamed* of, and you've tried to twist them into a cold, logical excuse for your ugly murder. Well, they never were that, Brandon, and you can't make them that. There must have been something deep inside you from the very start that let you do this thing, but there's always been something deep inside me that would *never* let me do it, and would never let me be a party to it now.
>
> BRANDON: What do you mean?
>
> RUPERT: I mean that tonight you've made me ashamed of every concept I ever had of superior or inferior beings, but I thank you for that shame because now I know that we are each of us a separate human being, Brandon, with the right to live and work and think as individuals, but with an obligation to the society we live in.

At this point, Rupert's strident speech—perhaps the most significant in the entire film—is interrupted by the sound of a vehicle horn, by the sound of something that is not here in the apartment (**E**). He continues his denunciation of Brandon and Phillip:

> RUPERT: By what right do you *dare* say that there's a superior few to which you belong? By what right did you *dare* decide that that boy in there (*pointing with the gun towards the wooden chest*) was inferior and therefore could be killed?

Brandon's face is visible during this part of Rupert's speech. He looks somewhat confused—and it is not difficult to see why. Rupert's lengthy, moralizing speech is rather puzzling, for the simple reason that earlier in the film, as all the guests gathered with their hosts by the main window and discussed Rupert's philosophy, we watched as he upheld precisely the values that have led Brandon and Phillip to kill David. When Mr. Kentley remarked that Rupert could not possibly be serious about the desirability of murder "in season," moreover, Cadell stood his ground. "But I am," he insisted, "I'm a very serious fellow." Here, however, in the final few minutes of the film, Rupert retreats completely from his beliefs and suddenly becomes a very serious advocate of responsibility towards the society about which he earlier spoke with such contempt. He fails, in short, to be a man who stands by his words. As Michael Wood puts it, Rupert essentially becomes a humanist as the end of *Rope* approaches.[7]

Rupert did not kill David Kentley, of course, and he was, as we know perfectly well, not present when the crime was committed. Brandon suggests in shot 3, meanwhile, that Rupert "never could have acted" upon his theories if invited actually to partake in the killing of David. But Rupert's attempt in *Rope*'s dying minutes to insist upon a distance and, moreover, an essential difference between himself and the murderers rings rather hollow: the abstract values that he earlier upheld with such conviction are precisely the values that sanctioned the killing of David Kentley. Rupert, in short, as various critics have pointed out, is at least partly complicit in the crime.[8]

Robin Wood, who was one of the first to comment on this complicity, sees a weakness in the film's treatment of Rupert's philosophies: "[T]he spectator wants—and I think needs—to know," he wrote in 1965, "just how Rupert *did* mean his teaching to be taken."[9] This judgment comes in the introduction to the first edition of *Hitchcock's Films*—a book that went through various radical rewritings over the years and is now more commonly known by its later title of *Hitchcock's Films Revisited*. This early belief that the film fails to some degree because it does not deliver clear moral guidance is one of the ways in which Wood's youthful allegiance to F. R. Leavis leaves its mark upon his groundbreaking study of Hitchcock's work.[10] The later material in Wood's book often revises the author's earlier readings and assumptions, so I see no need here to offer a lengthy critique of Leavis's (or Wood's) approach to culture and criticism in terms of morality and value judgments. What does interest me, though, in a book about *Rope*'s perpetual movement and undecidability, is the very problem that Wood identifies: just how did Rupert mean his teaching to be taken? Of what meaning for his words did he dream?

As I see it, the film never allows us to answer with certainty. In having Rupert discover his complicity as he discovers the truth about David, *Rope* raises a troubling question about the role of his teaching in the crime—but it leaves that question open and beyond settling. Rupert both stands by and stands back from his beliefs about the art of murder, and this duplicity—in the literal sense of the term—remains in play when the film's final credits begin to roll. As Amy Lawrence puts it, he "must renounce himself while remaining the hero."[11] Even in the case of Rupert—the detective figure and the summoner of justice—*Rope* is a film of perpetual movement.

## Opening the Window

Rupert's newfound commitment to dominant social values surfaces again when he refers to "what society's going to do" to Brandon and Phillip. "I don't know what that'll be but I can guess, and I can help: you're going to *die*, Brandon—*both of you*." Rupert is not now merely defending the *doxa* that he once mocked; he is actively helping to bring the killers to justice. They will, with his assistance, stand before the law that he earlier dismissed with such casual contempt. He makes the precise nature of this assistance clear when he walks over to the apartment's main windows, opens one, and fires the gun three times into the air. (Brandon and Phillip turned "an ordinary household article" into a weapon when they used a length of rope to strangle David Kentley; Rupert now does the opposite by using a lethal weapon not to shoot anyone, but merely to act as a signal—which will, of course, lead indirectly in time to possible death by execution.) Because the window is no longer closed, the sounds of the city outside are suddenly far clearer: a vehicle's horn is heard immediately after the shots have been fired, and it is much louder than the horn that sounds just before Rupert throws the window open **(E)**. Then, for the very first time in *Rope*, we hear footsteps and even voices from the street below, together with ongoing urban sounds **(E)**. The people whose words we hear are never seen, but we can make out that they are referring acousmatically to the gunshots and how they came from "up there," as one voice puts it. The police, we hear, are to be called.[12] These exterior voices "represent society," as William Rothman observes; they are, in effect, working with Rupert to bring about the corrective, normative demise of Brandon and Phillip.[13]

In the light of Gaston Bachelard's work on the poetics of space, the eleventh shot of *Rope* can be read as one in which the distinction between inside and outside is dramatically disturbed twice over. "Chests, especially small caskets," Bachelard observes, "[. . .] are objects *that may be opened*. When a chest is closed, it is returned to the general community of objects; it takes its place in exterior space."[14] But, anticipating one of the book's later chapters on the dialectics of outside and inside, Bachelard then considers what happens when such an object ceases to be sealed: "[F]rom the moment the casket is opened, dialectics no longer exist. The outside is effaced with one stroke, an atmosphere of novelty and surprise reigns. The outside has no more meaning" (p. 85). This is precisely what happens in *Rope* when Rupert lifts the lid of the *cassone*: the body of David is no longer secreted within the trunk but is instead known and visible to the figure who stands outside it in the apartment. This unsettling of the distinction between inside and outside—a distinction that, at the level of the *cassone*, has animated much of the film—is mirrored in Rupert's actions at the window. When he throws it open, the noise of the external world that *Rope* has kept at a distance suddenly returns and floods into the space of the penthouse (where the characters and camera remain); when he fires the gun, he sends three projectiles from inside to outside and thereby summons the latter to the former.

The camera tracks back slowly from the window to show the three men inside the apartment; Phillip is standing at the piano, leaning forwards. We hear a police siren approaching. (The effect was achieved by recording a real police car in the vicinity of Mariposa and Riverside Drive, Los Angeles, on March 5, 1948. For the use of the squad car and motorcycle riders, the studio made a donation of $50 to the Burbank Police Buck of the Month Association.[15]) "Here comes the squad car now," says a voice at street level. "They're coming," adds Phillip from the piano.[16] The outside world that *Rope* has kept at a distance for an hour and a quarter is moving closer and closer; the distinction between inside and outside is collapsing. As the sound of the siren comes to dominate the soundtrack, Rupert sits with his back to the camera and his arm resting protectively on the *cassone*; he is still holding the gun.[17] Brandon stands and mixes himself another drink. The rope used to kill David lies upon the floor, reminding us, in the wake of Rupert's comment about how Brandon and Phillip are "going to *die*," that "the rope" was once a shorthand phrase for execution by hanging.[18] Phillip takes a seat at the piano and begins to play the first of Poulenc's *Mouvements perpétuels* once again. The tempo is extremely slow, possibly because he plays with just one hand, and the notes are difficult to hear due to the siren. It is, David Schroeder proposes, as though Poulenc's piece "has become a march to the scaffold."[19] The mise-en-scène is perhaps better described as a *misère-en-scene*, to borrow a lovely term from Alan Hollinghurst.[20] As "THE END" appears upon the screen and the credits begin to roll, a loud orchestral version of Poulenc's composition takes over triumphantly from Phillip's pale performance.

In a fascinating essay on Hitchcock's "narrative modernism," Thomas Hemmeter identifies a curious resistance to conventional Hollywood resolution in these final moments of *Rope*:

> But far from providing closure to the film's narrative, the discovery [of the body] leads to a different sort of suspense when Rupert (. . .) sits waiting for the outside world to ring down the curtain. After he fires several shots out the window to attract the police, the camera pulls back to a long shot to reveal a geometric composition placing Rupert at the apex of a triangle whose other points are Brandon (. . .) and Phillip (. . .). The mise-en-scène creates a modernist tableau, visually reinscribing Rupert into the story more as co-perpetrator of the crime than as amateur detective. The shot holds and holds across narrative time as an exhausted Rupert awaits a conclusion that does not and cannot come. (. . .) The suspense built through Rupert's detection and discovery becomes a suspense built upon his proclaimed innocence, a suspense whose burdensome waiting reopens the film's narrative as we recall that he provoked the killers' actions by advocating the rights of supermen to kill others.[21]

Phillip's final words—"They're coming"—contribute further to this sense of openness and perpetual movement where closure and settling ought to occur. His present participle defers the actual moment of arrival, the point at which the police reach the building and the apartment. "They're coming" is qualitatively different from, say, "They're here." Brandon utters the film's first line—"Open it," he says, referring to the *cassone*—and thereby sets in motion a movement towards discovery and disclosure. But this opening at the level of deed and discourse is not answered, at the other end of *Rope*, by a complete closing. "They're coming" gestures towards an event that is not actually depicted in the film. The movement from beginning to end, from opening to closure, is a perpetual movement.

## Reworking Poulenc

The nondiegetic orchestral rendering of Poulenc that takes over from Phillip's one-handed performance tries to enforce closure, however, by taking two notable liberties with the original composition of 1918.[22] First, as Scott D. Paulin notes, Phillip never gets to play "the piece through to its conclusion," even though this is the conclusion of the film, which means that he never reaches the strikingly open, unresolved final notes of Poulenc's work.[23] Had he played on, he would have reached a point at which the composition, as Kevin Clifton explains, "not so much ends, but simply stops and fades away into nothingness"[24] because the pianist's right hand "ultimately resists melodic closure" and thereby "undermines a complete sense of balanced resolution since it is left totally open-ended on the dissonant high A on beat 4."[25]

But *Rope* does more than merely cut Phillip's one-handed performance short, and here lies the second of the film's challenges to the spirit of Poulenc. As Paulin puts it so well in his discussion of the relationship between sound and sexuality in *Rope*, the music being played forlornly by Phillip as the sirens approach is suddenly silenced as

> the theme is taken up by brass and strings and given an emphatic and triumphant tonal cadence in a major key over the words "The End." Such a cadence is impossible within the harmonic language of Poulenc's work—just as such an "end," a productive goal, is often considered to be absent from gay sexuality—and this cadence or goal is quite literally imposed from outside here, with Poulenc's harmonic freedom reinterpreted as sterility. This nondiegetic closure "corrects" Poulenc's deviation from the prescribed norms, but it also assimilates the music to the dominant paradigm, as if to deny that such deviance ever existed.[26]

What interests me about Paulin's commentary here is his recognition that the resolution imposed by the reworked Poulenc is, in his phrase, "a nondiegetic closure." It is, in other words, a closure that is at odds with what has happened diegetically, in the apartment, in the world of *Rope*. It has to be "quite literally imposed from outside," I would suggest, because what occurs "inside" is too undecidable, too fluid, too much a case of perpetual movement ever to be capable of coming to firm closure and convenient, conventional resolution. The orchestral music that heralds the arrival of the words "THE END" is an awkward imposition that comes too late, an attempt from elsewhere to tie an anchoring knot in a rope that coils, recoils, and refuses ever to be still.

# Postscript

THE OFFICIAL PREMIERE OF *Rope* took place at the Globe Theater in New York on August 26, 1948. A sixty-foot-high sign featuring an image of James Stewart as Rupert sat on top of the building for the occasion, a length of rope swinging dramatically from the figure's hands.[1] The film received somewhat mixed reviews, as various commentators have noted, and although there were (as I discussed in chapter 1) various troubles with censors, a modest profit was generated at the box office.[2] Financial statements prepared by Warner Bros. show that, by late 1959, the film had enjoyed particular financial success in the United States, the United Kingdom, Australia, Brazil, France, and Italy.[3] But the income did not always reach its destination: in 1954, Transatlantic Pictures sued Warner Bros. over withheld earnings; the court ruled in favor of the plaintiffs and ordered Warner to pay $34,206.54 plus costs.[4]

By the time *Rope* appeared in cinemas in the summer of 1948, Hitchcock and Bernstein were at work on the next Transatlantic Pictures production, *Under Capricorn*, which was shot largely in England. The latter would in effect mark the end of Transatlantic for it was so spectacularly unpopular with audiences that it was repossessed by Bankers Trust in lieu of unrecovered advances.[5] For his next four films—*Stage Fright* (1950), *Strangers on a Train* (1951), *I Confess* (1953), and *Dial "M" for Murder* (1954)—Hitchcock moved on to work directly with Warner Bros., which had, of course, been involved with *Rope* at the level of production and distribution.[6] There would never be another Transatlantic Pictures film after *Under Capricorn* in 1949, though the archives reveal that the company was not formally liquidated until February 22, 1962.[7]

Although *Rope*'s set made an uncanny reappearance in 1949 in *My Dream Is Yours*—a Michael Curtiz film made at Warner Bros. and starring

Doris Day, who would go on to feature in Hitchcock's *The Man Who Knew Too Much* in 1956—the film has not always been available for revisiting in the years since its release.[8] When, for instance, Sidney Bernstein wrote to the head of booking at Warner Bros. in July 1957 to suggest screening the film on television alongside a small-screen adaptation of Patrick Hamilton's original play that was planned for October of that year, he was told that Hitchcock's *Rope* had been withdrawn from circulation in the United States.[9] No explanation was given, but the situation had apparently changed by the summer of 1962 because the archives contain scripts by Arthur Houseman for a trailer to publicize the film's rerelease in cinemas.[10] But then *Rope* vanished again, along with several of Hitchcock's other films, as Walter Raubicheck and Walter Srebnick explain:

> *Rope* was the first of two films Hitchcock made for his own production company [. . .] and he retained his rights to the film. In 1953, Hitchcock signed an agreement with Paramount Pictures which gave him the rights to five future films and ultimately gave Paramount the rights to only one (*To Catch a Thief*). Hitchcock went on to make *Rear Window, The Trouble with Harry, The Man Who Knew Too Much, Vertigo* and *Psycho* for Paramount between 1953 and 1960, and under the agreement Hitchcock retained the rights to these films. In 1962 he sold the rights to *Psycho* to MCA/Universal for a significant amount of corporate stock. By 1973 [*Rear Window, The Trouble with Harry, The Man Who Knew Too Much, Vertigo*, and *Rope*] were removed from circulation as the director's lawyers began to negotiate new financial arrangements for their showing in theaters and on television. The process took almost ten years, during which time Hitchcock died and interest in his complete works intensified.[11]

Throughout all these developments, these comings and goings, there has been a steady interest in *Rope*. In the realm of criticism, discussions of the film have been particularly significant in opening up Hitchcock studies—and the analysis of Hollywood cinema more generally—to queer theory.[12] As *Perpetual Movement* has discussed from chapter to chapter, other analyses have sought to address, among other things: *Rope*'s place in the culture of the Cold War, its portrayal of hospitality, its use of music, its experimental qualities, its depiction of masculinity, its presentation of food, and its architectural elements.[13] In the summer of 2001, meanwhile, *Rope* moved from the screen back to the footlights when Arthur Laurents's script—not Patrick Hamilton's play—was used for a stage version performed in California to mark the fifty-third anniversary of the film's release.[14] *Rope*, it seems, is a film that sometimes goes away without ever really going away.

I have written these pages to address *Rope*'s resonance, its hold, its staying power—in short, the qualities that prevent it from becoming a rope of sand. For Kevin Clifton, the first of Francis Poulenc's *Mouvements perpétuels* "fits well with the restrictive visual world created and sustained" in Hitchcock's film.[15] I do not disagree, but I have called this book *Perpetual Movement* and turned often to the phrase for a slightly different reason. Poulenc's composition, as Clifton explains, effectively moves in two directions as it unfolds: the left hand of the pianist is constant, predictable, tied to the "excessive repetition" of the *ostinato*; the right hand, meanwhile, is given to striking tonal shifts and "ultimately resists melodic closure."[16] Poulenc's piece pulls against itself and, in doing so, remains undecidable, open, perpetually on the move. Hitchcock's film, as I see it, shares these qualities.

On the one hand (the left hand), it is a Hollywood narrative that is bound to what Roland Barthes called the "hermeneutic code" and to the dominant cultural conventions of its time. It follows and repeats a familiar formula, then, by moving steadily and surely towards revelation, restoration, and preservation of the (hetero)normative values demanded by the Production Code Administration. It also, with its regally roaming camera, ropes off a position of knowledge and intimate access for its audience: we see and we know with privileged clarity, and the film, in making this so effortlessly possible, constructs a viewing position in which, as Jean-François Lyotard puts it in his account of the therapeutic pleasures of realism, consciousness is protected from doubt.[17]

But there is another hand; this is not the end of the story. (If it were, I would not have written.) While all of this fostering flattery is underway, *Rope*, like Poulenc's composition, pulls in another direction, away from its *ostinato*. As I have noted in my obsessive analysis, every shot of the film is marked by moments at which we are reminded that we are not seeing and knowing something. These eruptions of an "elsewhere" have escaped the attention of critics to date and are often marginal, but they exist within the film and call out for consideration. Meanwhile, *Rope* makes it possible for us to interpret the relationship between Brandon and Phillip in two contradictory ways: they are lovers who sleep together in the apartment's only bedroom; they are merely friends who live in a penthouse that contains more than one bedroom. Because it refuses to be consistent on this count, *Rope* provides evidence for both understandings of its central and animating relationship; its narrative, as Kevin Clifton puts it, "supports contradictory readings"—a situation that leaves Hitchcock's adaptation with "one foot inside and one foot outside the celluloid closet."[18]

Let me move in conclusion from feet back to hands. *Rope* often invites us to consider what hands can do, what can be done to them, and what they might signify. When the camera cuts inside the apartment at the beginning of its second shot, we see gloved hands pulling a rope around the neck of David Kentley; one of those same hands is wounded when Phillip breaks a glass upon being mistaken by Mrs. Atwater for David; Mrs. Atwater reads the lines in Phillip's palms and announces that they will bring him "great fame." Hands often reach out from Hitchcock's body of work, of course, and I am handing readers nothing new when I merely point this out.[19] ("I am close to an ending, and turning to obvious things," writes T. J. Clark in the dying pages of *The Sight of Death*.[20]) If we wish to understand the bind of *Rope*, we need to handle things slightly differently. In the first of Poulenc's *Mouvements perpétuels*, we find the pianist's hands at odds with each other. While each finger and thumb works ultimately in the name of the composition, there is a tension, a manual duplicity, a "difference which does not stop," as Barthes puts it.[21] Poulenc's piece can never come to conventional closure, can never be unified, because of this handiwork; what we find in the end is enigma, an opening.

My sense, after spending a year tangled up in *Rope*, is that Hitchcock's film follows suit, takes its lead from Poulenc. "Very fond of that little tune, aren't you?" says Rupert while he listens to Phillip playing the piano. It is easy to fathom such fondness: pleasure, in the end, is about perpetual movement. This, in Clark's phrase, is "what compels the return."[22] This is what holds us, what reels us back in. This is the bliss to which we are bound. This is Alfred Hitchcock's rope trick.

# Notes

## Introduction

1. Thomas Mann, "Death in Venice," in *Death in Venice, Tristan, Tonio Kröger*, trans. H. T. Lowe-Porter (Harmondsworth: Penguin, 1955), p. 47.

2. Many discussions of *Rope* give the name of the one murderer as "Philip," but the end credits clearly refer to "Phillip," as do all versions of the screenplay.

3. Philip Roth, *The Ghost Writer* (London: Vintage, 2005), p. 18.

4. Henry David Thoreau, *Walden* (Princeton: Princeton University Press, 1971), p. 3.

5. Roland Barthes, *Roland Barthes by Roland Barthes*, trans. Richard Howard (Berkeley and Los Angeles: University of California Press, 1994), p. 179.

6. Stephen Benson and Clare Connors, "Introduction," in *Creative Criticism: An Anthology and Guide*, ed. Stephen Benson and Clare Connors (Edinburgh: Edinburgh University Press, 2014), pp. 1–47.

7. Neil Badmington, *Hitchcock's Magic* (Cardiff: University of Wales Press, 2011). For my discussion in that book of the textual link between *Rope* and *Rebecca*, see pp. 81–83.

8. A publicity slogan used in 1948 actually read: "IF YOU MISS THE BEGINNING OF ROPE REMEMBER . . . THERE'S A BODY IN THE BOX." For a photograph of the line on a display board from the period, see folder 14503A2, Warner Bros. Archive.

9. For a consideration specifically of the relationship between "real time" and space in the film, see Peter J. Dellolio, "Filmic Space and Real Time in *Rope*," *Midwest Quarterly* 50.1 (2008), 87–101.

10. Colin MacCabe, "Realism and the Cinema: Notes on Some Brechtian Theses," in *Theoretical Essays: Film, Linguistics, Literature* (Manchester: Manchester University Press, 1985), p. 39.

11. The film's credits identify Leo F. Forbstein as *Rope*'s musical director, but the adaptation of Poulenc was undertaken by the uncredited David Buttolph. See Kevin Clifton, "The Anatomy of Aural Suspense in *Rope* and *Vertigo*," in

*Partners in Suspense: Critical Essays on Bernard Herrmann and Alfred Hitchcock*, ed. Steve Rawle and K. J. Donnelly (Manchester: Manchester University Press, 2017), p. 38.

12. Henri Hell, *Francis Poulenc*, trans. Edward Lockspeiser (London: John Calder, 1959), p. 8. See also Francis Poulenc, *My Friends and Myself*, ed. Stéphane Audel, trans. James Harding (London: Dobson, 1978), p. 38. Although the *Trois mouvements perpétuels* were originally written for solo piano, Poulenc later produced—in 1944 and, in revised form, in 1946—an arrangement for nine instruments. See Carl B. Schmidt, *Entrancing Muse: A Documented Biography of Francis Poulenc* (Hillsdale, NY: Pendragon Press, 2001), p. 324.

13. Hell, *Poulenc*, p. 74.

14. Hitchcock's insistence is mentioned in a Warner Bros. interdepartmental memo from Joseph McLaughlin to Helen Schoen dated January 21, 1948. The payment of $1500 is noted in another indepartmental memo from Leo F. Forbstein to C.H. Wilder dated January 24, 1948. Both documents can be found in folder 1057B, Warner Bros. Archive.

15. Francis Poulenc, *"Echo and Source": Selected Correspondence 1915–1963*, ed. and trans. Sidney Buckland (London: Victor Gollancz, 1991), p. 33. Reinforcing the point, Poulenc added not long after in the same letter that the pieces were "ultra easy" (p. 34).

16. For Poulenc's own explicit acknowledgment of his debt to Satie, see his *My Friends and Myself*, pp. 63–71. The influence is mentioned often in writing about Poulenc; see, for example, Hell, *Poulenc*, pp. 8–9; Schmidt, *Entrancing Muse*, p. 67.

17. Scott D. Paulin, "Unheard Sexualities: Queer Theory and the Soundtrack," in *Spectatorship: Shifting Theories of Gender, Sexuality, and Media*, ed. Roxanne Samer and William Whittington (Austin: University of Texas Press, 2017), pp. 79–80. Wilfrid Mellers offers the following more technical account in his *Francis Poulenc* (Oxford and New York: Oxford University Press, 1993), p. 9: "No. 1, "assez modere" in speed, adheres unchangingly to its ostinato which, in one bar of 4/4, combines oscillating tonics and dominants with a rising and falling scale [. . .] The four-bar tune droops pentatonically, as though "singing itself"; but the answering three-bar phrase melodically shifts to an undulating scale of C, while the ostinato remains in its initial B flat. The first two bars are repeated, but the second two are dissonantly mutated into the minor while the ostinato remains major. Bell-like major ninths resonate over the ostinato and the tune, repeated, is chromaticized and tickled with acciacaturas, similar to those in Satie's exotic *Gnossiennes*. All the music is recapitulated "sans nuances," and the piece dissipates in a five-bar coda: two bars of the original ditty, two in which the melody wavers between D and C, slowing down by way of its own weight, and a final very slow bar in which pitch and movement dissolve in pianissimo bitonality. Only in the final bar does the ostinate cease, chromaticized in unresolved appoggiaturas."

18. Schmidt, *Entrancing Muse*, p. 343. Schmidt writes: "Poluenc realized that the only music used in the film was a three-fold repetition of his *Trois mouvements*

*perpétuels*. Following the advice of George Middleton in New York, Poulenc asked Robert Douglas Gibson at Chester for the appropriate letter so that he could collect royalties. Mme. Salabert granted him 50% of moneys accrued from films, and he suggested Gibson do likewise" (p. 343). (Salabert and Chester published Poulenc's work in France and the United Kingdom, respectively; Gibson worked for Chester in London.) It is not quite accurate to say that Poulenc's movement is "the only music used in the film": in Shots 6 and 7, a radio broadcast plays light music in the background.

19. Murray Pomerance, *A Dream of Hitchcock* (Albany: SUNY Press, 2019), p. 2.

20. See, for instance: Murray Pomerance, *Marnie* (London: BFI, 2014) and *The Man Who Knew Too Much* (London: BFI, 2016); Steffan Sharff, *The Art of Looking in Hitchcock's* Rear Window (New York: Limelight, 1997); Raymond Durgnat, *A Long Hard Look at* Psycho (London: BFI, 2002); Camille Paglia, *The Birds* (London: BFI, 1998); Tom Ryall, *Blackmail* (London: BFI, 2003); and Charles Barr, *Vertigo* (London: BFI, 2002).

21. Murray Pomerance, "Some Hitchcockian Shots," in *A Companion to Alfred Hitchcock*, ed. Thomas Leitch and Leland Poague (Malden, MA, and Oxford: Wiley-Blackwell, 2011), p. 238.

22. Roland Barthes, *The Neutral: Lecture Course at the Collège de France (1977–1978)*, ed. Thomas Clerc, trans. Rosalind E. Krauss and Denis Hollier (New York: Columbia University Press, 2005), p. 11.

23. Vladimir Nabokov, *Pale Fire* (New York: Lancer Books, 1963), p. 19.

24. T. J. Clark, *The Sight of Death: An Experiment in Art Writing* (New Haven and London: Yale University Press, 2006), p. vii.

25. Indeed, Maggie Nelson has called the book "obsessive" in her "All That Is the Case: Some Thoughts on Fact in Nonfiction and Documentary Poetry," in *Lit from Within: Contemporary Masters on the Art and Craft of Writing*, ed. Kevin Haworth and Dinty W. Moore (Athens: Ohio University Press, 2011), p. 162.

26. George Gissing, *New Grub Street* (Harmondsworth: Penguin, 1968), p. 82.

27. Roland Barthes, Sarrasine *de Balzac: Séminaires à l'École pratique des hautes études 1967–1968, 1968–1969*, ed. Claude Coste and Andy Stafford (Paris: Seuil, 2011), p. 55. As no English translation of this text exists at present, all translations here are my own.

28. I take the title of this later course from the list of Barthes's lecture courses and seminars provided in Lucy O'Meara, *Roland Barthes at the Collège de France* (Liverpool: Liverpool University Press, 2012), pp. 205–06.

29. Roland Barthes, *S/Z*, trans. Richard Miller (Oxford: Blackwell, 1990), p. 3.

30. Barthes, *S/Z*, p. 6. I have modified the published English translation typographically slightly here for Richard Miller adds a hyphen ("in-different") to the straightforward "indifférence" found in Barthes's original French. For the latter, see Roland Barthes, *Oeuvres Complètes*, rev. ed., ed. Eric Marty (Paris: Seuil, 2002), 5 vols., vol. 3, p. 123.

31. Barthes, *S/Z*, p. 12.

32. Roland Barthes, "On *S/Z* and *Empire of Signs*," in *The Grain of the Voice: Interviews 1962–1980*, trans. Linda Coverdale (Berkeley and Los Angeles: University of California Press, 1991), p. 69.

33. Don DeLillo, *White Noise* (London: Picador, 1985), p. 81.

34. D. A. Miller, "Anal *Rope*," *Representations* 32 (1990), p. 114.

35. The list of those who have made incorrect claims of one sort or another about the form of *Rope* is considerable. See, for instance: Gilles Deleuze, *Cinema 1: The Movement-Image*, trans. Hugh Tomlinson and Barbara Habberjam (London and New York: Continuum, 2005), p. 204; Slavoj Žižek, *Looking Awry: An Introduction to Jacques Lacan through Popular Culture* (Cambridge, MA, and London: MIT Press, 1991), p. 41; Peter Conrad, *The Hitchcock Murders* (London: Faber and Faber, 2000), p. 151; Robin Wood, *Hitchcock's Films Revisited*, rev. ed. (New York: Columbia University Press, 2002), p. 78 (though the error is then corrected on p. 349 of the same book); Walter Raubicheck and Walter Srebnick, "Introduction: Hitchcock's Rereleased Films and Cinema Studies," in *Hitchcock's Rereleased Films: From* Rope *to* Vertigo, ed. Walter Raubicheck and Walter Srebnick (Detroit: Wayne State University Press, 1991), p. 18; Kristin L. Matthews, "Reading, Guidance, and Cold War Consensus in Alfred Hitchcock's *Rope*," *The Journal of Popular Culture* 43.4 (2010), p. 738; Antonio R. Damasio, "How Hitchcock's *Rope* Stretches Time," *Scientific American*, 16.1 (2006), p. 38; Michel Chion, *Audio-Vision: Sound on Screen*, ed. and trans. Claudia Gorbman (New York: Columbia University Press, 1994), p. 42.

36. For a fascinating discussion of the intertextual relationship between *Shadow of a Doubt* and *Rope*, see Susan Smith, *Hitchcock: Suspense, Humour and Tone* (London: BFI, 2000), pp. 54–55. See also Michael Wood's excellent *Alfred Hitchcock: The Man Who Knew Too Much* (New York: Amazon, 2015), p. 70.

37. François Truffaut, *Hitchcock*, updated ed. (London: Paladin, 1978), p. 217.

38. The timings here are taken from the Region 2 DVD release of the film, played on an iMac; other formats and systems might produce slightly different timings.

39. I will discuss the temporary unavailability of the film between 1973 and 1983–84 in the postscript to this book.

40. Stefan Sharff lists all 796 shots that make up *Rear Window* in his *The Art of Looking in Hitchcock's* Rear Window, pp. 104–75.

41. Geoff Dyer, *Zona* (Edinburgh: Canongate, 2013), p. 31.

42. Barthes, *S/Z*, p. 13.

43. Tobias Wolff, *Old School* (London: Bloomsbury, 2004), p. 53.

44. Blaise Pascal, *Pensées*, trans. A. J. Krailsheimer, rev. ed. (Harmondsworth: Penguin, 1995), p. 192.

# Chapter 1

1. I take the phrase "Operation *Rope*" from Hitchcock himself, who used it to describe the detailed technical planning required for the film in a booklet

produced by Warner Bros. to mark the release of the film in 1948. See Warner Bros. Pictures, *A Photographic Production Notebook on Alfred Hitchcock's* Rope (Los Angeles: Warner Bros., 1948), n.p. Paperback and spiral-bound hardback copies of this booklet can be found in folder 630 of the Alfred Hitchcock Collection, Margaret Herrick Library.

2. While all of Hitchcock's films before *Rope* had been in black and white, it should not be forgotten that the violent climax of *Spellbound* (1945) included a very brief flash of red, created by the "hand coloring of four frames of film (to yield a sixth-of-a-second explosion of red on screen)" when a point-of-view captures the moment at which Dr Murchison fires a gun into his own face. Leonard J. Leff, *Hitchcock and Selznick: The Rich and Strange Collaboration of Alfred Hitchcock and David O. Selznick in Hollywood* (London: Weidenfeld and Nicolson, 1988), p. 162. Leff's book provides an excellent account of Hitchcock's time working under contract to Selznick; see also Thomas Schatz, *The Genius of the System: Hollywood Filmmaking in the Studio Era* (London: Faber and Faber, 1998), especially chapters 11, 15, and 20.

3. Patrick McGilligan, *Alfred Hitchcock: A Life in Darkness and Light* (New York: HarperCollins, 2003), p. 393.

4. While Hitchcock was under contract to David O. Selznick, *Foreign Correspondent* (1940), *Mr. and Mrs. Smith* (1941), *Suspicion* (1941), *Saboteur* (1942), *Shadow of a Doubt* (1943), *Lifeboat* (1944), *Aventure Malgache* (1944), *Bon Voyage* (1944), *Notorious* (1946), and the Holocaust documentary *Memory of the Camps* (also known as *F3080)*, which was made in 1945 but not shown publicly until 1984, were all made away from Selznick International. Selznick played a key role in the development of *Notorious*, but, as Leonard J. Leff explains (*Hitchcock and Selznick*, p. 220), his name did not actually appear in the credits of the RKO production for legal reasons.

5. The date of the signing of the deeds is taken from Carolyn Moorhead, *Sidney Bernstein: A Biography* (London: Jonathan Cape, 1984), p. 175. For discussions of Hitchcock's involvement with the London Film Society, see, among others, Tom Ryall, *Alfred Hitchcock and the British Cinema*, (London: Athlone, 1996), pp. 10–13; Donald Spoto, *The Dark Side of Genius: The Life of Alfred Hitchcock*, new ed. (London: Plexus, 1994), pp. 71–73; McGilligan, *Alfred Hitchcock*, pp. 76–77. According to David Sterritt, Hitchcock and Bernstein first met each other in 1923; Moorhead's biography offers no information about this encounter. David Sterritt, "From Transatlantic to Warner Bros.," in *A Companion to Alfred Hitchcock*, ed. Thomas Leitch and Leland Poague (Malden, MA and Oxford: Wiley-Blackwell, 2011), p. 313.

6. Moorhead's biography of Bernstein dates the beginning of his acquaintance with Selznick to the mid-1920s (pp. 40–41).

7. Moorhead, *Bernstein*, p. 170.

8. Moorhead, *Bernstein*, p. 172.

9. Hitchcock and Bernstein originally wished to make *Under Capricorn* the first Transatlantic film, but production was delayed (and *Rope* chosen instead) because Ingrid Bergman was unavailable. *Under Capricorn* was eventually released

in 1949—one year after *Rope*. See Spoto, *The Dark Side of Genius*, p. 302 and McGilligan, *Alfred Hitchcock*, p. 399. There were also discussions about Transatlantic making as its first film a modern-day version of *Hamlet*, with Cary Grant as star, or an adaptation of Margaret Wilson's novel *The Dark Duty* featuring Ronald Colman; rights for the latter had been obtained by Transatlantic by November 1947, and Hitchcock was still considering the project as late as 1963. For full information about the *Hamlet* discussions, see folder 1124 of the Alfred Hitchcock Collection at the Margaret Herrick Library; details of the plans to adapt *The Dark Duty* can be found in folders 1050 and 1051 of the same collection. For a more readily accessible discussion of several projects considered but never actually completed by Hitchcock, see Sidney Gottlieb, "Unknown Hitchcock: The Unrealized Projects," in *Hitchcock: Past and Future*, ed. Richard Allen and Sam Ishii-Gonzáles (London and New York: Routledge, 2004), pp. 85–106. For more about the discussions surrounding the launch of Transatlantic, see chapter 8 of Moorhead, *Sidney Bernstein* and Sterritt, "From Transatlantic to Warner Bros."

10. Moorhead, *Bernstein*, p. 174.

11. Bernstein is listed nowhere in the credits of *Rope*, but an undated staff and cast sheet held in folder 2812 at the Warner Bros. Archive confirms his involvement with the film in the capacity of producer.

12. Sean French, *Patrick Hamilton: A Life* (London: Faber and Faber, 1993), p. 104. The first American staging of Hamilton's play took place at the Masque Theater, New York, under the title *Rope's End*, on September 19, 1929. It was revived (as *Rope*) at the Playhouse in Cedarhurst, Long Island, on August 9, 1945 and then at the Community Center Auditorium in New York on October 28, 1951. All this information is taken from a letter, dated December 8, 1972, from E. Fulton Brylawksi of the Fulton Brylawski law firm, Washington, D.C., to Samuel Taylor of Taylor, Winokur and Schoenberg in San Francisco. See folder 630 of the Alfred Hitchcock Collection, Margaret Herrick Library.

13. French, *Patrick Hamilton*, p. 104. See chapter 10 of French's fine book for an overview of the place of *Rope* in Hamilton's wider work and career. *Rope* ran for 131 performances in London and 100 performances in New York in 1929. See Amnon Kabatchnik, *Blood on the Stage, 1925–1950: Milestone Plays of Crime, Mystery, and Detection: An Annotated Repertoire* (Lanham, MD: Scarecrow Press, 2010), p. 247.

14. Quoted in French, *Patrick Hamilton*, p. 104.

15. Patrick Hamilton, *Rope: A Play* (London: Constable and Co. Ltd., 1929), p. 13. It is often stated that Rupert is or was the boys' teacher in the play, but Hamilton's text nowhere specifies this. We are told that Rupert has known Brandon since he was an infant (p. 49), but not that this was in the capacity of teacher.

16. McGilligan, *Alfred Hitchcock*, p. 400.

17. My summary here of the Leopold and Loeb case draws extensively from the concise overview given in Jordan Schildcrout, "Queer Justice: The Retrials of Leopold and Loeb," *The Journal of American Culture* 34.2 (2011), 167–77. For more lengthy accounts, see Hal Higdon, *Leopold and Loeb: The Crime of the Century* (Urbana and Chicago: University of Illinois Press, 1999) and Simon Baatz, *For the*

*Thrill of It: Leopold, Loeb, and the Murder that Shocked Jazz Age Chicago* (New York: HarperCollins, 2008). Folder number 1587 of the Alfred Hitchcock Collection at the Margaret Herrick Library contains a copy of Maureen McKernan's *The Amazing Crime and Trial of Leopold and Loeb* (Chicago: Plymouth Court Press, 1924). It is possible that this detailed book was consulted during the development of *Rope*, but the archive contains no specific confirmation of this.

18. Hamilton, "Preface on Thrillers," in *Rope*, p. ix.

19. French, *Patrick Hamilton*, p. 101. For an excellent discussion of how the Leopold and Loeb case has been taken up in different ways in a variety of dramatic narratives, see Schildcrout, "Queer Justice."

20. All the Balaban-Warner correspondence to which I refer in this paragraph can be found in folder 2198, Warner Bros. Archive.

21. French, *Patrick Hamilton*, p. 196.

22. French, *Patrick Hamilton*, pp. 141, 196. The American adaptation of Hamilton's *Gas Light* was eventually directed by George Cukor and released in 1944 as *Gaslight*.

23. Carolyn Moorhead describes Bernstein's seeing of *Rope* in 1929 in her *Sidney Bernstein*, p. 175. David Sterritt claims in passing that Hitchcock and Bernstein watched the play together in London, but he offers no supporting evidence or further details. See David Sterritt, "Morbid Psychologies and So Forth: The Fine Art of *Rope*," in *Hitchcock at the Source: The Auteur as Adaptor*, ed. R. Barton Palmer and David Boyd (Albany: SUNY Press, 2011), p. 161.

24. See the contract in folder 2812, Warner Bros. Archive. No more specific date than the year (1947) is given on the document.

25. Copies of both contracts can be found in folder 2812, Warner Bros. Archive. In his *Patrick Hamilton*, Sean French gives incorrect information about how much Hamilton was paid for the adaptation rights (p. 197).

26. Moorhead, *Sidney Bernstein*, p. 176; McGilligan, *Alfred Hitchcock*, p. 401.

27. French, *Patrick Hamilton*, pp. 196–97.

28. Alfred Hitchcock to Joseph Breen, September 4, 1946. Letter contained in the 38-page Production Code Administration (PCA) file on *Rope* held at the Margaret Herrick Library.

29. Joseph Breen to Alfred Hitchcock, September 9, 1946. Letter, *Rope* PCA file, Margaret Herrick Library. What Breen saw as the "derisive" treatment of the Ten Commandments can be found in Act II of the play and comes from the mouth of Rupert (Hamilton, *Rope*, pp. 66–67); there is no equivalent moment in Hitchcock's film. Although he urged Hitchcock to lighten the play's emphasis upon alcohol, Breen nonetheless accepted that it was necessary to the development of the plot for Granillo to become inebriated.

30. French, *Patrick Hamilton*, p. 198.

31. French, *Patrick Hamilton*, p. 203. See also McGilligan, *Alfred Hitchcock*, p. 408. It is not clear precisely what in Hitchcock's adaptation upset Patrick Hamilton. The film is based fairly closely on his play and is far more faithful to its source material than many of Hitchcock's other adaptations. It does, however, move the setting of the tale from London to New York and depart in some

further ways from the stage version; I will discuss some of these textual differences elsewhere in this book as they become relevant. For a useful summary of the main differences between Hamilton's *Rope* and Hitchcock's *Rope*, see Sterritt, "Morbid Psychologies," pp. 166–68, and Amy Lawrence, "American Shame: *Rope*, James Stewart, and the Postwar Crisis in American Masculinity," in *Hitchcock's America*, ed. Jonathan Freedman and Richard Millington (New York and Oxford: Oxford University Press, 1999), pp. 65–67.

32. Arthur Laurents, *Original Story By: A Memoir of Broadway and Hollywood* (New York and London: Applause, 2000), p. 126.

33. Laurents, *Original Story By*, p. 127.

34. Hume Cronyn, *A Terrible Liar: A Memoir* (New York: William Morrow, 1991), pp. 205–10.

35. Spoto, *The Dark Side of Genius*, p. 303. François Truffaut, *Hitchcock*, updated ed. (London: Paladin, 1978), p. 216.

36. Arthur Laurents, *Rope*, screenplay dated November 22, 1947. Folder 2198A, Warner Bros. Archive.

37. Fred Ahern to Joseph Breen, December 1, 1947. Letter, *Rope* PCA file, Margaret Herrick Library.

38. Stephen S. Jackson to Fred Ahern, December 15, 1947. Letter, *Rope* PCA file, Margaret Herrick Library. Peers is wrongly called "Peer" in this letter; Shurlock and Hodenfield are identified only by their surnames. Shurlock would go on to succeed Joseph Breen as head of the PCA when the latter stepped down in 1954.

39. Jackson to Ahern, December 15, 1947.

40. Fred Ahern to Stephen S. Jackson, December 17, 1947. Letter, *Rope* PCA file, Margaret Herrick Library. For the revised script itself, see Arthur Laurents, *Rope*, screenplay dated December 16, 1947 (with additional pages dated January 13, 1948), folder 2198A, Warner Bros. Archive.

41. Stephen S. Jackson to Fred Ahern, December 22, 1947. Letter, *Rope* PCA file, Margaret Herrick Library.

42. The unattributed novelization of the film published in 1948 to accompany the film's release omits the strangling altogether and simply opens with the slamming of the lid of the wooden chest. See *Alfred Hitchcock's* Rope (New York: Dell, 1948), p. 5.

43. Strangely, Brandon is very clearly seen wiping the glass in question in the completed film. The gesture is missing, however, from the novelization. See *Alfred Hitchcock's* Rope, p. 7.

44. The finished film incorporates this change: Brandon says, "All the better: it's much more dangerous." Other references explicitly to excitement, however, remain in the completed version of *Rope*.

45. The finished film incorporates this change: at the very end of the second shot, Brandon utters the line, "We have a very simple excuse."

46. The PCA once again, echoing Breen's letter to Hitchcock on September 9, 1946, accepted that the drunken behavior of Phillip was important to the plot

and stressed that the censors' concerns were with what Jackson called "the casual drinking among other guests."

47. Fred Ahern to Stephen S. Jackson, January 19, 1948. Letter, *Rope* PCA file, Margaret Herrick Library.

48. Stephen S. Jackson to Fred Ahern, January 23, 1948. Letter, *Rope* PCA file, Margaret Herrick Library.

49. Fred Ahern to Stephen S. Jackson, January 24, 1948. Letter, *Rope* PCA file, Margaret Herrick Library.

50. A copy of the complete contract can be found in folder 12723B, Warner Bros. Archive.

51. Information about the use of the different stages at the studio is taken from folder 1490, Warner Bros. Archive.

52. Bill Krohn, *Hitchcock at Work* (London: Phaidon, 2000), p. 106. Although Krohn's discussion of the making of *Rope* is somewhat brief, it reproduces a wonderful photograph of the main room of the apartment while filming is underway (pp. 106–07).

53. Warner Bros. Pictures, *A Photographic Production Notebook*, n.p. So that the walls could slide out of the way silently, they were mounted on Vaseline-greased rollers. See Alfred Hitchcock, "My Most Exciting Picture," in *Hitchcock on Hitchcock: Selected Writings and Interviews*, ed. Sidney Gottlieb (London Faber and Faber, 1997), p. 276.

54. Truffaut, *Hitchcock*, p. 222.

55. Hitchcock, "My Most Exciting Picture," pp. 276–77.

56. Hitchcock, "My Most Exciting Picture," pp. 277–78.

57. Hitchcock, "My Most Exciting Picture," p. 278.

58. Hitchcock, "My Most Exciting Picture," p. 278.

59. Hitchcock, "My Most Exciting Picture," pp. 278–79.

60. Hitchcock, "My Most Exciting Picture," p. 279.

61. Hitchcock, "My Most Exciting Picture," p. 279.

62. Hitchcock, "My Most Exciting Picture," p. 280. Celotex, which is still in production and widely used, is a type of insulation board.

63. Hitchcock, "My Most Exciting Picture," p. 280. Munaw is not named in Hitchcock's article, but he is identified on a photograph (and shown wielding his bamboo pole) in folder 14503A4, Warner Bros. Archive. For further photographs of the numbered floor markers used on set, see folder 597A. For another account of this element of the filming process, see Truffaut, *Hitchcock*, pp. 221–22.

64. Hitchcock, "My Most Exciting Picture," p. 276.

65. Laurents, *Original Story By*, p. 128.

66. All these detailed reports can be found in folder 1490, Warner Bros. Archive.

67. The production and progress sheets only record when close-up shots of Stewart, Collier, Chandler, and Hardwicke were filmed for the trailer. Nothing in the archives specifies when similar footage of the other actors was shot.

68. Truffaut, *Hitchcock*, p. 217. See also Hitchcock, "My Most Exciting Picture," p. 283.

69. The PCA file on *Rope* held at the Margaret Herrick Library contains the analysis chart completed during assessment by the censors, along with a two-page synopsis of the film. Both are dated March 16, 1948.

70. While the PCA file on *Rope* held at the Margaret Herrick Library includes Stephen S. Jackson's covering letter of March 22 to Peers, it does not contain the certificate itself.

71. In Maryland, the censors demanded that all glimpses of the strangulation of David be eliminated, along with two lines spoken by Brandon: 1) "Well, murder can be an art, too. The power to kill can be just as satisfying as the power to create"; 2) "And then I felt tremendously exhilarated! How did you feel?" The same cuts were required in Ohio, along with the "And then?" uttered by Phillip just before Brandon says, "And then I felt tremendously exhilarated!" Pennsylvania was a touch more forgiving: its local censors asked only for the removal of the shots of David's strangulation. All information here is taken from the *Rope* PCA file, Margaret Herrick Library, and folder 2701B, Warner Bros. Archive.

72. Motion Picture Association of America reports relating to Italy, India, and Holland can be found in the *Rope* PCA file, Margaret Herrick Library. Information about the situation in Germany is taken from folder number 630 of the Alfred Hitchcock Collection at the same library, in which letters from March and April 1960 describe the ongoing inability to have *Rope* approved for distribution in Germany. The archives do not reveal precisely when the Italian, Indian, and Dutch censors relented, but the ban in each country must have been lifted before late 1958 because Warner Bros. financial statements relating to film, covering receipts up until September 28, 1958, show income received from each of the countries in question. See folder 629 of the Alfred Hitchcock Collection, Margaret Herrick Library. The German prohibition, meanwhile, seems to have been lifted in 1963: a letter, dated May 31, 1963, from George Sharf of M.G.M.'s New York office to Herman Citron at the Park-Citron Agency in Los Angeles states that *Rope* has temporarily passed the German censors. Sharf goes on to say that he is worried that the decision will be reversed before the planned release of the film in July, but the archives do not contain anything that implies that his fears had foundation. See folder number 630 of the Alfred Hitchcock Collection, Margaret Herrick Library.

73. See folder 2701B, Warner Bros. Archive.

74. Sol E. Zwicker to H. Bareford, Warner Bros. internal memo, November 10, 1948. Folder 12670A, Warner Bros. Archive.

75. One of these "tradeshow" screenings took place at Warner Bros. Studios in California on August 20, 1948, as is made clear in a brief review entitled "Rope" which was published in *Variety*, August 26, 1948: 3.

76. *Under Capricorn* was shot at Elstree from July 21 to October 18, 1948, with exteriors filmed sometime later in California. Information taken from an official document entitled "Motion Pictures Made by Mr. Alfred Hitchcock from 1939 to 1957," folder 1425, Alfred Hitchcock Collection, Margaret Herrick Library.

77. I take the figure of $450,000 from Sterritt, "Morbid Psychologies," p. 169. The "Nothing Ever Held . . ." tagline was used widely in publicity materials at the time of the film's release. A large-format booklet entitled *Warner Bros' Plans for Your Presentation of Rope* produced by the studio in 1948 shows the phrase in question employed in advertisements for cooking, sports, and finance, for instance. On occasions, the phrase was modified to reflect the support of well-known individuals; one of the examples given in the booklet is "Nothing Ever Held J. Edgar Hoover Like Alfred Hitchcock's Rope." See Warner Bros. Pictures, *Warner Bros' Plan for Your Presentation of Rope* (Los Angeles: Warner Bros., 1948), p. 32. A copy of this publication is held at the Margaret Herrick Library.

78. See folder 597A, Warner Bros. Archive.

79. See folder 14503A3, Warner Bros. Archive.

80. See the anonymously published *Alfred Hitchcock's* Rope. Information about the print run is taken from Warner Bros. Pictures, *Warner Bros' Plan for Your Presentation of Rope*, p. 32.

81. See Location Expenses Report #2144, February 24, 1948, folder 1434, Warner Bros. Archive.

82. In *The Encyclopedia of Alfred Hitchcock* (New York: Checkmark Books, 2002), for instance, Thomas Leitch claims that Hitchcock is not the man walking along the street after the opening credits (p. 47); Maurice Yacowar comes to the same conclusion in the chapter entitled "Hitchcock's Appearances" in his *Hitchcock's British Films*, 2nd ed. (Detroit: Wayne State University Press, 2010), p. 225. By way of contrast, critics such as James Holt, D. A. Miller, and François Truffaut believe that the strolling figure is indeed the director of the film. See James Holt, "The Hitchcock Cameo: Aesthetic Considerations," in *Hitchcock and Philosophy: Dial M for Metaphysics*, ed. David Baggett and William A. Drumin (Chicago and La Salle, IL: Open Court, 2007), p. 235; D. A. Miller, *Hidden Hitchcock* (Chicago and London: University of Chicago Press, 2016); and Truffaut, *Hitchcock*, p. 187.

83. Peter J. Dellolio, "Filmic Space and Real Time in *Rope*," *Midwest Quarterly* 50.1 (2008), p. 91. For more on the various ways in which figures of law and authority in Hitchcock's work are unreliable or untrustworthy (or both), see chapter 4 of Eric San Juan and Jim McDevitt, *Hitchcock's Villains: Murderers, Maniacs, and Mother Issues* (New York: Scarecrow Press, 2013).

84. Examples of advertising materials on which this phrase was used can be found in Warner Bros. Pictures, *Warner Bros' Plan for Your Presentation of Rope*; see, for instance, pp. 34–35.

85. The *OED* also records an obsolete intransitive verb form: "to rope"—"to utter a cry or shout; to cry out."

# Chapter 2

1. Michael Wood, *Alfred Hitchcock: The Man Who Knew Too Much* (New York: Amazon, 2015), p. 70.

2. Warner Bros. Pictures, *A Photographic Production Notebook on Alfred Hitchcock's Rope*, 1948, n.p. Folder 630, Alfred Hitchcock Collection, Margaret Herrick Library.

3. Arthur Laurents, *Original Story By: A Memoir of Broadway and Hollywood* (New York and London: Applause, 2000), p. 128.

4. Peter Conrad, *The Hitchcock Murders* (London: Faber and Faber, 2000), p. 127; D. A. Miller, *Hidden Hitchcock* (Chicago and London: University of Chicago Press, 2016), p. 19; Raymond Durgnat, *The Strange Case of Alfred Hitchcock or the Plain Man's Hitchcock* (London: Faber and Faber, 1974), p. 208.

5. Richard Allen, *Hitchcock's Romantic Irony* (New York: Columbia University Press, 2007), p. 143; Lesley Brill, *The Hitchcock Romance: Love and Irony in Hitchcock's Films* (Princeton: Princeton University Press, 1988), p. 274.

6. Peter J. Dellolio, "Filmic Space and Real Time in *Rope*," *Midwest Quarterly* 50.1 (2008), pp. 94 and 95; William Rothman, *Hitchcock—The Murderous Gaze* (Cambridge, MA, and London: Harvard University Press, 1982), p. 247.

7. Charles Barr, "Hitchcock and Early Filmmakers," in *A Companion to Alfred Hitchcock*, ed. Thomas Leitch and Leland Poague (Malden, MA, and Oxford: Wiley-Blackwell, 2011), p. 57; Angelo Restivo, "Hitchcock and the Postmodern," in *A Companion to Alfred Hitchcock*, ed. Thomas Leitch and Leland Poague (Malden, MA, and Oxford: Wiley-Blackwell, 2011), p. 567. Barr's point about Murnau was anticipated by Raymond Durgnat several decades earlier in *The Strange Case of Alfred Hitchcock*, p. 202. More recently, writing with Alain Kerzoncuf, Barr has referred to "a restlessly moving camera at the expense of cutting" in *Rope* and added to his earlier claim about Murnau with a suggestion that Graham Cutts's *The Rat* (1925) might also have been a stylistic influence upon Hitchcock's film. See Alain Kerzoncuf and Charles Barr, *Hitchcock Lost and Found* (Lexington: University Press of Kentucky, 2015), pp. 69–70.

8. Allen, *Hitchcock's Romantic Irony*, p. 144.

9. Allen, *Hitchcock's Romantic Irony*, p. 143.

10. Dellolio, "Filmic Space and Real Time in *Rope*," p. 100.

11. Kristin L. Matthews, "Reading, Guidance, and Cold War Consensus in Alfred Hitchcock's *Rope*," *The Journal of Popular Culture* 43.4 (2010), p. 744. See also Wood, *Alfred Hitchcock*, p. 72. Richard Allen locates an echo of *Rope*'s beginning in the opening sequence of *Blue Velvet* (dir. by David Lynch, 1986)—another film in which terror hides beneath the surface of polite everyday American life. Richard Allen, "Hitchcock's Legacy," in *A Companion to Alfred Hitchcock*, ed. Thomas Leitch and Leland Poague (Malden, MA, and Oxford: Wiley-Blackwell, 2011), p. 586.

12. Laurents discusses his life with Granger during the time of *Rope* in *Original Story By*, p. 130. He notes that he and Granger were not actually living together when the latter was cast in the film and that Hitchcock was probably unaware of their relationship at that point.

13. A copy of Dall's contract of employment with Warner Bros. can be found in folder 2827A, Warner Bros. Archive. It was signed on July 26, 1943, and Dall was released from its terms on May 6, 1946.

14. In *Hitchcock—The Murderous Gaze*, William Rothman notes that "[o]pening a film with a hallucinatory fragment of a murder scene is one of Hitchcock's characteristic strategies. He uses it, for example, in *Murder! Young and Innocent, Rope, and I Confess*" (p. 349 n. 1). This wooden trunk will later be identified by Brandon as a "*cassone*"—an Italian signifier whose connotations I will discuss in chapter 5 of this book. In *Hitchcock's Romantic Irony* (p. 150), Richard Allen sees in the characters' exhausted recovery a foreshadowing of the aftermath of the brutal murder of Gromek in Hitchcock's *Torn Curtain* (1966).

15. Patrick Hamilton, *Rope* (London: Constable & Co., 1929), p. 13.

16. Hamilton, *Rope*, p. 13. More recent editions of the play reword these stage directions—and others—partly, I suspect, in the name of modernizing the original interwar English. Granillo's name is changed to Phillip in the film.

17. The script for this planned trailer was written by Arthur Houseman and is dated June 4, 1962. See folder 630 of the Alfred Hitchcock Collection, Margaret Herrick Library. Arthur Laurents, incidentally, was not keen on this aspect of the film: "I thought it better," he wrote in his autobiography (*Original Story By*, p. 127), "to let the audience guess whether there really was a body in the chest." Another detail in Laurents's memoir at this point should be treated with a degree of scepticism. He claims that Hitchcock "inserted a scene of the actual murder" only "[a]fter the picture was shot" (p. 127), but the screenplay opened with a close-up of the rope used to strangle David from its first draft onwards. See Arthur Laurents, *Rope*, screenplay dated November 22, 1947, n.p. Folder 2198A, Warner Bros. Archive.

18. D. A. Miller, "Anal *Rope*," *Representations* 32 (1990), p. 124.

19. For the Hamilton quote, see Sean French, *Patrick Hamilton: A Life* (London: Faber and Faber, 1993), p. 114. For more on the role of the Lord Chamberlain in British theater censorship, see, for instance: Dominic Shellard and Steve Nicholson with Miriam Handley, *The Lord Chamberlain Regrets: A History of British Theatre Censorship* (London: British Library, 2004); David Carlson, David Carlton, and Anne Etienne, *Theatre Censorship: From Walpole to Wilson* (Oxford: Oxford University Press, 2007); and John Johnston, *The Lord Chamberlain's Blue Pencil* (London: Hodder and Stoughton, 1990). I thank Irene Morra for ushering me through this theatrical material.

20. Laurents, *Original Story By*, p. 124. Several pages later, Laurents confirms that he is including Rupert in this figure of three (p. 130).

21. Laurents, *Original Story By*, p. 127.

22. I take the phrase "compulsory heterosexuality" from Adrienne Rich's classic essay, "Compulsory Heterosexuality and Lesbian Existence," *Signs* 5.4 (1980), pp. 631–60. *Rope*'s careful coding of homosexuality has been discussed often in criticism. See, most notably, chapter 16 of Robin Wood, *Hitchcock's Films Revisited*, rev. ed. (New York: Columbia University Press, 2002) and Miller, "Anal *Rope*."

23. Miller, "Anal *Rope*," p. 118. As Miller makes clear, he is drawing in his discussion of connotation and denotation upon Roland Barthes's *S/Z*, trans. Richard Miller (Oxford: Blackwell, 1990). See, above all, pp. 6–11 of the book, where Barthes discusses connotation at length.

24. Miller, "Anal *Rope*," p. 118.
25. Miller, "Anal *Rope*," p. 119.
26. John Orr, *Hitchcock and Twentieth-Century Cinema* (London and New York: Wallflower Press, 2005), pp. 81–82.
27. Miller, "Anal *Rope*," p. 118.
28. Conrad, *The Hitchcock Murders*, p. 259.
29. Conrad, *The Hitchcock Murders*, p. 258.
30. Edith Wharton, *The Age of Innocence* (Harmondsworth: Penguin, 1974), p. 142. My mind has also been known to wander during this charged moment in the film to Katherine Mansfield's short story "A Dill Pickle," in which a fondled glove marks both the intimacy and the distance between two former lovers. Katherine Mansfield, "A Dill Pickle," in *Bliss and Other Stories* (Harmondsworth: Penguin, 1962), pp. 181–88.
31. David Greven, *Intimate Violence: Hitchcock, Sex, and Queer Theory* (New York: Oxford University Press, 2017), p. 121; Eric San Juan and Jim McDevin, *Hitchcock's Villains: Murderers, Maniacs, and Mother Issues* (New York: Scarecrow Press, 2013), p. 61. Lee Wallace discusses how *Rope* "maintains the forensic deniability of its homosexual subject" in "Continuous Sex: The Editing of Homosexuality in *Bound* and *Rope*," *Screen* 41.4 (2000), p. 376.
32. Adriana Cavarero, *Inclinations: A Critique of Rectitude*, trans. Amanda Minervini and Adam Sitze (Stanford, CA: Stanford University Press, 2016), p. 6.
33. There is a sense, in fact, in which the height of trunk will require characters to lean forward when they wish to handle objects placed upon its lid, as if the mere act of approaching the marker of a terrible crime were enough often to inspire inclination.
34. Wood, *Hitchcock's Films Revisited*, p. 350.
35. Hamilton's play goes one step further with this darkness. The opening stage directions refer to a room that is "completely darkened save for the pallid gleam from lamplight in the street below, which comes through the window" (p. 13), but, following the loud closing of the chest, Brandon "goes over to window and draws the heavy curtains to. Complete black out" (p. 13). There is no equivalent moment of total darkness in Hitchcock's adaptation.
36. For a Lacanian analysis of this window and its function in the film, see Thomas J. Connelly, "Big Window, Big Other: Enjoyment and Spectatorship in Alfred Hitchcock's *Rope*," *Quarterly Review of Film and Video* 31 (2014), pp. 779–88. For an illuminating discussion of the fact that Brandon and Phillip's apartment is specifically a penthouse, see Steven Jacobs, *The Wrong House: The Architecture of Alfred Hitchcock* (Rotterdam: 010 Publishers, 2007), pp. 268–70.
37. There are fainter noises of distant horns *before* the curtains are opened (just before Brandon lights his cigarette, for instance, and then again moments later, immediately prior to Brandon's saying of the line: "Phillip, we don't have too much time"), but the external sound is much clearer, louder, and longer when Brandon pulls the curtains back and says "There, that's much better."
38. We even see that we are *not seeing* the thoroughfares from which the sounds arise: when Brandon opens the main curtains, he looks out of the window

and can presumably gaze down at the Manhattan streets below, but the film provides no point-of-view shot that would allow us to share his vision.

39. Dellolio is completely wrong to suggest that Rupert's opening of the window at the very end of the film "introduc[es] natural sounds for only the second time in the film" ("Filmic Space and Real Time in *Rope*," p. 90). To claim, on the same page, that *Rope* features "Hitchcock's most insulated soundtrack" is, I think, completely to misread the film, and to state that "[t]he first time we hear distinct street sounds is while Phillip plays the piano" (p. 91) is to be guilty of a glaring critical oversight.

40. Virginia Woolf, *Mrs. Dalloway* (London: Penguin, 1992), p, 22.

41. Alfred Hitchcock, "My Most Exciting Picture," in *Hitchcock on Hitchcock: Selected Writings and Interviews*, ed. Sidney Gottlieb (London: Faber and Faber, 1997), p. 282.

42. See the set drawings in box 5687, Warner Bros. Archive. The sketches in question were produced by Russell Menzer of the Warner Bros. art department on January 6, 1948 on the following sheets: sheet 14 (S); sheet 15 (T); sheet 16 (O); sheet 17 (R); sheet 18 (A). Each letter was approximately 60 inches high and 38 inches wide and was made out of four separate neon tubes of 5/8-inch thickness in the following colors: white (two tubes), red, and green. While Menzer drew these sketches, the art direction of *Rope* was the overall responsibility of Perry Ferguson, whose contract of employment with Transatlantic stated that he was to be paid $750 per week for at least seven weeks. For a copy of this contract, which was signed on December 2, 1947, see folder 2812, Warner Bros. Archive.

43. Arthur Laurents, *Rope*, screenplay dated November 22, 1947, pp. 20, 21. Folder 2198A, Warner Bros. Archive. Kenneth is also described as a student of Princeton in the unpaginated section at the start of the screenplay, in which brief descriptions of the characters are offered.

44. Laurents, *Rope*, screenplay dated November 22, 1947, p. 67. The Princeton Club is located on West 43rd Street in midtown Manhattan.

45. Arthur Laurents, *Rope*, screenplay dated December 16, 1947 (with additional pages dated January 13, 1948), pp. 4, 67. Folder 2198A, Warner Bros. Archive. The Harvard Club is still, as in 1948, on West 44th Street in midtown Manhattan, just a few minutes' walk from the Princeton Club.

46. President Conant's request is outlined in telegrams dated July 13, 1948 from Albert S. Howson to Joseph Hummel of the French Warner Bros. office and to Hitchcock himself, copies of which are kept in folder 2812, Warner Bros. Archive. A letter dated July 17, 1948 from Transatlantic Pictures to A.E. Carlson of Technicolor, giving permission for the word "Harvard" to be removed from the phrase "the Harvard Club" in all prints of the film, can be found in folder 2701B.

47. See, for instance, *Dial "M" for Murder* (1954), *Rear Window* (1954), and *Vertigo* (1958), where, in each case, a husband's carefully planned murder of his wife eventually unravels.

48. In Patrick Hamilton's original play, the wooden chest is locked until the climax of the tale (p. 86).

49. Gaston Bachelard, *The Poetics of Space*, trans. Maria Jolas (Boston: Beacon Press, 1969), p. 81.

50. Christopher Isherwood, *Christopher and His Kind: 1929–1939* (New York: Avon Books, 1977), p. 104.

51. I will refer to the room beyond the door as the kitchen throughout this book, largely because that is how it is identified in the film itself. However, all the set drawings from the time of production call this part of the apartment the pantry. See box 5687, Warner Bros. Archive.

52. Information taken from an undated, unsigned publicity document in folder 706, Warner Bros. Archive.

53. Miller, *Hidden Hitchcock*, p. 57.

54. The troublesome candle was part of *Rope*'s screenplay as early as Arthur Laurents's first draft of November 1947. In the beginning there was perfectly planned imperfection. See Laurents, *Rope*, screenplay dated November 22, 1947, p. 9.

55. Six years later, in Hitchcock's *Rear Window*, the composer who lives across from Jefferies also has trouble with a canted candle, as we can see when the camera sweeps around the courtyard for the last time in the film's final minutes to show him in the company of Miss Lonelyhearts. The leaning object can be seen on the mantelpiece between the two characters.

## Chapter 3

1. V. F. Perkins, "*Rope*," *Movie* 7 (1963), p. 11.

2. D. A. Miller, *Hidden Hitchcock* (Chicago and London: University of Chicago Press, 2016), p. 74.

3. Miller, *Hidden Hitchcock*, p. 56.

4. *Alfred Hitchcock's* Rope (New York: Dell, 1948), p. 14.

5. Information taken from an untitled publicity document by Bill Rice and Ken Whitmore, folder 706, Warner Bros. Archive. Edith Evanson would go on to play the minor role of an office cleaner named Rita in Hitchcock's *Marnie* (1964). I will discuss her brief appearance in the later film in chapter 8 of this book.

6. Both the novelization and Arthur Laurents's screenplay explicitly call the chest, in a moment not found in the actual film, a bier. See *Alfred Hitchcock's* Rope, p. 23 and Arthur Laurents, *Rope*, screenplay dated December 16, 1947 (with additional pages dated January 13, 1948), p. 15. A copy of the latter can be found in folder 2198A, Warner Bros. Archive.

7. Susan Smith, *Hitchcock: Suspense, Humour and Tone* (London: BFI, 2000), p. 34.

8. Richard Allen, *Hitchcock's Romantic Irony* (New York: Columbia University Press, 2007), p. 62; Michael Wood, *Alfred Hitchcock: The Man Who Knew Too Much* (New York: Amazon, 2015), p. 72. Allen goes on to refer to an essay by Thomas M. Bauso which is a useful further point of reference here: "*Rope*: Hitchcock's Unkindest Cut," in *Hitchcock's Rereleased Films: From* Rope *to* Vertigo,

ed. Walter Raubicheck and Walter Srebnick (Detroit: Wayne State University Press, 1991), pp. 226–39.

9. Released six years after *Rope*, *Rear Window* marked the second of Hitchcock's four collaborations with James Stewart; *The Man Who Knew Too Much* and *Vertigo* followed in 1956 and 1958, respectively.

10. Information about the physical qualities of the rope used in the film is taken from an undated, unsigned publicity document in folder 706, Warner Bros. Archive.

11. Peter J. Dellolio, "Filmic Space and Real Time in *Rope*," *Midwest Quarterly* 50.1 (2008), p. 93.

12. Lee Edelman, *No Future: Queer Theory and the Death Drive* (Durham, NC: Duke University Press, 2004), p. 131. One of the examples from Hitchcock's work that Edelman goes on to give, in fact, is "a dangling piece of rope."

13. For more on the place and purchase of objects in Hitchcock's films, see Mladen Dolar, "Hitchcock's Objects," in *Everything You Always Wanted to Know about Lacan (But Were Afraid to Ask Hitchcock)*, ed. Slavoj Žižek (London and New York: Verso, 1992), pp. 31–46; Marc Raymond Strauss, *Hitchcock's Objects and Subjects: The Significance of Things on Screen* (Jefferson, NC: McFarland, 2016); and, more briefly, John Orr, *Hitchcock and Twentieth-Century Cinema* (London and New York: Wallflower Press, 2005), p. 37.

14. Although *Rope* concerns itself with the passing of time, nothing in the film visibly ties the action to a particular day or date. However, one of the set stills held in folder 3229B of the Warner Bros. Archive shows a calendar on the wall in the kitchen that clearly displays the month of January 1948. The calendar is just about visible in the film itself, notably when Brandon drops the rope into the drawer, but is impossible to read.

15. Eric Rohmer and Claude Chabrol, *Hitchcock: The First Forty-Four Films*, trans. Stanley Hochman (New York: Ungar, 1979), p. 91; Arthur Laurents, *Rope*, screenplay dated November 22, 1947, p. 17. Folder 2198A, Warner Bros. Archive.

16. *Alfred Hitchcock's* Rope, p. 30.

17. Kenneth's surname is given as "Turner" in Arthur Laurents's first two drafts of the screenplay, but it was changed to "Lawrence" when the studio discovered that a real-life Kenneth Turner lived in Manhattan (at 21 E 87th Street, to be precise). See the memo from Carl Milliken (Research Department at Warner Bros.) to Fred Ahern (Transatlantic) dated January 5, 1948, folder 2812, Warner Bros. Archive.

18. Michel Chion, "The Impossible Embodiment," in *Everything You Always Wanted to Know About Lacan (But Were Afraid to Ask Hitchcock)*, ed. Slavoj Žižek (London and New York: Verso, 1992), p. 195. Chion also discusses acousmatic sound in his *Audio-Vision: Sound on Screen*, ed. and trans. Claudia Gorbman (New York: Columbia University Press, 1994), pp. 71–73, 82–83, and 128–31.

19. All information here concerning the replacement of Crane with Dick is taken from the daily production and progress reports in folder 1490, Warner Bros. Archive. Crane appears to have worked on *Rope* for the final time on January

17, but he officially remained in employment on the production until January 19.

20. In the novelization, when Phillip refers to being locked up, the narrative discourse adds: "It was Brandon's tongue speaking through him, he thought" (p. 32).

21. Smith, *Hitchcock: Suspense, Humour and Tone*, p. 57.

22. Henri Bergson, *Laughter: An Essay on the Meaning of the Comic*, trans. Cloudesley Brereton and Fred Rothwell (London: Macmillan, 1911), p. 6.

23. Joan Chandler's original contract of employment with Warner Bros. was signed on April 5, 1945 and stated that she would begin work on August 15, 1945 for a period of 52 weeks, with possibilities for renewal annually. The studio chose, however, not to renew her contract when this initial period came to an end in August 1946. For the relevant legal documents, see folder 2738A, Warner Bros. Archive.

24. All of these legal materials can be found in folder 2738A, Warner Bros. Archive.

25. V. F. Perkins sees the triangle as "a central compositional motif" in *Rope*. Perkins, "*Rope*," p. 13.

26. Perkins, "*Rope*," p. 11.

# Chapter 4

1. D. A. Miller, *Hidden Hitchcock* (Chicago and London: University of Chicago Press, 2015), pp. 5 and 4.

2. D. A. Miller, "Anal *Rope*," *Representations* 32 (1990), 114–33.

3. The bookcase is so far to the edge of the frame at this point that it is not visible on some screens.

4. See the memo from Carl Milliken to Fred Ahern dated January 5, 1948, folder 2812, Warner Bros. Archive. On January 12, Victor Peers wrote to Milliken to say that *Allure* could be used instead of *CHIC* (folder 2812), but news of this change seems not to have made it to Arthur Laurents, as his final screenplay of January 13 leaves the magazine unnamed altogether. Arthur Laurents, *Rope*, screenplay dated December 16, 1947 (with additional pages dated January 13, 1948), folder 2198A, Warner Bros. Archive.

5. The image in question sits in a grey frame or mount by the window. It is particularly clear when, in the very first scene set in Midge's apartment, Scottie sits in the chair with his walking stick.

6. Adriana Cavarero, *Inclinations: A Critique of Rectitude*, trans. Amanda Minervini and Adam Sitze (Stanford, CA: Stanford University Press, 2016), p. 33. In Laurents's first draft of the script, there was a snide reference at this point in the dialogue to Mondrian, but the line was removed for fear of a lawsuit. See the memo from Carl Milliken to Fred Ahern dated January 5, 1948, folder 2812, Warner Bros. Archive. For the offending Mondrian reference itself,

see Arthur Laurents, *Rope*, screenplay dated November 22, 1947, p. 27. Folder 2198A, Warner Bros. Archive.

7. Some years ago, in chapter 2 of *Hitchcock's Magic* (Cardiff: University of Wales Press, 2011), I discussed at length the place and the significance of frames in *Rear Window*, but it did not occur to me at the time that *Rope* is engaged in a related consideration.

8. The novelization adds a historical detail present nowhere in the film: "Brandon had pursued her vigorously," Phillip recalls. *Alfred Hitchcock's* Rope (New York: Dell, 1948), p. 35. Meanwhile, several publicity photographs from the period actually show John Dall and Joan Chandler in a passionate embrace upon a couch (albeit in clothes that they wear at no point in *Rope* and, in the case of Chandler, with a completely different hairstyle). See folder 597A, Warner Bros. Archive.

9. Laurents, *Rope*, screenplay dated November 22, 1947, n.p. The reference here to "400" is to Ward McAllister's list—first published in 1892—of key representatives of "old money" in fashionable New York society. For a concise summary, see C. Wright Mills, *The Power Elite*, new ed. (New York: Oxford University Press, 2000), pp. 54–55. I thank Carl Distefano for pointing me in the right direction here from his 400-level vantage point on fashionable Staten Island.

10. Laurents, *Rope*, screenplay dated November 22, 1947, p. 9.

11. Life is much easier for the novelization and Arthur Laurents's screenplay, however, which both handle this moment rather differently and, in doing so, make the ongoing conversation in the main room perfectly clear. "A privilege for what few?" Janet asks when Brandon has left the room—a line which is just about discernible in the film. But the book then has Kenneth replying, "Oh, the supermen or something—," to which Janet responds, "Schoolboy talk!" and then adds, "Why, if all you moppets really did everything you talked about in prep school and college, this world would be a bedlam." "Isn't it?" answers Phillip. *Alfred Hitchcock's* Rope, p. 42; Arthur Laurents, *Rope*, screenplay dated December 16, 1947 (with additional pages dated January 13, 1948), p. 30. I have quoted the phrasing from the novelization here. Laurents's screenplay is worded ever so slightly differently: Kenneth says "The supermen. Or something," to which Janet replies, "Schoolboy talk. If all you moppets really did everything you talked about in prep school, this world would be bedlam."

12. Both actors wrote autobiographies, but Collier's was published too early to cover her starring in *Rope*, and Hardwicke's says nothing at all about his being cast as Mr. Kentley. See Constance Collier, *Harlequinade: The Story of My Life* (London: John Lane, the Bodley Head, 1929) and Sir Cedric Hardwicke, *A Victorian in Orbit: The Irreverent Memoirs of Sir Cedric Hardwicke as Told to James Brough* (London: Methuen, 1961).

13. Throughout my year tangled up in *Rope*, I wondered obsessively if the actors in the background or offscreen were, when speaking lines that were indistinct, following a script or ad-libbing. What were they saying when they knew that their

words would come across as no more than vague sounds? And then, towards the end of the project, I discovered Arthur Laurents's fascinating autobiography, *Original Story By: A Memoir of Broadway and Hollywood* (New York and London: Applause, 2000), in which he reports that he was present on set to add background dialogue (p. 127). I could find no record of this additional work by Laurents in the archives, so, as always with Hitchcock, something of the mystery remains.

14. I use the term "tracks" rather loosely here and elsewhere in this book: the camera actually moved around the set of *Rope* on wheels, not conventional fixed tracks.

15. Marc Raymond Strauss, *Hitchcock's Objects as Subjects: The Significance of Things on Screen* (Jefferson, NC: McFarland, 2016), p. 123.

16. An entry in *The Encyclopedia of Alfred Hitchcock* records that "Dick Hogan [. . .] was too claustrophobic to remain in the chest where he had been placed even for length of a single long take, so a special release had to be built into the bottom of the chest to allow him to escape." Thomas Leitch, *The Encyclopedia of Alfred Hitchcock* (New York: Checkmark Books, 2002), p. 285.

17. "Dick Hogan; Big Band Singer, Movie Actor," *Los Angeles Times*, August 26, 1995. Available online at: http://articles.latimes.com/1995-08-26/news/mn-39162_1_dick-hogan.

18. See the memo from Roy Obringer to T. J. Martin dated May 10, 1948, folder 2812, Warner Bros. Archive. Further filming for the trailer took place between 1:00 p.m. and 7:10 p.m. on June 14, 1948 at the Warner Bros. studio in Burbank (Stage 7). On this latter date, footage of Janet and David on the park bench was captured, as was an interior shot of the apartment. Hitchcock himself was on set throughout, while Joan Chandler and Dick Hogan were present from 1:00 p.m. until 4:30 p.m. James Stewart attended for just twenty minutes (6:50 p.m.–7:10 p.m.) and filmed his contribution to the trailer in two takes. See the daily production and progress report for June 14, 1948 in folder 1490, Warner Bros. Archive.

19. For a discussion specifically of this use of Poulenc in the trailer, see Kevin Clifton, "The Anatomy of Aural Suspense in *Rope* and *Vertigo*," in *Partners in Suspense: Critical Essays on Bernard Herrmann and Alfred Hitchcock*, ed. Steve Rawle and K. J. Donnelly (Manchester: Manchester University Press, 2017), pp. 38–40.

20. Kristin L. Matthews, "Reading, Guidance, and Cold War Consensus in Alfred Hitchcock's *Rope*," *The Journal of Popular Culture* 43.4 (2010), p. 746.

21. David Greven is wrong to claim that the color of Kenneth's clothing establishes a visual link between him and David Kentley: "They wear the same brown suit," he writes in his *Intimate Violence: Hitchcock, Sex, and Queer Theory* (New York: Oxford University Press, 2017), p. 131. While David's appearance in the film is extremely brief, if it long enough for us to see quite clearly that his suit is grey.

22. If we know that the neon sign spells out "STORAGE"—a textual secret that I discussed in chapter 2 of this book—we can also just about detect a fragment of the letter "T" through the left-hand window and an even smaller piece of the "R" through the other. I think, however, that these two elements are so

small that they are all but impossible to understand without help from the article by Hitchcock that appeared in *Popular Photography* in November 1948. For this reason, my discussion here in chapter 4 focusses only on the juxtaposition of the "S" and the "A," both of which are easy to read without extratextual assistance.

23. Jacques Derrida, *Glas*, trans. John P. Leavey, Jr. and Richard Rand (Lincoln: University of Nebraska Press, 1986). The point is made as early as the very first page of the book: "*Sa* from now on will be the siglum of *savoir absolu*" (p. 1).

24. Richard Allen, *Hitchcock's Romantic Irony* (New York: Columbia University Press, 2007), p. 58.

25. Steven Jacobs, *The Wrong House: The Architecture of Alfred Hitchcock* (Rotterdam: 010 Publishers, 2007), p. 268.

26. Robin Wood, *Hitchcock's Films Revisited*, rev. ed. (New York: Columbia University Press, 2002), p. 351.

27. Miller, "Anal *Rope*," p. 119.

28. Wood, *Hitchcock's Films Revisited*, p. 351.

29. Laurents, *Rope*, screenplay dated November 22, 1947, p. 34; Laurents, *Rope*, screenplay dated December 16, 1947, p. 34.

30. See the letter from Stephen S. Jackson (PCA) to Fred Ahern (Transatlantic) dated December 15, 1947 in the *Rope* PCA file, Margaret Herrick Library. I discussed this letter and its wider context in more detail in chapter 1 of *Perpetual Movement*.

31. Laurents, *Rope*, screenplay dated December 16, 1947 (with additional pages dated January 13, 1948), p. 34. The archives contain no information about why the original "the bedroom" was restored during filming.

32. Angelo Restivo, "Hitchcock and the Postmodern," in *A Companion to Alfred Hitchcock*, ed. Thomas Leitch and Leland Poague (Malden, MA, and Oxford: Wiley-Blackwell, 2011), p. 568.

33. *Alfred Hitchcock's* Rope, p. 49.

## Chapter 5

1. The disappearance of Phillip's wound has sometimes been seen as a continuity error in the film. Its complete vanishing is certainly strange, but it is perhaps worth noting that as early as Laurents's first draft of the screenplay, it was specified that the cut should be dry by this point in proceedings. Arthur Laurents, *Rope*, screenplay dated November 22, 1947, p. 36. Folder 2198A, Warner Bros. Archive.

2. Roland Barthes, *Mythologies*, rev. ed., ed. Annette Lavers, trans. Annette Lavers and Siân Reynolds (London: Vintage, 2009), p. 113. *Mythologies* first appeared in book form in French in 1957.

3. For Barthes's brief, damning critique of *On the Waterfront*, see "A Sympathetic Worker," in *The Eiffel Tower and Other Mythologies*, trans. Richard Howard (Berkeley and Los Angeles: University of California Press, 1997), pp. 39–41.

4. Many critics have interpreted the wooden chest as a kind of coffin. See, for instance: Peter J. Dellolio, "Filmic Space and Real Time in *Rope*," *Midwest Quarterly* 50.1 (2008), p. 90; David Greven, *Intimate Violence: Hitchcock, Sex, and Queer Theory* (New York: Oxford University Press, 2017), p. 117; Kristin L. Matthews, "Reading, Guidance, and Cold War Consensus in Alfred Hitchcock's *Rope*," *The Journal of Popular Culture* 43.4 (2010), p. 746.

5. For an illuminating discussion of the piano as an instrument in Hitchcock's films, including *Rope*, see chapter 7 of David Schroeder, *Hitchcock's Ear: Music and the Director's Art* (New York and London: Continuum, 2012).

6. See the second page of the document entitled "BUDGET OF 'ROPE'" and dated January 9, 1948, folder 12723B, Warner Bros. Archive.

7. In the anonymous novelization published at the time of the film's release, we are told that Phillip plays "a crashing discord" on hearing Rupert's voice. *Alfred Hitchcock's* Rope (New York: Dell, 1948), p. 52. This does not happen in the film itself.

8. A copy of Stewart's contract of employment can be found in folder 2812, Warner Bros. Archive. The same folder also reveals that a 16mm print of *Rope* (for personal use only) was sent as a gift from Lew Wasserman to James Stewart in December 1955. Letter from Harold Berkowitz of Warner Bros. to P.R.M., Inc. (New York), June 13, 1956.

9. Patrick Hamilton's *Rope* also uses the term "*cassone*" just once, contrary to Heath A. Diehl's claim that it appears nowhere in the play; Diehl is also wrong to claim that Hamilton's play is set in Oxford. (On the latter count, he is probably thinking of the city to which the killers reveal that they are planning to flee.) See Heath A. Diehl, "Reading Hitchcock/Reading Queer: Adaptation, Narrativity, and a Queer Mode of Address in *Rope*, *Strangers on a Train*, and *Psycho*," *Clues: A Journal of Detection* 31.1 (Spring 2013), p. 35. The play's use of the word "Cassone," which Hamilton capitalizes and does not italicize, comes in Act I, when Sir Johnstone Kentley (the father of the murdered man) looks at the wooden chest in the room and asks, "That's not a Cassone, is it?" to which Brandon replies, "No, sir. It's not genuine, it's a reproduction. But it's rather a nice piece. I got it in Italy." Patrick Hamilton, *Rope: A Play* (London: Constable and Co. Ltd., 1929), p. 30.

10. Cristelle L. Baskins, Cassone *Painting: Humanism and Gender in Early Modern Italy* (Cambridge: Cambridge University Press, 1998), p. 4. For a more detailed discussion of the uses of the terms "*cassone*," "*forzieri*," "*goffani*," and "*cassette*," see Peter Thornton, "*Cassoni, Forzieri, Goffani* and *Cassette*: Terminology and its Problems," *Apollo* 120.272 (October 1984), 246–51.

11. Readers in search of such a thing might consult Baskins's Cassone *Painting*, which gives a very good historical overview, or, alternatively, her later text *The Triumph of Marriage: Painted Cassoni of the Renaissance* (Boston: Isabella Stewart Gardner Museum, 2008).

12. Diehl, "Reading Hitchcock/Reading Queer," p. 35.

13. Thornton, "*Cassoni*," p. 251. Thornton's article contains illustrations of such designs. The possibility of the transformation of a wedding chest into a coffin is, of course, always present in the "Legend of the Mistletoe Bough."

14. In Patrick Hamilton's original play, there is a reference to Brandon's "chest complex" (p. 49).

15. "Ginevra" can be found in Samuel Rogers, *Italy: A Poem* (London: Edward Moxton, 1852), pp. 110–14.

16. The Hitchcock films for which Stannard wrote screenplays are the following: *The Pleasure Garden* (1926), *The Mountain Eagle* (1926), *The Lodger: A Story of the London Fog* (1926), *Downhill* (1927), *Easy Virtue* (1927), *Champagne* (1928), *The Farmer's Wife* (1928), and *The Manxman* (1929). For a concise overview of Stannard's professional association with Hitchcock, see chapter 7 of Ian W. Macdonald, *Screenwriting Poetics and the Screen Idea* (Basingstoke: Palgrave Macmillan, 2013) and also the chapter entitled "The Silent Films: Eliot Stannard" in Charles Barr, *English Hitchcock* (Moffat: Cameron and Hollis, 1999).

17. Just after Mr. Kentley makes this remark, Brandon leans into the shot from the left to reach the food on the *cassone*.

18. Roland Barthes, "The Death of the Author," in *The Rustle of Language*, trans. Richard Howard (Berkeley and Los Angeles: University of California Press, 1989), p. 53.

19. Rogers, "Ginevra," pp. 112 ("And in her fifteenth year became a bride") and 113.

20. Rogers, "Ginevra," p. 114.

21. Rogers, "Ginevra," p. 114.

22. Baskins, Cassone *Painting*.

23. The design on the *cassone* in the film is not particularly easy to make out, but is much clearer in a series of reference photographs from the set that can be found in folder 3229B, Warner Bros. Archive.

24. All details in this paragraph, along with the quotation from *New York Call*, are taken from Steven J. Ross, *Working-class Hollywood: Silent Film and the Shaping of Class in America* (Princeton: Princeton University Press, 1998), p. 31. For further information about the Strand, see Ken Bloom, *Broadway: Its History, People and Places: An Encyclopedia*, 2nd ed. (New York and London: Routledge, 2012), pp. 504–06. Bloom gives a slightly lower figure for the number of seats in the theater.

25. In the first draft of Arthur Laurents's screenplay, this entire discussion about the new film is between Kenneth and Janet, and eventually Rupert; Mrs Atwater is not involved at all in the conversation, which refers to the Rialto instead of the Strand. The dialogue at this point in the initial draft referred to Humphrey Bogart, Lauren Bacall, and Gary Cooper, moreover. Laurents, *Rope*, screenplay dated November 22, 1947, pp. 41–44. A memo from Carl Milliken (Research Department, Warner Bros.) to Fred Ahern (Transatlantic) dated January 5, 1948 noted that written permission would need to be obtained from all

actors mentioned in this scene. See folder 2812, Warner Bros. Archive. (A blank copy of the necessary consent form can also be found in this file.) Meanwhile, a photograph in folder 597A of the Warner Bros. Archive shows Ingrid Bergman and Humphrey Bogart visiting the set of *Rope* during filming.

26. The novelization has "The-Something-and-the-Something" at this point, while the script of December 1947 specifies "The Something and The Something." See *Alfred Hitchcock's* Rope, p. 63 and Arthur Laurents, *Rope*, screenplay dated December 16, 1947 (with additional pages dated January 13 1948), p. 43. Folder 2198A, Warner Bros. Archive. In the film itself, however, Mrs. Atwater very clearly says "of," not "and." When she recalls and then rejects *The Something of the Something* as a title, meanwhile, it is possible that she is thinking of Hitchcock's *Shadow of a Doubt*, released by Universal in 1943. It starred neither Grant nor Bergman, but the role of Herb was played by Hume Cronyn, who would go on, as I discussed in chapter 1, to write the initial treatment for *Rope*.

27. Brandon leans into the frame again at this point, as he does a little later in the conversation, when Rupert mischievously repeats the phrase "just plain *Something*."

28. *Alfred Hitchcock's* Rope, p. 62.

29. Colin MacCabe, "Realism and the Cinema: Notes on Some Brechtian Theses," in *Theoretical Essays: Film, Linguistics, Literature* (Manchester: Manchester University Press, 1985), p. 39.

30. Patricia Waugh, *Metafiction: The Theory and Practice of Self-conscious Fiction* (London: Methuen, 1984), p. 6.

31. Waugh, *Metafiction*, p. 95.

32. This line was present as early as the first draft of the screenplay. Laurents, *Rope*, screenplay dated November 22, 1947, p. 45.

33. The reclaimed, affirmative, enabling use of the term was still some decades in the future when *Rope* was released, of course. In Laurents's first draft of *Rope*'s screenplay, Brandon refers to Rupert's "queer mood tonight" when the latter returns to the apartment, but the phrase had disappeared by the time the second draft was finished. Laurents, *Rope*, screenplay dated November 22, 1947, p. 86.

34. A reference photograph taken on set during filming shows a book entitled *Doctor Freud* on the small stand to the right of the drinks table in the apartment. The words on the spine of the volume cannot be seen at any point in the film itself, however. For the photograph, which is dated January 24, 1948, see folder 3229B, Warner Bros. Archive.

35. The novelization (*Alfred Hitchcock's* Rope, p. 66) adds that "his tone [was] intended to convey not only that he meant it but would very much like to have the whole subject dropped."

36. Indeed, the novelization makes the link between the two acts even more explicit by having Phillip remember that he wore gloves to strangle the chicken, as he later did when murdering David. *Alfred Hitchcock's* Rope, pp. 68–69.

## Chapter 6

1. The novelization of *Rope* has Janet saying "tense," not "intense," during this exchange. See *Alfred Hitchcock's* Rope (New York: Dell, 1948), p. 70. In the film, Janet's laughter here sounds remarkably chicken-like to my ears.

2. *Alfred Hitchcock's* Rope, p. 69.

3. Robin Wood, *Hitchcock's Films Revisited*, rev. ed. (New York: Columbia University Press, 2002), p. 78.

4. Wood, *Hitchcock's Films Revisited*, pp. 79–80.

5. When Arthur Laurents included this memorable phrase in his screenplay, could he perhaps have been thinking of the moment in Patrick Hamilton's 1941 novel *Hangover Square: A Story of Darkest Earl's Court* (London: Penguin, 2001) at which George Harvey Bone contemplates the use of a "blunt instrument" in the act of murder (p. 184)?

6. As this exchange makes clear, Peter Conrad is wrong to claim that Nietzsche's name is never mentioned in *Rope*. See his *The Hitchcock Murders* (London: Faber and Faber, 2000), p. 294. One critic has claimed that what we find in Hitchcock's film is a "vulgarised Nietzsche." See John Orr, *Hitchcock and Twentieth-Century Cinema* (London and New York: Wallflower Press, 2005), p. 104. For a related discussion, see chapter 10 of Tom Cohen, *Hitchcock's Cryptonymies: Volume I: Secret Agents* (Minneapolis and London: University of Minnesota Press, 2005).

7. Peter J. Dellolio, "Filmic Space and Real Time in *Rope*," *Midwest Quarterly* 50.1 (2008), p. 93; Eric Rohmer and Claude Chabrol, *Hitchcock: The First Forty-Four Films*, trans. Stanley Hochman (New York: Ungar, 1979), p. 60. For more on *Rope*'s engagement with Nazism, see Robin Wood, "Hitchcock and Fascism," *Hitchcock Annual* 13 (2004–05), 25–63.

8. The music heard at this point in *Rope* is Mack David's "Candlelight Café" and then "I'm Looking Over a Four-Leaf Clover." A total of $600 ($300 per song) was paid by Transatlantic for the necessary clearance to use these compositions in the film. See the memo from Herman Starr (of Witmark and Sons) to Warner Bros. dated July 21, 1948, folder 1057B, Warner Bros. Archive. For more on the music played on the radio in *Rope*, see Jack Sullivan, *Hitchcock's Music* (New Haven and London: Yale University Press, 2006), p. 146. In both the novelization and the shooting script, Janet and Kenneth listen to a record on the phonograph instead of a radio broadcast. See *Alfred Hitchcock's* Rope, p. 77, and Arthur Laurents, *Rope*, screenplay dated December 16, 1947 (with additional pages dated January 13, 1948), p. 51. Folder 2198A, Warner Bros. Archive. A sketch produced by the Art Department at the studio on January 14, 1948 confirms, however, that a radio panel was constructed for the bookcase behind the piano in the apartment, and it is possible to see the object clearly at various moments in the completed film. See Sheet 12, set 2, box 5687, Warner Bros. Archive.

9. Susan Sontag, *Regarding the Pain of Others* (London: Penguin, 2003), p. 46.

10. Conrad, *The Hitchcock Murders*, p. 200. According to Conrad, this "sense of entitlement" took Patrick Hamilton by surprise when he first saw the film.

11. *Alfred Hitchcock's* Rope, p. 84.

## Chapter 7

1. D. A Miller, *Hidden Hitchcock* (Chicago and London: University of Chicago Press, 2016), pp. 78–79.

2. The photograph in question can be found in folder 3329B, Warner Bros. Archive.

3. Miller, *Hidden Hitchcock*, pp. 80–81.

4. The novelization tells us that from where Phillip stands, all he can hear in turn of the conversation between Rupert and Mrs Wilson is "an indistinguishable murmur." *Alfred Hitchcock's* Rope (New York: Dell, 1948), p. 87. In the final draft of the script, the phrase "an indistinct murmur" is used instead. Arthur Laurents, *Rope*, screenplay dated December 16, 1947 (with additional pages dated January 13, 1948), p. 59. Folder 2198A, Warner Bros. Archive.

5. Jacques Derrida, "Mallarmé," in *Acts of Literature*, ed. Derek Attridge (New York and London: Routledge, 1992), p. 122.

6. See, for instance, Jacques Derrida, *Of Grammatology*, corrected ed., trans. Gayatri Chakravorty Spivak (Baltimore and London: Johns Hopkins University Press, 1997), pp. 20, 23, 49–50, 158.

7. John Orr, *Hitchcock and Twentieth-Century Cinema* (London and New York: Wallflower Press, 2005), p. 164.

8. *Alfred Hitchcock's* Rope, p. 85.

9. Arthur Laurents's screenplay, in fact, is explicit about this, for, when Mrs. Wilson says, "I'm like the grave," a note adds: "As a matter of fact she is at the grave now—clearing plates from the chest on to her tray." Laurents, *Rope*, screenplay dated December 16, 1947 (with additional pages dated January 13, 1948), p. 58.

10. Peter J. Dellolio thinks that Phillip is beginning to mouth Brandon's name at this point. See his "Filmic Space and Real Time in *Rope*," *Midwest Quarterly* 50.1 (2008), p. 99.

11. V. F. Perkins, "*Rope*," *Movie* 7 (1963), p. 12.

12. *Alfred Hitchcock's* Rope, p. 88.

13. Randolph Quirk, Sidney Greenbaum, Geoffrey Leech, and Jan Svartvik, *A Comprehensive Grammar of the English Language* (London and New York: Longman, 1985), p. 350. I was led to this source by a discussion of the use of "we" to mean "you" in Nigel Harwood, "'We Do Not Seem to Have a Theory . . . The Theory I Present Here Attempts to Fill This Gap': Inclusive and Exclusive Pronouns in Academic Writing," *Applied Linguistics* 26.3 (2005), p. 348. I thank my colleague Dawn Knight for her help here.

14. Quirk et al., *A Comprehensive Grammar*, p. 350.

15. Quirk et al., *A Comprehensive Grammar*, p. 350.

16. *Alfred Hitchcock's* Rope, p. 90. The sudden eruption of the siren was present as early as the first draft of the screenplay. See Arthur Laurents, *Rope*, screenplay dated November 22, 1947, p. 60. Warner Bros. Archive, folder 2198A. Phillip's response in all versions of the screenplay is to play the piano more loudly.

17. Kevin Clifton, "Unravelling Music in Hitchcock's *Rope*," *Horror Studies* 4.1 (2013), p. 69.

18. Paula Marantz Cohen, *Alfred Hitchcock: The Legacy of Victorianism* (Lexington: University of Kentucky Press, 1995), p. 88.

19. Laurents, *Rope*, screenplay dated December 16, 1947 (with additional pages dated January 13, 1948), p. 63.

20. Clifton, "Unravelling Music," p. 70.

21. Miller, *Hidden Hitchcock*, p. 57. This moment is given added dramatic weight in Arthur Laurents's screenplay by having the lights in the darkened room suddenly switched on as Mr. Kentley arrives. Laurents, *Rope*, screenplay dated December 16, 1947 (with additional pages dated January 13, 1948), pp. 63–64. The film itself does not feature such a change in lighting.

22. In the novelization (*Alfred Hitchcock's* Rope, p. 95) we are told that Rupert "made mental note" of the fact that Phillip is staring at the rope in horror.

## Chapter 8

1. The novelization of 1948 presents matters in a significantly different way here: "'Come this way, dear,' Mrs. Wilson said; 'I'll take you to the phone.' She escorted Mrs Atwater to the door as the other woman said 'Thank you.'" *Alfred Hitchcock's* Rope (New York: Dell, 1948), p. 99.

2. Arthur Laurents, *Rope*, screenplay dated November 22, 1947, p. 66. Folder 2198A Warner Bros. Archive.

3. Arthur Laurents, *Rope*, screenplay dated December 16, 1947, p. 66 and *Rope*, screenplay dated December 16, 1947 (with revised pages dated January 13, 1948), p. 66. Both drafts can be found in folder 2198A of Warner Bros. Archive.

4. Letter from Stephen S. Jackson to Fred Ahern, December 15, 1947, p. 1. *Rope* PCA file, Margaret Herrick Library. Jackson must have been referring to Laurents's first draft of November 22, 1947, which had been sent to the censors for consideration on December 1, 1947; see the letter from Fred Ahern to Joseph Breen dated December 1, 1947 in the *Rope* PCA file at the Margaret Herrick Library.

5. Steven Jacobs, *The Wrong House: The Architecture of Alfred Hitchcock* (Rotterdam: 010 Publishers, 2007), p. 268.

6. Jacobs, *The Wrong House*, p. 268. For a related point, see Robin Wood, *Hitchcock's Films Revisited*, rev. ed. (New York: Columbia University Press, 2002), p. 351. Indeed, no bedroom appears anywhere in the art department's drawings for the set at the Warner Bros. soundstage where was *Rope* was filmed. See the various sketches in box 5687, Warner Bros. Archive.

7. D. A. Miller, "Anal *Rope*," *Representations* 32 (1990), p. 119.

8. This, incidentally, is the section of dialogue from which a reference to the Harvard Club was removed at the request of the university's president. When Rupert wonders where David might be, Brandon originally said that he could be at "[t]he Harvard Club, or the Bradleys are having a party." For more on this alteration, see my discussion of the moment in question in chapter 2 of this book.

9. When Edith Evanson reappeared briefly as Rita in Hitchcock's *Marnie* sixteen years later, she found herself involved in a rather similar scenario: while she cleans the office floor on the left of the screen, Marnie steals from the safe on the right-hand side. For most of the sequence, Marnie is completely unaware that Rita is getting closer and closer to discovering her crime. We, however, are perfectly, agonizingly positioned to be aware of what is happening.

10. V. F. Perkins, "*Rope*," *Movie* 7 (1963), p. 11.

11. In the novelization, by way of contrast, we are told that Phillip is watching Mrs. Wilson as she clears the *cassone*. He tries to warn Brandon "but the fool had not noticed" (*Alfred Hitchcock's* Rope, p. 103).

12. D. A. Miller, *Hidden Hitchcock* (Chicago and London: University of Chicago Press, 2016), pp. 167–68, n. 18.

13. In *The Encyclopedia of Alfred Hitchcock* (New York: Checkmark Books, 2002), Thomas Leitch insists, having consulted production records in the Warner Bros. Archive in Los Angeles, that this is Hitchcock's only confirmed cameo appearance in *Rope* (p. 47). I am inclined to side with the many other critics who believe that Hitchcock is also seen from behind walking down the street in the film's opening shot. Meanwhile, I am not at all persuaded by Leitch's claim, made in his earlier book *Find the Director and Other Hitchcock Games* (Athens: University of Georgia Press, 1991), that Hitchcock also "appears briefly in the background in the costume and manner of Mr. Kentley. Mr. Kentley is a character, but Hitchcock is not playing this character, for he does nothing in the role but walk away from the camera for a few seconds (p. 3). I have studied carefully every scene of *Rope* in which Mr. Kentley appears, and I can see no evidence to support Leitch's claim that Hitchcock briefly performs the role. Leitch does not repeat his suggestion about Hitchcock pretending to Mr. Kentley in his later *Encyclopedia of Alfred Hitchcock*; perhaps he had had a change of heart by 2002.

14. For a revealing discussion of the relationship between the two films, see Amy Lawrence, "American Shame: *Rope*, James Stewart, and the Postwar Crisis in American Masculinity," in *Hitchcock's America*, ed. Jonathan Freedman and Richard Millington (New York and Oxford: Oxford University Press, 1999), p. 57.

15. For a rich, succulent discussion of "Reduco" in the context of food and fatness in Hitchcock, see chapter 1 of Jan Olsson, *Hitchcock à la Carte* (Durham: Duke University Press, 2015).

16. Alfred Hitchcock, "My Most Exciting Picture," in *Hitchcock on Hitchcock: Selected Writings and Interviews*, ed. Sidney Gottlieb (London: Faber and Faber, 1997), p. 282. Hitchcock was not always the most reliable of raconteurs, and he apparently forgets here that he had not appeared in all of his films prior to *Rope*.

There are, for instance, no known cameo appearances in *The Pleasure Garden* (1926), *Downhill* (1927), and, closer to 1948, *Jamaica Inn* (1939).

17. Miller, *Hidden Hitchcock*, pp. 167–68, n. 18.

18. Box 5687, Warner Bros. Archive. I thank Brett Service at the archive for having the patience to unfold this large-scale and highly delicate drawing twice while I gasped and swooned at what I was seeing.

19. Casey McKittrick, *Hitchcock's Appetites: The Corpulent Plots of Desire and Dread* (New York and London: Bloomsbury, 2016), p. 57.

20. When I have discussed *Rope* with my students over the years, they have sometimes found the presence of these initials inside the hat unrealistic, too much of an artificial plot device. What needs to be remembered, of course, is that in an era when the wearing of hats was much more common and uniform than it is now, stamping one's initials inside an everyday grey fedora would not have been at all unusual. (Traditional hatters, such as Lock and Co. of London, still offer this service, in fact.) I tip my hat to the senior salesman, close to retirement, in the now-vanished Calders of Cardiff for talking me through the technical details of the monogramming process and for reminiscing about the "more elegant days."

21. Thomas J. Connelly, "Big Window, Big Other: Enjoyment and Spectatorship in Alfred Hitchcock's *Rope*," *Quarterly Review of Film and Video* 31 (2014), p. 785.

22. Laurents, *Rope*, screenplay dated November 22, 1947, p. 74.

23. Susan Smith wonders if the decision to change the victim's name from Ronald to David was a reference to Hitchcock at last "killing off" his professional relationship with David O. Selznick. Susan Smith, *Hitchcock: Suspense, Humour and Tone* (London: BFI, 2000), p. 58.

24. The script was written by Arthur Houseman and is dated June 4, 1962. (Was this striking line an allusion to the moment in Hitchcock's then-recent *North by Northwest* [1959] at which the Professor says, "We're all in the same alphabet soup" to Thornhill?) By the time a revised version of the trailer's script was sent to Hitchcock on September 17, 1962, the line in question had been cut. Houseman's first draft also had Hitchcock himself repeating the line, spoken by Brandon in the film itself, about David's death being "justifiable homicide" on account of his being a student at Harvard. See folder 630 of the Alfred Hitchcock Collection, Margaret Herrick Library.

25. Laurents, *Rope*, screenplay dated December 16, 1947, p. 74.

26. I take the second part of the title of this final section of chapter 8 from the 1948 novelization, which refers to "the smile of the satisfied host" on Brandon's face when he leans against the closed door following the departure of the guests (*Alfred Hitchcock's* Rope, p. 110).

## Chapter 9

1. *Alfred Hitchcock's* Rope (New York: Dell, 1948), p. 116.

2. The element of menace is even clearer in the novelization, which refers to the "threatening step" that Brandon takes towards Phillip when the latter refuses to return to the telephone to continue the conversation with Rupert. *Alfred Hitchcock's* Rope, p. 117.

3. There is no such wondering on Phillip's part in the novelization, as he watches "Brandon's hands crack [the gun] open, check the cartridges" (*Alfred Hitchcock's* Rope, p. 120). The final version of the screenplay is similarly clear: we are told that "Brandon's hands crack open the gun to check the bullets." Arthur Laurents, *Rope*, screenplay dated December 16, 1947 (with additional pages dated January 13, 1948), p. 81. Folder 2198A, Warner Bros. Archive.

4. Does this at least in part explain why the screenplay wavered uncertainly at this point as it evolved through different drafts? In Arthur Laurents's first version, there is no reference at all to psychoanalysis in this scene (*Rope*, screenplay dated November 22, 1947, p. 82); for this, we must wait until the second draft, which adds Rupert's remark about "what a psychoanalyst would say" (*Rope*, screenplay dated December 16, 1947, p. 81). These words survive Laurents's revisions of January 1948 (*Rope*, screenplay dated December 16, 1947, with additional pages dated January 13, 1948, p. 81) and obviously make it into the completed film. All three versions of the script can be found in folder 2198A, Warner Bros. Archive.

5. Sigmund Freud, *The Psychopathology of Everyday Life*, trans. Anthea Bell (London: Penguin, 2002), p. 204. The unfortunate man also leaves behind his glasses and handkerchief, Freud tells us. "Translated into words," he explains, "his actions meant: well, you thieves, you've well and truly fleeced me."

6. The dropping of the ice is not mentioned in any of the drafts of the screenplay. In the anonymous novelization, meanwhile, we are told that Phillip spills some whisky "down the outside of the tall glass" shortly after this moment (*Alfred Hitchcock's* Rope, p. 122).

7. The novelization leaves no doubt that Phillip has indeed seen through Rupert's act (*Alfred Hitchcock's* Rope, p. 122).

8. Indeed, in the novelization, after Rupert uses the phrase "things to do," we read: "The pause which followed these words seemed to Phillip laden with significance" (*Alfred Hitchcock's* Rope, p. 124).

9. Eleven years later, in Hitchcock's *North by Northwest*, Roger Thornhill will tell Eve that he needs to be covered in olive oil if he is to be packed "like a sardine" into an overhead locker in her train compartment to avoid detection. The moment is light, played for laughs; there is no such levity in *Rope*'s presentation of a body packed into a similarly confined space.

10. When Brandon asks this question in the novelization, we are told that Phillip thinks to himself: "*Why, when the victim, a member of the well-known inferior class, was liquidated by the dictatorship of the non-proletariat*" (*Alfred Hitchcock's* Rope, p. 125; italics in original).

11. Rupert's gaze, according to the novelization, "seemed to be directed to the bulge in Brandon's pocket" (*Alfred Hitchcock's* Rope, p. 126).

12. Barthes writes: "Let us designate as *hermeneutic code* (HER) all the units whose function it is to articulate in various ways a question, its response, and the variety of chance events which can either formulate the question or delay its answer; or even, constitute an enigma and lead to its solution. [. . .] Under the hermeneutic code we list the various (formal) terms by which an enigma can be distinguished, suggested, formulated, held in suspense, and finally disclosed." Roland Barthes, *S/Z*, trans. Richard Miller (Oxford: Blackwell, 1990), pp. 17–19. See also Sarrasine *de Balzac: Séminaires à l'École pratique des hautes études 1967–1968, 1968–1969*, ed. Claude Coste and Andy Stafford (Paris: Seuil, 2011), pp. 519–24. With this quotation from *S/Z* in mind, I should perhaps explain where I locate *Rope*'s enigma, as the identity of David Kentley's killers is clearly not a mystery: we know from the beginning of the film's second shot precisely who is guilty. The enigma, rather, relates to the following questions: will the crime be discovered? when? by whom? As the film unfolds, it must delicately delay answering the questions that it has raised.

13. The sequence makes its first appearance in the revised pages dated January 13, 1948 that were added to the second draft of December 16, 1947.

14. Sam Ishii-Gonzáles, "Hitchcock with Deleuze," in *Hitchcock: Past and Future*, ed. Richard Allen and Sam Ishii-Gonzáles (London and New York: Routledge, 2004), p. 132.

15. The precise, unusual movements of the camera during Rupert's hypothetical account were mapped out in the final revisions to the screenplay. See Laurents, *Rope*, screenplay dated December 16, 1947 (with additional pages dated January 13, 1948), pp. 86–87. Both of these pages are pink (signifying that they have been changed since the previous draft) and bear the date January 13, 1948.

16. Up until this point in Rupert's narration, the novelization features italicized passages in which Phillip, listening to the account, remembers what actually happened when David arrived at the apartment earlier that day. These passages add details not present in the film and, above all, confirm that Rupert has correctly determined the basic chain of events. See *Alfred Hitchcock's* Rope, pp. 128–29.

17. Ned Schantz, "Hospitality and the Unsettled Viewer: Hitchcock's Shadow Scenes," in *Alfred Hitchcock*, ed. Neil Badmington (London and New York: Routledge, 2014), 4 vols., vol. 4, pp. 218–21.

18. Schantz, "Hospitality and the Unsettled Viewer," p. 220.

19. See chapter 3 of Neil Badmington, *Hitchcock's Magic* (Cardiff: University of Wales Press, 2011). As I pointed out in one of the book's footnotes, Schantz's essay first appeared in print in 2010 when *Hitchcock's Magic* was already in production, so my engagement with it there was reduced to what could be added at proof stage.

20. Lesley Brill, *The Hitchcock Romance: Love and Irony in Hitchcock's Films* (Princeton: Princeton University Press, 1988), p. 274.

21. Schantz, "Hospitality and the Unsettled Viewer," p. 220.

## Chapter 10

1. In the final version of Arthur Laurents's screenplay, the change of direction in Rupert's narration brings a smile of relief to Brandon's face. Arthur Laurents, *Rope*, screenplay dated December 16, 1947 (with additional pages dated January 13, 1948), p. 90. Folder 2198A, Warner Bros. Archive. Brandon certainly looks pleased at this point in the completed film, but it is hard to know if his expression is meant specifically to signify relief.

2. Phillip smashes the glass in the fireplace in the final version of Laurents's screenplay. Laurents, *Rope*, screenplay dated December 16, 1947 (with additional pages dated January 13, 1948), p. 88. In the film itself, however, we see no fireplace in the apartment, and Phillip throws the glass instead onto the floor near the table by the small window on the right-hand side of the main room.

3. The screenplay specifies that Rupert "toys with the rope" at this point. Laurents, *Rope*, screenplay dated December 16, 1947 (with additional pages dated January 13, 1948), p. 90.

4. There is no mention of this detail in the screenplay.

5. This dramatic flashing of the neon sign was specified as early as the first version of the script. In fact, the effect was even clearer in this draft because Phillip has just knocked over a lamp while trying to run from the room, thus making the scene much darker. Arthur Laurents, *Rope*, screenplay dated November 22, 1947, p. 87. Folder 2198A, Warner Bros. Archive.

6. We do not see precisely how or when Rupert removes the rope from the books, but when he leaves the apartment with Mr Kentley and Mrs Atwater in shot 8 we hear him say, "Can I help you with those books, Mr Kentley?"; he must have untied the bundle shortly afterwards.

7. Richard Allen, *Hitchcock's Romantic Irony* (New York: Columbia University Press, 2007), p. 235. The whole of chapter 6 of Allen's book addresses color design in Hitchcock's films, and the chromatic connection between *Rope* and *Vertigo* is mentioned at one point (p. 235). For a related discussion of this textual link, see Steven Jacobs, *The Wrong House: The Architecture of Alfred Hitchcock* (Rotterdam: 010 Publishers, 2007), p. 276.

8. William Rothman, *Hitchcock—The Murderous Gaze* (Cambridge, MA and London: Harvard University Press, 1982), p. 335.

9. D. A. Miller, *Hidden Hitchcock* (Chicago and London: University of Chicago Press, 2016), pp. 56–57.

10. Joseph Breen to Alfred Hitchcock, September 9, 1946. Letter, *Rope* PCA file, Margaret Herrick Library.

11. Don DeLillo, *White Noise* (London: Picador, 1985), p. 298.

12. In the drafts of November 22, 1947 and December 16, 1947, the final part of the film unfolds very differently; indeed, the screenplay of January 13, 1948 has an unbroken mass of pink pages, signifying that earlier text has been altered, running from pp. 80 through 95 (the end of the script). In both of the earlier versions, there is no struggle at all between Phillip and Rupert; instead,

Phillip tries to strangle Brandon, who throws his gun to Rupert and asks to be killed. Rupert chooses instead to open the window and fire three shots into the air (pp. 88 and 95 in both drafts). For all three versions of the screenplay, see Folder 2198A, Warner Bros. Archive.

13. Laurents, *Rope*, screenplay dated December 16, 1947 (with additional pages dated January 13, 1948) p. 91; *Alfred Hitchcock's Rope*, p. 137.

14. V. F. Perkins discusses the way in which Rupert and Phillip are linked via their injured hands in his *"Rope," Movie* 7 (1963), p. 13.

15. These technical details are explained in an unsigned, undated document in folder 698, Warner Bros. Archive.

16. In Arthur Laurents's script, after the bullet is fired Phillip falls partly onto the keys of the piano, "which clatter thinly." Laurents, *Rope*, screenplay dated December 16, 1947 (with additional pages dated January 13, 1948), p. 91. The same thing happens in the novelization (*Alfred Hitchcock's* Rope, p. 137), but there is no sound from the instrument at this point in the film itself.

17. Laurents's final version of the screenplay explains that Brandon had been trying to "edge closer" to Rupert until he is told to step away. Laurents, *Rope*, screenplay dated December 16, 1947 (with additional pages dated January 13, 1948), p. 91.

18. Laurents, *Rope*, screenplay dated December 16, 1947 (with additional pages dated January 13, 1948), p. 93; *Alfred Hitchcock's* Rope, p. 139.

19. Robin Wood, *Hitchcock's Films Revisited*, rev. ed. (New York: Columbia University Press, 2002), p. 80.

## Chapter 11

1. I take the title of this chapter from the Production Code Administration's official assessment of *Rope* in March 1948. (See chapter 1 of this book for more information about the production history of the film.) On the standard "analysis chart" completed by PCA officials during the review process, the censor responds to the prompt "FATE OF CRIMINAL(S)" with the phrase "Arrest indicated." *Rope* PCA file, Margaret Herrick Library.

2. V. F. Perkins, *"Rope," Movie* 7 (1963), p. 11.

3. Perkins was, after all, writing in the year of Hitchcock's *The Birds*, which makes Lydia's traumatic discovery of the body of Dan Fawcett even more shocking by having the camera leap progressively closer to the mutilated corpse with a series of rapid, jarring cuts.

4. Murray Pomerance, *The Man Who Knew Too Much* (London: BFI/Palgrave, 2016), p. 27.

5. Arthur Laurents, *Rope*, screenplay dated December 16, 1947 (with amended pages dated January 13, 1948), p. 93. Folder 2198A, Warner Bros. Archive.

6. Amy Lawrence, "American Shame: *Rope*, James Stewart, and the Postwar Crisis in American Masculinity," in *Hitchcock's America*, ed. Jonathan Freedman

and Richard Millington (New York and Oxford: Oxford University Press, 1999), p. 70.

7. Michael Wood, *Alfred Hitchcock: The Man Who Knew Too Much* (New York: Amazon, 2015), p. 72.

8. For discussions of this complicity, see, for instance: Richard Allen, *Hitchcock's Romantic Irony* (New York: Columbia University Press, 2007), p. 58; Robin Wood, *Hitchcock's Films Revisited*, rev. ed. (New York: Columbia University Press, 2002), p. 356; Perkins, "Rope," 13.

9. Wood, *Hitchcock's Films Revisited*, p. 80.

10. See, notably, Wood, *Hitchcock's Films Revisited*, pp. x–xi and xl–xlii.

11. Lawrence, "American Shame," p. 71.

12. In the original play, Rupert blows a police whistle out of the window in order to alert an officer to whom he has already spoken about his suspicions. Patrick Hamilton, *Rope* (London: Constable & Co., 1929), p. 90.

13. William Rothman, *Must We Kill the Thing We Love? Emersonian Perfectionism and the Films of Alfred Hitchcock* (New York: Columbia University Press, 2014), p. 104.

14. Gaston Bachelard, *The Poetics of Space*, trans. Maria Jolas (Boston: Beacon Press, 1969), p. 85.

15. See location expense report #2150, dated March 8, 1948, folder 1434, Warner Bros. Archive. Meanwhile, Hitchcock told François Truffaut that the sound of the people talking at ground level was achieved by placing a microphone six storeys up and asking a group down below to talk about the gunshot. François Truffaut, *Hitchcock*, updated ed. (London: Paladin, 1978), p. 223. I am not sure how much faith to place in this account, however, for moments later in the interview Hitchcock—who was not always the most reliable interviewee—added that the siren was that of a real ambulance (p. 224); the production files in the Warner Bros. Archive record very clearly that the vehicle was a police car.

16. In both the novelization and Arthur Laurents's script, Phillip speaks further words that are not present in the film: "It's all over . . . I'm glad." See *Alfred Hitchcock's* Rope (New York: Dell, 1948), p. 144; Arthur Laurents, *Rope*, screenplay dated December 16, 1947 (with additional pages dated January 13, 1948), p. 95. The script specifies that he says this phrase "to himself, really."

17. The protective quality of Rupert's pose here is mentioned in Perkins, "Rope," p. 13.

18. See, for instance, William Cowper, "Retirement," in *Poems* (Edinburgh: William Blair, 1818), 2 vols, vol. 1, p. 207: "At length, when all had long supposed him dead, / By cold submersion, razor, rope or lead."

19. David Schroeder, *Hitchcock's Ear: Music and the Director's Art* (New York and London: Continuum, 2012), p. 174.

20. Alan Hollinghurst, *The Swimming-Pool Library* (London: Vintage, 2006), p. 161.

21. Thomas Hemmeter, "Hitchcock's Narrative Modernism: Ironies of Fictional Time," in *A Companion to Alfred Hitchcock*, ed. Thomas Leitch and Leland Poague (Malden, MA and Oxford: Wiley-Blackwell, 2011), p. 79. As I noted in

chapter 3, V. F. Perkins, writing nearly half a century before Hemmeter, saw the triangle as "a central compositional motif" in *Rope*. Perkins, "Rope," 13.

22. There were plans to use Edward Elgar's "Variations on an Original Theme (Enigma)" to accompany the final credits, but the Elgar estate refused permission. See the memo from Helen Schoen of the Copyright and Music Clearance Division in the New York office of Warner Bros. to Joseph McLaughlin at the Los Angeles office of the studio, March 10, 1948, folder 1057B, Warner Bros. Archive.

23. Scott D. Paulin, "Unheard Sexualities: Queer Theory and the Soundtrack," in *Spectatorship: Shifting Theories of Gender, Sexuality, and Media*, ed. Roxanne Samer and William Whittington (Austin: University of Texas Press, 2017), p. 80.

24. Kevin Clifton, "Unravelling Music in Hitchcock's *Rope*," *Horror Studies* 4.1 (2013), p. 68.

25. Clifton, "Unravelling Music in Hitchcock's *Rope*," p. 70.

26. Paulin, "Unheard Sexualities," pp. 80–81.

## Postscript

1. Memo from Mort Blumenstock to Roy Obringer, May 10, 1948, folder 2812, Warner Bros. Archive.

2. See, for instance, James M. Vest, *Hitchcock and France: The Forging of an Auteur* (Westport, CT and London: Praeger, 2003), p. 14; Joel W. Finler, *Alfred Hitchcock: The Hollywood Years* (London: B. T. Batsford, 1992), p. 85; John Russell Taylor, *Hitch: The Life and Work of Alfred Hitchcock* (London: Abacus, 1981), p. 188; David Sterritt, "Morbid Psychologies and So Forth: The Fine Art of Rope," in *Hitchcock at the Source: The Auteur as Adaptor*, ed. R. Barton Palmer and David Boyd (Albany: SUNY Press, 2011), pp. 168–69.

3. For these detailed financial statements, see folder 629 of the Alfred Hitchcock Collection, Margaret Herrick Library. The records also show income from Argentina, Australia, Belgium, Bolivia, Brazil, Burma, Canada, Chile, Colombia, Cuba, Denmark, Ecuador, Egypt, Finland, Formosa (Taiwan), France, Ghana, Greece, Holland, Hong Kong, India, Israel, Italy, Jamaica, Japan, Lebanon, Malta, Mexico, New Zealand, Nigeria, Norway, Pakistan, Panama, Paraguay, Peru, the Philippines, Portugal, Puerto Rico, Singapore, South Africa, Sweden, Switzerland, Thailand, Trinidad, Turkey, Uruguay, and Venezuela.

4. See the letter from Gordon L. Files to F. E. Witt of Warner Bros. dated December 16, 1954, folder 12934B, Warner Bros. Archive. This folder contains various other documents relating to the lawsuit, as do folders 12670 and 12670A.

5. For information relating to this development, see folder 949 of the Alfred Hitchcock Collection, Margaret Herrick Library.

6. Hitchcock's contract of employment with Warner Bros. was actually signed *before* the disastrous release of *Under Capricorn*. For a copy of the 63-page document, which is dated October 13, 1948, see folder 2847, Warner Bros. Archive.

The contract, which emerged from discussions that had been underway since at least April 1948, specified that Hitchcock would be paid $3000 per week plus ten percent of gross receipts over $4,000,000. It also stated that Hitchcock's term of employment would begin on January 3, 1949 or on the day after principal photography on *Under Capricorn* was completed (whichever was earlier).

7. See folder 630 of the Alfred Hitchcock Collection, Margaret Herrick Library. The date of liquidation is given in a letter from Jacqueline H. Johnstone of Price Waterhouse and Co., Los Angeles, to Herman Citron at the Park-Citron Agency, Beverly Hills, December 20, 1962. Another letter in the file—dated February 4, 1963 and from Robert Winokur of the Taylor and Winokur law firm, San Francisco, to George Sharf of M.G.M. in New York—specifies how the Transatlantic assets were distributed on liquidation: 50 percent went to Sidney Bernstein, 25 percent went to Alfred Hitchcock, and 25 percent went to Alma Reville Hitchcock (the director's wife).

8. The set can be seen roughly 65 minutes into the film, when it features as the residence of Gary Mitchell. Elements of the set have clearly been altered since *Rope* was filmed—the spectacular Manhattan cyclorama has gone, for instance, while a bar has been added in the corner (Phillip would surely approve)—but details such as the painted pillars in the foyer are still identifiable.

9. Memo from Sidney Bernstein to Mr. Chapman, July 18, 1957, folder 630 of the Alfred Hitchcock Collection, Margaret Herrick Library.

10. See folder 630 of the Alfred Hitchcock Collection, Margaret Herrick Library. The scripts are dated June 4 and September 17, 1962.

11. Walter Raubicheck and Walter Srebnick, "Introduction: Hitchcock's Rereleased Films and Cinema Studies," in *Hitchcock's Rereleased Films: From Rope to Vertigo*, ed. Walter Raubicheck and Walter Srebnick (Detroit: Wayne State University Press, 1991), pp. 19–20.

12. I am thinking above all of groundbreaking work such as chapter 16 ("The Murderous Gays: Hitchcock's Homophobia") of Robin Wood, *Hitchcock's Films Revisited*, rev. ed. (New York: Columbia University Press, 2002) and D. A. Miller, "Anal *Rope*," *Representations* 32 (1990), 114–33. For a concise summary of the relationship between queer theory and Hitchcock's work, see Alexander Doty, "Queer Hitchcock," in *A Companion to Alfred Hitchcock*, ed. Thomas Leitch and Leland Poague (Malden, MA and Oxford: Wiley-Blackwell, 2011), pp. 473–89. For a more *Rope*-centric overview, see chapter 4 of David Greven, *Intimate Violence: Hitchcock, Sex, and Queer Theory* (New York: Oxford University Press, 2017).

13. See, for instance: Kristin L. Matthews, "Reading, Guidance, and Cold War Consensus in Alfred Hitchcock's *Rope*," *The Journal of Popular Culture* 43.4 (2010), 738–60; Ned Schantz, "Hospitality and the Unsettled Viewer: Hitchcock's Shadow Scenes," in *Alfred Hitchcock*, ed. Neil Badmington (London and New York: Routledge, 2014), 4 vols, vol. 4, pp. 215–32; Kevin Clifton, "Unravelling Music in Hitchcock's *Rope*," *Horror Studies* 4.1 (2013), 63–74; Thomas Hemmeter, "Twisted Writing: *Rope* as an Experimental Film," in *Hitchcock's Rereleased Films: From Rope to Vertigo*, ed. Walter Raubicheck and Walter Srebnick (Detroit: Wayne State

University Press, 1991), pp. 253–65; Amy Lawrence, "American Shame: *Rope*, James Stewart, and the Postwar Crisis in American Masculinity," in *Hitchcock's America*, ed. Jonathan Freedman and Richard Millington (New York and Oxford: Oxford University Press, 1999), pp. 55–76; Casey McKittrick, *Hitchcock's Appetites: The Corpulent Plots of Desire and Dread* (New York and London: Bloomsbury, 2016); Steven Jacobs, *The Wrong House: The Architecture of Alfred Hitchcock* (Rotterdam: 010 Publishers, 2007), pp. 266–76.

14. See Michael Phillips, "With Staging 'Rope' Comes Full Circle," *Los Angeles Times*, August 28, 2001, https://www.latimes.com/archives/la-xpm-2001-aug-28-ca-39132-story.html and Philip Brandes, "Hitchcock without the Camera," *Los Angeles Times*, August 19, 2001, https://www.latimes.com/archives/la-xpm-2001-aug-19-ca-35756-story.html. These performances took place in Solvang and Santa Maria, CA.

15. Clifton, "Unravelling Music," p. 68.

16. Clifton, "Unravelling Music," pp. 68 and 70.

17. Jean-François Lyotard, "Answer to the Question: What Is the Postmodern?" in *The Postmodern Explained to Children: Correspondence 1982–1985*, trans. Don Barry et al. (London: Turnaround, 1992), p. 15.

18. Clifton, "Unravelling Music," p. 69.

19. For a relevant discussion of this theme, see Sabrina Barton, "Hitchcock's Hands," in *Framing Hitchcock: Selected Essays from the* Hitchcock Annual, ed. Sidney Gottlieb and Christopher Brookhouse (Detroit: Wayne State University Press, 2002), pp. 159–78.

20. T. J. Clark, *The Sight of Death: An Experiment in Art Writing* (New Haven and London: Yale University Press, 2006), p. 239.

21. Roland Barthes, *S/Z*, trans. Richard Miller (Oxford: Blackwell, 1990), p. 3.

22. Clark, *The Sight of Death*, p. 142.

# Bibliography

## Books, Essays, Articles

*Alfred Hitchcock's* Rope (New York: Dell, 1948).
Allen, Richard, "Hitchcock's Legacy," in *A Companion to Alfred Hitchcock*, ed. Thomas Leitch and Leland Poague (Malden, MA and Oxford: Wiley-Blackwell, 2011), pp. 572–91.
——, *Hitchcock's Romantic Irony* (New York: Columbia University Press, 2007).
Baatz, Simon, *For the Thrill of It: Leopold, Loeb, and the Murder that Shocked Jazz Age Chicago* (New York: HarperCollins, 2008).
Bachelard, Gaston, *The Poetics of Space*, trans. Maria Jolas (Boston: Beacon Press, 1969).
Badmington, Neil, *Hitchcock's Magic* (Cardiff: University of Wales Press, 2011).
Barr, Charles, *English Hitchcock* (Moffat: Cameron and Hollis, 1999).
——, "Hitchcock and Early Filmmakers," in *A Companion to Alfred Hitchcock*, ed. Thomas Leitch and Leland Poague (Malden, MA and Oxford: Wiley-Blackwell, 2011), pp. 49–66.
——, *Vertigo* (London: BFI, 2002).
Barthes, Roland, "The Death of the Author," in *The Rustle of Language*, trans. Richard Howard (Berkeley and Los Angeles: University of California Press, 1989), pp. 49–55.
——, *Mythologies*, rev. ed., ed. Annette Lavers, trans. Annette Lavers and Siân Reynolds (London: Vintage, 2009).
——, *The Neutral: Lecture Course at the Collège de France (1977–1978)*, ed. Thomas Clerc, trans. Rosalind E. Krauss and Denis Hollier (New York: Columbia University Press, 2005).
——, "On S/Z and *Empire of Signs*," in *The Grain of the Voice: Interviews 1962–1980*, trans. Linda Coverdale (Berkeley and Los Angeles: University of California Press, 1991), pp. 68–87.
——, *Roland Barthes by Roland Barthes*, trans. Richard Howard (Berkeley and Los Angeles: University of California Press, 1994).

———, Sarrasine de Balzac: Séminaires à l'École pratique des hautes études 1967–1968, 1968–1969, ed. Claude Coste and Andy Stafford (Paris: Seuil, 2011).

———, "A Sympathetic Worker," in *The Eiffel Tower and Other Mythologies*, trans. Richard Howard (Berkeley and Los Angeles: University of California Press, 1997), pp. 39–41.

———, *S/Z*, trans. Richard Miller (Oxford: Blackwell, 1990).

Barton, Sabrina, "Hitchcock's Hands," in *Framing Hitchcock: Selected Essays from the Hitchcock Annual*, ed. Sidney Gottlieb and Christopher Brookhouse (Detroit: Wayne State University Press, 2002), pp. 159–78.

Baskins, Cristelle L., Cassone *Painting: Humanism and Gender in Early Modern Italy* (Cambridge: Cambridge University Press, 1998).

———, *The Triumph of Marriage: Painted Cassoni of the Renaissance* (Boston: Isabella Stewart Gardner Museum, 2008).

Bauso, Thomas M., "*Rope*: Hitchcock's Unkindest Cut," in *Hitchcock's Rereleased Films: From Rope to Vertigo*, ed. Walter Raubicheck and Walter Srebnick (Detroit: Wayne State University Press, 1991), pp. 226–39.

Benson, Stephen, and Clare Connors, "Introduction," in *Creative Criticism: An Anthology and Guide*, ed. Stephen Benson and Clare Connors (Edinburgh: Edinburgh University Press, 2014), pp. 1–47.

Bergson, Henri, *Laughter: An Essay on the Meaning of the Comic*, trans. Cloudesley Brereton and Fred Rothwell (London: Macmillan, 1911).

Bloom, Ken, *Broadway: Its History, People and Places: An Encyclopedia*, 2nd ed. (New York and London: Routledge, 2012).

Brandes, Philip, "Hitchcock without the Camera," *Los Angeles Times*, August 19, 2001, https://www.latimes.com/archives/la-xpm-2001-aug-19-ca-35756-story.html.

Brill, Lesley, *The Hitchcock Romance: Love and Irony in Hitchcock's Films* (Princeton: Princeton University Press, 1988).

Carlson, David, David Carlton, and Anne Etienne, *Theatre Censorship: From Walpole to Wilson* (Oxford: Oxford University Press, 2007).

Cavarero, Adriana, *Inclinations: A Critique of Rectitude*, trans. Amanda Minervini and Adam Sitze (Stanford, CA: Stanford University Press, 2016).

Chion, Michel, *Audio-Vision: Sound on Screen*, ed. and trans. Claudia Gorbman (New York: Columbia University Press, 1994).

———, "The Impossible Embodiment," in *Everything You Always Wanted to Know about Lacan (But Were Afraid to Ask Hitchcock)*, ed. Slavoj Žižek (London and New York: Verso, 1992), pp. 195–207.

Clark, T. J., *The Sight of Death: An Experiment in Art Writing* (New Haven and London: Yale University Press, 2006).

Clifton, Kevin, "The Anatomy of Aural Suspense in *Rope* and *Vertigo*," in *Partners in Suspense: Critical Essays on Bernard Herrmann and Alfred Hitchcock*, ed. Steve Rawle and K. J. Donnelly (Manchester: Manchester University Press, 2017), pp. 37–49.

——, "Unravelling Music in Hitchcock's *Rope*," *Horror Studies* 4.1 (2013), 63–74.
Cohen, Paula Marantz, *Alfred Hitchcock: The Legacy of Victorianism* (Lexington: University of Kentucky Press, 1995).
Cohen, Tom, *Hitchcock's Cryptonymies: Volume I: Secret Agents* (Minneapolis and London: University of Minnesota Press, 2005).
Collier, Constance, *Harlequinade: The Story of My Life* (London: John Lane, the Bodley Head, 1929).
Connelly, Thomas J., "Big Window, Big Other: Enjoyment and Spectatorship in Alfred Hitchcock's *Rope*," *Quarterly Review of Film and Video* 31 (2014), 779–88.
Conrad, Peter, *The Hitchcock Murders* (London: Faber and Faber, 2000).
Cowper, William, "Retirement," in *Poems* (Edinburgh: William Blair, 1818), 2 vols, vol. 1, pp. 186–215.
Cronyn, Hume, *A Terrible Liar: A Memoir* (New York: William Morrow, 1991).
Damasio, Antonio R., "How Hitchcock's *Rope* Stretches Time," *Scientific American* 16.1 (2006), 38–39.
Deleuze, Gilles, *Cinema 1: The Movement-Image*, trans. Hugh Tomlinson and Barbara Habberjam (London and New York: Continuum, 2005).
DeLillo, Don, *White Noise* (London: Picador, 1985).
Dellolio, Peter J., "Filmic Space and Real Time in *Rope*," *Midwest Quarterly* 50.1 (2008), 87–101.
Derrida, Jacques, *Glas*, trans. John P. Leavey Jr. and Richard Rand (Lincoln and London: University of Nebraska Press, 1986).
——, "Mallarmé," in *Acts of Literature*, ed. Derek Attridge (New York and London: Routledge, 1992), pp. 110–26.
——, *Of Grammatology*, corrected ed., trans. Gayatri Chakravorty Spivak (Baltimore and London: Johns Hopkins University Press, 1997).
"Dick Hogan; Big Band Singer, Movie Actor," *Los Angeles Times*, August 26, 1995, http://articles.latimes.com/1995-08-26/news/mn-39162_1_dick-hogan.
Diehl, Heath A., "Reading Hitchcock/Reading Queer: Adaptation, Narrativity, and a Queer Mode of Address in *Rope*, *Strangers on a Train*, and *Psycho*," *Clues: A Journal of Detection* 31.1 (Spring 2013), 33–43.
Dolar, Mladen, "Hitchcock's Objects," in *Everything You Always Wanted to Know About Lacan (But Were Afraid to Ask Hitchcock)*, ed. Slavoj Žižek (London and New York: Verso, 1992), pp. 31–46.
Doty, Alexander, "Queer Hitchcock," in *A Companion to Alfred Hitchcock*, ed. Thomas Leitch and Leland Poague (Malden, MA, and Oxford: Wiley-Blackwell, 2011), pp. 473–89.
Durgnat, Raymond, *A Long Hard Look at* Psycho (London: BFI, 2002).
——, *The Strange Case of Alfred Hitchcock or the Plain Man's Hitchcock* (London: Faber and Faber, 1974).
Dyer, Geoff, *Zona* (Edinburgh: Canongate, 2013).
Edelman, Lee, *No Future: Queer Theory and the Death Drive* (Durham, NC: Duke University Press, 2004).

Finler, Joel W., *Alfred Hitchcock: The Hollywood Years* (London: B.T. Batsford, 1992).
French, Sean, *Patrick Hamilton: A Life* (London: Faber and Faber, 1993).
Freud, Sigmund, *The Psychopathology of Everyday Life*, trans. Anthea Bell (London: Penguin, 2002).
Gissing, George, *New Grub Street* (Harmondsworth: Penguin, 1968).
Gottlieb, Sidney, "Unknown Hitchcock: The Unrealized Projects," in *Hitchcock: Past and Future*, ed. Richard Allen and Sam Ishii-Gonzáles (London and New York: Routledge, 2004), pp. 85–106.
Greven, David, *Intimate Violence: Hitchcock, Sex, and Queer Theory* (New York: Oxford University Press, 2017).
Hamilton, Patrick, *Hangover Square: A Story of Darkest Earl's Court* (London: Penguin, 2001).
———, *Rope: A Play* (London: Constable and Co. Ltd., 1929).
Hardwicke, Sir Cedric, *A Victorian in Orbit: The Irreverent Memoirs of Sir Cedric Hardwicke as Told to James Brough* (London: Methuen, 1961).
Harwood, Nigel, "'We Do Not Seem to Have a Theory . . . The Theory I Present Here Attempts to Fill This Gap': Inclusive and Exclusive Pronouns in Academic Writing," *Applied Linguistics* 26.3 (2005), 343–75.
Hell, Henri, *Francis Poulenc*, trans. Edward Lockspeiser (London: John Calder, 1959).
Hemmeter, Thomas, "Hitchcock's Narrative Modernism: Ironies of Fictional Time," in *A Companion to Alfred Hitchcock*, ed. Thomas Leitch and Leland Poague (Malden, MA, and Oxford: Wiley-Blackwell, 2011), pp. 67–85.
———, "Twisted Writing: *Rope* as an Experimental Film," in *Hitchcock's Rereleased Films: From* Rope *to* Vertigo, ed. Walter Raubicheck and Walter Srebnick (Detroit: Wayne State University Press, 1991), pp. 253–65.
Higdon, Hal, *Leopold and Loeb: The Crime of the Century* (Urbana and Chicago: University of Illinois Press, 1999).
Hitchcock, Alfred, "My Most Exciting Picture," in *Hitchcock on Hitchcock: Selected Writings and Interviews*, ed. Sidney Gottlieb (London Faber and Faber, 1997), pp. 275–84.
Hollinghurst, Alan, *The Swimming-Pool Library* (London: Vintage, 2006).
Holt, James, "The Hitchcock Cameo: Aesthetic Considerations," in *Hitchcock and Philosophy: Dial M for Metaphysics*, ed. David Baggett and William A. Drumin (Chicago and La Salle, IL: Open Court, 2007), pp. 229–38.
Isherwood, Christopher, *Christopher and His Kind: 1929–1939* (New York: Avon Books, 1977).
Ishii-Gonzáles, Sam, "Hitchcock with Deleuze," in *Hitchcock: Past and Future*, ed. Richard Allen and Sam Ishii-Gonzáles (London and New York: Routledge, 2004), pp. 128–45.
Jacobs, Steven, *The Wrong House: The Architecture of Alfred Hitchcock* (Rotterdam: 010 Publishers, 2007).
Johnston, John, *The Lord Chamberlain's Blue Pencil* (London: Hodder and Stoughton, 1990).
Kabatchnik, Amnon, *Blood on the Stage, 1925–1950: Milestone Plays of Crime, Mystery, and Detection: An Annotated Repertoire* (Lanham, MD: Scarecrow Press, 2010).

Kerzoncuf, Alain, and Charles Barr, *Hitchcock Lost and Found* (Lexington: University Press of Kentucky, 2015).
Krohn, Bill, *Hitchcock at Work* (London: Phaidon, 2000).
Laurents, Arthur, *Original Story By: A Memoir of Broadway and Hollywood* (New York and London: Applause, 2000).
Lawrence, Amy, "American Shame: *Rope*, James Stewart, and the Postwar Crisis in American Masculinity," in *Hitchcock's America*, ed. Jonathan Freedman and Richard Millington (New York and Oxford: Oxford University Press, 1999), pp. 55–76.
Leff, Leonard J., *Hitchcock and Selznick: The Rich and Strange Collaboration of Alfred Hitchcock and David O. Selznick in Hollywood* (London: Weidenfeld and Nicolson, 1988).
Leitch, Thomas, *The Encyclopedia of Alfred Hitchcock* (New York: Checkmark Books, 2002).
——, *Find the Director and Other Hitchcock Games* (Athens, GA, and London: University of Georgia Press, 1991).
Lyotard, Jean-François, "Answer to the Question: What Is the Postmodern?," in *The Postmodern Explained to Children: Correspondence 1982–1985*, trans. Don Barry et al. (London: Turnaround, 1992), pp. 9–25.
MacCabe, Colin, "Realism and the Cinema: Notes on Some Brechtian Theses," in *Theoretical Essays: Film, Linguistics, Literature* (Manchester: Manchester University Press, 1985), pp. 33–57.
Macdonald, Ian W., *Screenwriting Poetics and the Screen Idea* (Basingstoke: Palgrave Macmillan, 2013).
Mann, Thomas, "Death in Venice," in *Death in Venice, Tristan, Tonio Kröger*, trans. H. T. Lowe-Porter (Harmondsworth: Penguin, 1955), pp. 7–83.
Mansfield, Katherine, "A Dill Pickle," in *Bliss and Other Stories* (Harmondsworth: Penguin, 1962), pp. 181–88.
Matthews, Kristin L., "Reading, Guidance, and Cold War Consensus in Alfred Hitchcock's *Rope*," *The Journal of Popular Culture* 43.4 (2010), 738–60.
McGilligan, Patrick, *Alfred Hitchcock: A Life in Darkness and Light* (New York: HarperCollins, 2003).
McKernan, Maureen, *The Amazing Crime and Trial of Leopold and Loeb* (Chicago: Plymouth Court Press, 1924).
McKittrick, Casey, *Hitchcock's Appetites: The Corpulent Plots of Desire and Dread* (New York and London: Bloomsbury, 2016).
Mellers, Wilfrid, *Francis Poulenc* (Oxford and New York: Oxford University Press, 1993).
Miller, D. A., "Anal *Rope*," *Representations* 32 (1990), 114–33.
——, *Hidden Hitchcock* (Chicago and London: University of Chicago Press, 2016).
Mills, C. Wright, *The Power Elite*, new ed. (New York: Oxford University Press, 2000).
Moorhead, Carolyn, *Sidney Bernstein: A Biography* (London: Jonathan Cape, 1984).
Nabokov, Vladimir, *Pale Fire* (New York: Lancer Books, 1963).

Nelson, Maggie, "All That Is the Case: Some Thoughts on Fact in Nonfiction and Documentary Poetry," in *Lit from Within: Contemporary Masters on the Art and Craft of Writing*, ed. Kevin Haworth and Dinty W. Moore (Athens, OH: Ohio University Press, 2011), pp. 155–63.

Olsson, Jan, *Hitchcock à la Carte* (Durham: Duke University Press, 2015).

O'Meara, Lucy, *Roland Barthes at the Collège de France* (Liverpool: Liverpool University Press, 2012).

Orr, John, *Hitchcock and Twentieth-Century Cinema* (London and New York: Wallflower Press, 2005).

Paglia, Camille, *The Birds* (London: BFI, 1998).

Pascal, Blaise, *Pensées*, trans. A. J. Krailsheimer, rev. ed. (Harmondsworth: Penguin, 1995).

Paulin, Scott D., "Unheard Sexualities: Queer Theory and the Soundtrack," in *Spectatorship: Shifting Theories of Gender, Sexuality, and Media*, ed. Roxanne Samer and William Whittington (Austin: University of Texas Press, 2017), pp. 77–95.

Perkins, V. F., "Rope," *Movie* 7 (1963), 11–13.

Phillips, Michael, "With Staging 'Rope' Comes Full Circle," *Los Angeles Times*, August 28, 2001, https://www.latimes.com/archives/la-xpm-2001-aug-28-ca-39132-story.html.

Pomerance, Murray, *A Dream of Hitchcock* (Albany: SUNY Press, 2019).

———, *The Man Who Knew Too Much* (London: BFI, 2016).

———, *Marnie* (London: BFI, 2014).

———, "Some Hitchcockian Shots," in *A Companion to Alfred Hitchcock*, ed. Thomas Leitch and Leland Poague (Malden, MA, and Oxford: Wiley-Blackwell, 2011), pp. 237–52.

Poulenc, Francis, *"Echo and Source": Selected Correspondence 1915–1963*, ed. and trans. Sidney Buckland (London: Victor Gollancz, 1991).

———, *My Friends and Myself*, ed. Stéphane Audel, trans. James Harding (London: Dobson, 1978).

Quirk, Randolph, Sidney Greenbaum, Geoffrey Leech, and Jan Svartvik, *A Comprehensive Grammar of the English Language* (London and New York: Longman, 1985).

Raubicheck, Walter, and Walter Srebnick, "Introduction: Hitchcock's Rereleased Films and Cinema Studies," in *Hitchcock's Rereleased Films: From* Rope *to* Vertigo, ed. Walter Raubicheck and Walter Srebnick (Detroit: Wayne State University Press, 1991), pp. 17–30.

Restivo, Angelo, "Hitchcock and the Postmodern," in *A Companion to Alfred Hitchcock*, ed. Thomas Leitch and Leland Poague (Malden, MA, and Oxford: Wiley-Blackwell, 2011), pp. 555–71.

Rich, Adrienne, "Compulsory Heterosexuality and Lesbian Existence," *Signs* 5.4 (1980), 631–60.

Rogers, Samuel, "Ginevra," in *Italy: A Poem* (London: Edward Moxton, 1852), pp. 110–14.

Rohmer, Eric, and Claude Chabrol, *Hitchcock: The First Forty-Four Films*, trans. Stanley Hochman (New York: Ungar, 1979).
"Rope," *Variety*, August 26, 1948, 3.
Ross, Steven J., *Working-class Hollywood: Silent Film and the Shaping of Class in America* (Princeton: Princeton University Press, 1998).
Roth, Philip, *The Ghost Writer* (London: Vintage, 2005).
Rothman, William, *Hitchcock—The Murderous Gaze* (Cambridge, MA, and London: Harvard University Press, 1982).
——, *Must We Kill the Thing We Love? Emersonian Perfectionism and the Films of Alfred Hitchcock* (New York: Columbia University Press, 2014).
Ryall, Tom, *Alfred Hitchcock and the British Cinema* (London: Athlone, 1996).
——, *Blackmail* (London: BFI, 2003).
San Juan, Eric, and Jim McDevitt, *Hitchcock's Villains: Murderers, Maniacs, and Mother Issues* (New York: Scarecrow Press, 2013).
Schantz, Ned, "Hospitality and the Unsettled Viewer: Hitchcock's Shadow Scenes," in *Alfred Hitchcock*, ed. Neil Badmington (London and New York: Routledge, 2014), 4 vols, vol. 4, pp. 215–32.
Schatz, Thomas, *The Genius of the System: Hollywood Filmmaking in the Studio Era* (London: Faber and Faber, 1998).
Schildcrout, Jordan, "Queer Justice: The Retrials of Leopold and Loeb," *The Journal of American Culture* 34.2 (2011), 167–77.
Schmidt, Carl B., *Entrancing Muse: A Documented Biography of Francis Poulenc* (Hillsdale, NY: Pendragon Press, 2001).
Schroeder, David, *Hitchcock's Ear: Music and the Director's Art* (New York and London: Continuum, 2012).
Sharff, Steffan, *The Art of Looking in Hitchcock's* Rear Window (New York: Limelight, 1997).
Shellard, Dominic, and Steve Nicholson with Miriam Handley, *The Lord Chamberlain Regrets: A History of British Theatre Censorship* (London: British Library, 2004).
Smith, Susan, *Hitchcock: Suspense, Humour and Tone* (London: BFI, 2000).
Sontag, Susan, *Regarding the Pain of Others* (London: Penguin, 2003).
Spoto, Donald, *The Dark Side of Genius: The Life of Alfred Hitchcock*, new ed. (London: Plexus, 1994).
Sterritt, David, "From Transatlantic to Warner Bros.," in *A Companion to Alfred Hitchcock*, ed. Thomas Leitch and Leland Poague (Malden, MA, and Oxford: Wiley-Blackwell, 2011), pp. 309–28.
——, "Morbid Psychologies and So Forth: The Fine Art of *Rope*," in *Hitchcock at the Source: The Auteur as Adaptor*, ed. R. Barton Palmer and David Boyd (Albany: SUNY Press, 2011), pp. 159–72.
Strauss, Marc Raymond, *Hitchcock's Objects and Subjects: The Significance of Things on Screen* (Jefferson, NC: McFarland, 2016).
Sullivan, Jack, *Hitchcock's Music* (New Haven and London: Yale University Press, 2006).

Taylor, John Russell, *Hitch: The Life and Work of Alfred Hitchcock* (London: Abacus, 1981).
Thoreau, Henry David, *Walden* (Princeton: Princeton University Press, 1971).
Thornton, Peter, "*Cassoni, Forzieri, Goffani* and *Cassette*: Terminology and its Problems," *Apollo* 120.272 (October 1984), 246–51.
Truffaut, François, *Hitchcock*, updated ed. (London: Paladin, 1978).
Vest, James M., *Hitchcock and France: The Forging of an Auteur* (Westport, CT and London: Praeger, 2003).
Wallace, Lee, "Continuous Sex: The Editing of Homosexuality in *Bound* and *Rope*," *Screen* 41.4 (2000), 369–87.
Waugh, Patricia, *Metafiction: The Theory and Practice of Self-conscious Fiction* (London: Methuen, 1984).
Wharton, Edith, *The Age of Innocence* (Harmondsworth: Penguin, 1974).
Wolff, Tobias, *Old School* (London: Bloomsbury, 2004).
Wood, Michael, *Alfred Hitchcock: The Man Who Knew Too Much* (New York: Amazon, 2015).
Wood, Robin, "Hitchcock and Fascism," *Hitchcock Annual* 13 (2004–05), 25–63.
———, *Hitchcock's Films Revisited*, rev. ed. (New York: Columbia University Press, 2002).
Woolf, Virginia, *Mrs. Dalloway* (London: Penguin, 1992).
Yacowar, Maurice, *Hitchcock's British Films*, 2nd ed. (Detroit: Wayne State University Press, 2010).
Žižek, Slavoj, *Looking Awry: An Introduction to Jacques Lacan through Popular Culture* (Cambridge, MA, and London: MIT Press, 1991).

## Archival Material

Ahern, Fred, to Joseph Breen, December 1, 1947. Letter, *Rope* PCA file, Margaret Herrick Library.
———, to Stephen S. Jackson, December 17, 1947. Letter, *Rope* PCA file, Margaret Herrick Library.
———, to Stephen S. Jackson, January 19, 1948. Letter, *Rope* PCA file, Margaret Herrick Library.
———, to Stephen S. Jackson, January 24, 1948. Letter, *Rope* PCA file, Margaret Herrick Library.
Berkowitz, Harold, to P.R.M., Inc. (New York), June 13, 1956. Memorandum, folder 2812, Warner Bros. Archive.
Bernstein, Sidney, to Mr. Chapman, July 18, 1957. Memorandum, folder 630, Alfred Hitchcock Collection, Margaret Herrick Library.
Blumenstock, Mort, to Roy Obringer, May 10, 1948. Memorandum, folder 2812, Warner Bros. Archive.
Box 5687, Warner Bros. Archive. (Art Department sketches.)

Breen, Joseph, to Alfred Hitchcock, September 9, 1946. Letter, *Rope* PCA file, Margaret Herrick Library.

Brylawksi, E. Fulton, to Samuel Taylor, December 8, 1972. Letter, folder 630, Alfred Hitchcock Collection, Margaret Herrick Library.

"BUDGET OF 'ROPE.'" Document dated January 9, 1948, folder 12723B, Warner Bros. Archive.

Contract of employment with Transatlantic Pictures, Perry Ferguson, December 2, 1947. Folder 2812, Warner Bros. Archive.

Contract of employment with, and assigning adaptation rights to, Transatlantic Pictures, Patrick Hamilton, March 20, 1947. Folder 2812, Warner Bros. Archive.

Contract of employment with Transatlantic Pictures for directing *Rope*, Alfred Hitchcock, 1947. Folder 2812, Warner Bros. Archive.

Contract of employment with Transatlantic Pictures, James Stewart, December 29, 1947. Folder 2812, Warner Bros. Archive.

Contract of employment with Warner Bros., John Dall, July 26, 1943. Folder 2827A, Warner Bros. Archive.

Contract of employment with Warner Bros., Alfred Hitchcock, October 13, 1948. Folder 2847, Warner Bros. Archive.

Contract of employment with Warner Bros., Joan Chandler, April 5, 1945. Folder 2738A, Warner Bros. Archive.

Daily production and progress reports for *Rope*, 1948. Folder 1490, Warner Bros. Archive.

Files, Gordon L., to F. E. Witt, December 16, 1954. Letter, folder 12934B, Warner Bros. Archive.

Forbstein, Leo F., to C. H. Wilder, January 24, 1948. Memorandum, folder 1057B, Warner Bros. Archive.

Hitchcock, Alfred, to Joseph Breen, September 4, 1946. Letter, *Rope* PCA file, Margaret Herrick Library.

Houseman, Arthur, script for *Rope* rerelease trailer, June 4, 1962. Folder 630, Alfred Hitchcock Collection, Margaret Herrick Library.

Howson, Albert S., to Alfred Hitchcock, July 13, 1948. Telegram, folder 2812, Warner Bros. Archive.

———, to Joseph Hummel, July 13, 1948. Telegram, folder 2812, Warner Bros. Archive.

Jackson, Stephen S., to Fred Ahern, December 15, 1947. Letter, *Rope* PCA file, Margaret Herrick Library.

———, to Fred Ahern, December 22, 1947. Letter, *Rope* PCA file, Margaret Herrick Library.

———, to Fred Ahern, January 23, 1948. Letter, *Rope* PCA file, Margaret Herrick Library.

Johnstone, Jacqueline H., to Herman Citron, December 20, 1962. Letter, folder 630, Alfred Hitchcock Collection, Margaret Herrick Library.

Laurents, Arthur, *Rope*, screenplay dated November 22, 1947. Folder 2198A, Warner Bros. Archive.

———, *Rope*, screenplay dated December 16, 1947. Folder 2198A, Warner Bros. Archive.

———, *Rope*, screenplay dated December 16, 1947 (with additional pages dated January 13, 1948). Folder 2198A, Warner Bros. Archive.

Location Expenses Report #2144, February 24, 1948. Folder 1434, Warner Bros. Archive.

Location Expenses Report #2150, March 8, 1948. Folder 1434, Warner Bros. Archive.

McLaughlin, Joseph, to Helen Schoen, January 21, 1948. Letter, folder 1057B, Warner Bros. Archive.

Milliken, Carl, to Fred Ahern, January 5, 1948. Memorandum, folder 2812, Warner Bros. Archive.

"Motion Pictures Made by Mr. Alfred Hitchcock from 1939 to 1957." Folder 1425, Margaret Herrick Library.

Obringer, Roy, to T. J. Martin, May 10, 1948. Memorandum, folder 2812, Warner Bros. Archive.

Peers, Victor, to Carl Milliken, January 12, 1948. Memorandum, folder 2812, Warner Bros. Archive.

Publicity document for *Rope*, undated, untitled, and unsigned. Folder 706, Warner Bros. Archive.

Rice, Bill, and Ken Whitmore, untitled publicity document. Folder 706, Warner Bros. Archive.

Schoen, Helen, to Joseph McLaughlin, March 10, 1948. Memorandum, folder 1057B, Warner Bros. Archive.

Sharf, George, to Herman Citron, May 31, 1963. Letter, folder 630, Alfred Hitchcock Collection, Margaret Herrick Library.

Staff and cast sheet for *Rope*, undated. Folder 2812, Warner Bros. Archive.

Transatlantic Pictures, to A. E. Carlson, July 17, 1948. Letter, folder 2701B, Warner Bros. Archive.

Warner Bros. Pictures, *A Photographic Production Notebook on Alfred Hitchcock's* Rope (Los Angeles: Warner Bros., 1948). Folder 630, Alfred Hitchcock Collection, Margaret Herrick Library.

———, *Warner Bros' Plan for Your Presentation of Rope* (Los Angeles: Warner Bros., 1948). Margaret Herrick Library.

Winokur, Robert, to George Sharf, February 4, 1963, Letter, folder 630, Alfred Hitchcock Collection, Margaret Herrick Library.

Zwicker, Sol E., to H. Bareford, November 10, 1948. Memorandum, folder 12670A, Warner Bros. Archive.

∾

Additionally, miscellaneous material from the following folders at the Warner Bros. Archive and the Alfred Hitchcock Collection at the Margaret Herrick Library was consulted (as is referenced contextually in the notes to this book): folders 629, 630, 1050, 1051, and 1124 (Margaret Herrick Library); folders 597, 597A, 698, 949, 1490, 2198, 2701B, 2738A, 3229B, 12670, 12670A, 12723B, 14503A2, and 14503A4 (Warner Bros. Archive).

# Index

Ahern, Fred, 24, 25, 26
Allen, Richard, 38, 56, 76, 164, 186
Alter, Dinsmore, 29
*Aventure Malgache* (Hitchcock film), 157

Bacall, Lauren, 175
Bachelard, Gaston, 47, 144
Balaban, Barney, 21–22
Balzac, Honoré de, 11–14, 16
Barr, Charles, 38, 164, 175
Barth, John, 91
Barthes, Roland, 8, 11–14, 16, 83, 88, 129, 151, 165, 183
Barton, Sabrina, 189
Baskins, Cristelle L., 86, 89
Bauso, Thomas M., 168–69
Bayly, T. H., 87
Benson, Stephen, 2, 3–5
Bergman, Ingrid, 90, 157, 176
Bergson, Henri, 60
Bernstein, Sidney, 19–20, 22, 23, 149, 150, 157, 158
*Birds, The* (Hitchcock film), 185
Bishop, Henry, 87
*Blue Velvet* (David Lynch film), 164
Bogart, Humphrey, 175, 176
*Bon Voyage* (Hitchcock film), 157
Brando, Marlon, 83
Breen, Joseph, 23, 24, 25, 159

Brill, Lesley, 38
Buttolph, David, 153

Calvert, C. C., 87
Cavarero, Adriana, 43–44, 51, 68
Chabrol, Claude, 58
*Champagne* (Hitchcock film), 175
Chandler, Joan, 60
Chion, Michel, 59, 156
Church, Hazel, 54
Clark, T. J., 9–10, 17, 38, 152
Clifton, Kevin, 110, 146, 151–52, 153–54, 188
Cohen, Paula Marantz, 110
Collier, Constance, 72
Collins, Edward J., 87
Conant, James Bryant, 47
Connelly, Thomas J., 119, 166
Connors, Clare, 2, 3–5
Conrad, Peter, 38, 42, 43, 99, 156, 177
Cooper, Gary, 175
Crane, Richard, 59, 169–70
Cronyn, Hume, 23–24, 117
Curtiz, Michael, 149–50
Cutts, Graham, 164

Dall, John, 39, 49
Damasio, Antonio R., 156
Dante Alighieri, 9

# Index

Darrow, Clarence, 21
David, Mack, 177
Day, Doris, 149–50
Deleuze, Gilles, 156
DeLillo, Don, 14, 138
Dellolio, Peter J., 34, 38, 57, 96, 153, 166, 178
Derrida, Jacques, 76, 103–05
*Dial "M" for Murder* (Hitchcock film), 57, 149, 167
Dick, Douglas, 59
Diehl, Heath A., 174
Doty, Alexander, 188
*Downhill* (Hitchcock film), 72, 175, 181
Durgnat, Raymond, 38
Dyer, Geoff, 15–16

*Easy Virtue* (Hitchcock film), 175
Edelman, Lee, 57
Elgar, Edward, 187
Evanson, Edith, 54, 167, 180

*Farmer's Wife, The* (Hitchcock film), 175
Ferguson, Perry, 167
Finler, Joel W., 187
Forbstein, Leo F., 153, 154
*Foreign Correspondent* (Hitchcock film), 57, 157
Franks, Robert, 21, 22
French, Sean, 21
Freud, Sigmund, 125–26, 176

Gielgud, John, 20
Gissing, George, 10
Gottlieb, Sidney, 158
Granger, Farley, 39, 84
Grant, Cary, 90
Greenbaum, Sidney, 108
Greven, David, 43, 188

Hamilton, Patrick, 20–21, 22–23, 24–25, 39–40, 40–41, 88, 119–20, 150, 158, 159–60, 166, 167, 174, 177, 186
Hardwicke, Cedric, 72
Harwood, Nigel, 178
Hegel, Georg Wilhelm Friedrich, 76
Hemmetter, Thomas, 145, 188
Hitchcock, Alfred: other films by. *See* individual entries by title of film
Hodenfield, Milton, 24
Hogan, Dick, 73–74
Hollinghurst, Alan, 145
Houseman, Arthur, 150, 181

*I Confess* (Hitchcock film), 149
Isherwood, Christopher, 48
Ishii-Gonzáles, Sam, 129

Jackson, Stephen S., 24, 25, 26, 114
Jacobs, Steven, 78, 166, 184, 189
*Jamaica Inn* (Hitchcock film), 181

Krohn, Bill, 27

Laurents, Arthur, 23–24, 29, 38, 39, 41, 46–47, 58, 68, 110, 113, 119, 120, 129, 151, 164, 165, 168, 169, 170, 171, 172, 173, 175, 176, 177, 178, 179, 182, 183, 184, 185, 186
Lawrence, Amy, 141, 143, 180, 189
Leavis, F. R., 142
Leech, Geoffrey, 108
Leitch, Thomas, 163, 180
Leff, Leonard J., 157
*Legend of the Mistletoe Bough, The*, 87–89, 90, 91
Leopold and Loeb case, 21–22, 25, 40, 68, 84, 88
Leopold, Nathan. *See* Leopold and Loeb case
*Lifeboat* (Hitchcock film), 116–18, 120, 157
*Lodger, The* (Hitchcock film), 175
Loeb, Allen, 21–22

Loeb, Ernie, 21–22
Loeb, Richard. *See* Leopold and Loeb case
Lyotard, Jean-François, 151

MacCabe, Colin, 6, 90
Macdonald, Ian W., 175
Mallarmé, Stéphane, 103–05
Mann, Thomas, 1
Mansfield, Katherine, 166
*Manxman, The* (Hitchcock film), 175
*Marnie* (Hitchcock film), 168, 180
Mather, Philippe, 101
McDevin, Jim, 43
McGilligan, Patrick, 19, 21
McKittrick, Casey, 118–19, 189
McLaughlin, Joseph, 154
*Man Who Knew Too Much, The* (Hitchcock film, 1956 version), 139–40, 150
Mason, James, 89–90
Matthews, Kristin L., 38–39, 74–75, 156, 188
Mellers, Wilfrid, 154
*Memory of the Camps* (Hitchcock film), 157
Miller, D. A., 14, 15, 38, 41–42, 50–51, 53, 63–64, 78, 101–02, 110, 114, 116, 118, 137, 188
Mills, C. Wright, 171
*Mistletoe Bough, The*. See *Legend of the Mistletoe Bough, The*
Moorhead, Caroline, 157, 158, 159
*Mountain Eagle, The* (Hitchcock film), 175
*Mr. and Mrs. Smith* (Hitchcock film), 157
Munaw, George, 29, 161
Murnau, F. W., 38
*My Dream is Yours* (Michael Curtiz film), 149–50

Nelson, Maggie, 155
Nietzsche, Friedrich, 21, 95

*North by Northwest* (Hitchcock film), 181, 182
*Notorious* (Hitchcock film), 57, 90, 116, 119, 157

Olsson, Jan, 180
*On the Waterfront* (Elia Kazan film), 83
Orr, John, 42, 106, 169, 177

*Paradine Case, The* (Hitchcock film), 19
Pascal, Blaise, 17
Paulin, Scott, 7, 146
PCA. *See* Production Code Administration
Peers, Victor, 24, 25, 32
Perkins, V. F., 53, 61, 107, 115, 139, 185, 186–87
*Pleasure Garden, The* (Hitchcock film), 175, 181
Poe, Edgar Allan, 57
Pomerance, Murray, 8, 139
Porter, Cole, 50
Poulenc, Francis, 6–7, 74, 84, 109–10, 144–47, 151–52, 153, 154, 155, 172
Poussin, Nicolas, 9–10
Production Code Administration, 23–26, 32–33, 41–42, 47, 79, 113–14, 137, 149–50, 151, 159–60, 162, 185
*Psycho* (Hitchcock film), 57, 59, 150

Quirk, Randolph, 108

*Rat, The* (Graham Cutts film), 164
Raubicheck, Walter, 150, 156
*Rear Window* (Hitchcock film), 15, 56, 57, 150, 167, 168
*Rebecca* (Hitchcock film), 4, 19, 130–31
Restivo, Angelo, 38, 79
Rich, Adrienne, 165
Rogers, Samuel, 87, 88

Rohmer, Eric, 58
*Rope*: adaptation process of, 22–26; bedroom(s) in, 78–81, 87, 91, 106, 113–14, 125, 151–52, 179; *cassone* in, 86–87, 89, 91, 109, 114–15, 120, 123, 125, 127, 130, 133, 134, 138, 139, 144, 145, 174, 175, 180; censorship and, 23–26, 32–33, 41–42, 47, 79, 113–14, 137, 149–50, 151, 162; cuts in, 14–16; filming and rehearsal of, 26–33; form of, 14–16; frames and framing in, 52, 64–66, 69, 72, 97–99; humor in, 55–56, 59–60, 95; metafiction in, 90–91; music in, 6–7, 34, 84, 97, 107, 109–10, 144–47, 151–52, 153–54, 154–55, 174, 177, 187; neon "Reduco" sign in, 116–19, 123, 180; neon "STORAGE" sign in, 45–46, 76, 103–05, 106, 108, 123, 135–36, 172–73, 184; novelization (anonymous, 1948) of, 33, 54, 58, 75–76, 79–80, 90, 94, 99, 106, 108, 109, 113, 124, 138, 160, 168, 170, 171, 174, 176, 177, 178, 179, 180, 181, 182, 183, 185, 186; production history of, 19–33; word "queer" in, 91, 176; queerness and, 57, 91, 106, 150, 188; release and marketing of, 32–33, 149–50; set design for, 27–29, 46, 103, 161, 167, 168, 179; sexuality in, 25, 40–44, 69–70, 77–81, 86–87, 89, 91, 105–06, 113–14, 146; sound in, 34–35, 45, 49, 50, 53, 54, 55, 60–61, 68–69, 71–72, 77, 83, 85, 96, 103, 108, 109, 114–15, 120, 123, 126, 128, 129, 134–35, 138, 140, 141, 143–44, 146, 166, 167, 169, 179, 186; trailer for, 31, 32, 74, 161, 172
Rosen, Morris, 29
Roth, Philip, 1
Rothman, William, 38, 136–37, 143, 165

*Saboteur* (Hitchcock film), 57, 157
San Juan, Eric, 43
Satie, Erik, 7
Schantz, Ned, 130–31, 188
Scharff, Stefan, 156
Schatz, Thomas, 157
Schoen, Helen, 154, 187
Schroeder, David, 145, 174
Schmidt, Carl B., 154, 155
Sedgwick, Eve Kosofsky, 5
Selznick, David O., 19, 20, 116–17, 157, 181
*Shadow of a Doubt* (Hitchcock film), 15, 157
Shurlock, Geoffrey, 24
Smith, Susan, 55–56, 59, 69, 156, 181
Sonnenschein, Hugo, 21–22
Sontag, Susan, 98
*Spellbound* (Hitchcock film), 125, 157
Spoto, Donald, 24
Srebnick, Walter, 150, 156
*Stage Fright* (Hitchcock film), 149
Stannard, Eliot, 87
Sterritt, David, 187
Stewart, James, 29, 85, 138, 139, 141
Stow, Percy, 87
*Strangers on a Train* (Hitchcock film), 57, 64–65, 149
Strauss, Marc Raymond, 73
Sullivan, Jack, 177
*Suspicion* (Hitchcock film), 57, 72, 157
Svartik, Jan, 108

Tarkovsky, Andrei, 16
Taylor, John Russell, 187
*To Catch a Thief* (Hitchcock film), 150
Transatlantic Pictures, 19–20, 22–27, 32, 39, 47, 60, 90, 114, 149, 157–58, 167, 177, 188
*Trouble with Harry, The* (Hitchcock film), 150
Truffaut, François, 15, 24, 32, 161, 163, 186

*Under Capricorn* (Hitchcock film), 33, 149, 157–58, 162, 187

*Vertigo* (Hitchcock film), 68, 135, 150, 167
Vest, James M., 187
Viñes, Ricardo, 6–7

Wallace, Lee, 166
Warner, Harry, 21–22
Warner, Jack, 22
Waugh, Patricia, 91
Wharton, Edith, 43
Wilder, C. H., 154
Wolff, Tobias, 16
Wood, Michael, 37, 56, 142, 156
Wood, Robin, 78–79, 94, 95, 138, 142, 156, 177, 179, 186, 188
Woolf, Virginia, 45
*Wrong Man, The* (Hitchcock film), 64

Žižek, Slavoj, 156

Also in the series

William Rothman, editor, *Cavell on Film*

J. David Slocum, editor, *Rebel Without a Cause*

Joe McElhaney, *The Death of Classical Cinema*

Kirsten Moana Thompson, *Apocalyptic Dread*

Frances Gateward, editor, *Seoul Searching*

Michael Atkinson, editor, *Exile Cinema*

Paul S. Moore, *Now Playing*

Robin L. Murray and Joseph K. Heumann, *Ecology and Popular Film*

William Rothman, editor, *Three Documentary Filmmakers*

Sean Griffin, editor, *Hetero*

Jean-Michel Frodon, editor, *Cinema and the Shoah*

Carolyn Jess-Cooke and Constantine Verevis, editors, *Second Takes*

Matthew Solomon, editor, *Fantastic Voyages of the Cinematic Imagination*

R. Barton Palmer and David Boyd, editors, *Hitchcock at the Source*

William Rothman, *Hitchcock: The Murderous Gaze, Second Edition*

Joanna Hearne, *Native Recognition*

Marc Raymond, *Hollywood's New Yorker*

Steven Rybin and Will Scheibel, editors, *Lonely Places, Dangerous Ground*

Claire Perkins and Constantine Verevis, editors, *B Is for Bad Cinema*

Dominic Lennard, *Bad Seeds and Holy Terrors*

Rosie Thomas, *Bombay before Bollywood*

Scott M. MacDonald, *Binghamton Babylon*

Sudhir Mahadevan, *A Very Old Machine*

David Greven, *Ghost Faces*

James S. Williams, *Encounters with Godard*

William H. Epstein and R. Barton Palmer, editors, *Invented Lives, Imagined Communities*

Lee Carruthers, *Doing Time*

Rebecca Meyers, William Rothman, and Charles Warren, editors, *Looking with Robert Gardner*

Belinda Smaill, *Regarding Life*

Douglas McFarland and Wesley King, editors, *John Huston as Adaptor*

R. Barton Palmer, Homer B. Pettey, and Steven M. Sanders, editors, *Hitchcock's Moral Gaze*

Nenad Jovanovic, *Brechtian Cinemas*

Will Scheibel, *American Stranger*

Amy Rust, *Passionate Detachments*

Steven Rybin, *Gestures of Love*

Seth Friedman, *Are You Watching Closely?*

Roger Rawlings, *Ripping England!*

Michael DeAngelis, *Rx Hollywood*

Ricardo E. Zulueta, *Queer Art Camp Superstar*

John Caruana and Mark Cauchi, editors, *Immanent Frames*

Nathan Holmes, *Welcome to Fear City*

Homer B. Pettey and R. Barton Palmer, editors, *Rule, Britannia!*

Milo Sweedler, *Rumble and Crash*

Ken Windrum, *From El Dorado to Lost Horizons*

Matthew Lau, *Sounds Like Helicopters*

Dominic Lennard, *Brute Force*

William Rothman, *Tuitions and Intuitions*

Michael Hammond, *The Great War in Hollywood Memory, 1918–1939*

Burke Hilsabeck, *The Slapstick Camera*

Niels Niessen, *Miraculous Realism*

Alex Clayton, *Funny How?*

Bill Krohn, *Letters from Hollywood*

Alexia Kannas, *Giallo!*

Homer B. Pettey, editor, *Mind Reeling*

Matthew Leggatt, editor, *Was It Yesterday?*

Merrill Schleier, editor, *Race and the Suburbs in American Film*

www.ingramcontent.com/pod-product-compliance
Lightning Source LLC
Chambersburg PA
CBHW030651230426
43665CB00011B/1038